Coming Through the Swamp

Coming Through the Swamp

The Nature Writings of
Gene Stratton Porter

Edited and with an introduction by

Sydney Landon Plum

University of Utah Press
Salt Lake City

© 1996 by the University of Utah Press
All rights reserved.
5   4   3   2   1
2000   1999   1998   1997   1996

Library of Congress Cataloging-in-Publication Data

Stratton-Porter, Gene, 1863–1924.
    Coming through the swamp : the nature writing of Gene Stratton
Porter / edited and with an introduction by Sydney Landon Plum.
        p.   cm.
    Includes bibliographical references (p.   ).
    ISBN 0-87480-497-3 (cloth : alk. paper). —ISBN 0-87480-498-1
(pbk. : alk. paper)
    1. Natural history. 2. Nature stories. I. Plum, Sydney Landon. II. Title.
QH81.S8725   1996
813'.52—dc20   95-48024

Paperback cover photograph: "Moths of the Carnival" (*Eacles imperiales*: the
Yellow Emperor)
Frontispiece: "Coming Through the Swamp"—Gene Stratton Porter
Book design by Richard Firmage

To Terry,
Trevor and Hilary
and Charity
who keep me moving on

Contents

MICHIGAN

OHIO

Rome City •

Wildflower Woods on Sylvan Lake

Gene Stratton Porter Country
Northeastern Indiana

St. Joseph River

Maumee River

Fort Wayne •

Wabash County

St. Mary's River

Wabash River

Wabash •

One inch = thirteen miles

Geneva •

• Limberlost Cabin

The Stratton family farm, where Geneva Stratton was born, was in Wabash County.

Wabash—The town which the Stratton family moved into in 1874.

Geneva—The town to which Gene Stratton moved with her husband, Charles Dorwin Porter, after their marriage in 1884.

Limberlost State Historic Site—In 1894 Gene and Charles had a log home built next to the Limberlost Swamp.

"Wildflower Woods"—In 1912 Gene bought a cottage on Sylvan Lake, and in 1914 she moved to the home she had built there. Gene lived there until her move to California in 1920. This home, its grounds and gardens, are now the Limberlost North State Historic Site.

Preface

This collection has been published in order to introduce the naturalist Gene Stratton Porter to a contemporary audience. Although a United States president (Theodore Roosevelt) acknowledged her importance to the conservation movement, an influential critic (William Lyon Phelps) hailed her as an institution, and millions of her contemporaries read her writings, seventy years after her death it is difficult to find copies of her work in print. Even when her books are found, her work as a naturalist continues to be overshadowed by the popularity of her novels. Bertrand F. Richards, one of her biographers, bemoans the neglect of her nature writings, particularly chastising Joseph Wood Krutch for leaving her out of his 1950 anthology of American nature writing. Only one naturalist, Annie Dillard, included a Stratton Porter work—*Moths of the Limberlost*—in her booklist that was part of the 1986 publication *On Nature: Nature, Landscape, and Natural History.*

I have selected the pieces included here because they represent the body of natural history writing produced by Gene Stratton Porter, because they mention or develop themes of interest to contemporary readers of natural history, and because of their quality. I have tried to represent the breadth of Stratton Porter's work while offering some assistance to those making their way through the quite extensive body of her writing. The essay which introduces the collection is intended as such a guide, not as a definitive biographical or critical study. I have taken the liberty of including lengthy excerpts in the essay from works—some of which are quite obscure—which I did not include in their entirety.

I have enjoyed making my own way through these works, and share Christopher Morley's appreciation (written to F. Nelson Doubleday) of *Homing With the Birds:* "Mrs. Porter's beautiful stories . . . are a kind of education in the art of wondering at the fulness of life." I would like to thank Becky Smith, Curator of the Limberlost State Historic Site in Geneva, Indiana, for her help; and Martha Schwartzlander at the Rome City site for her spritely and informed telephone conversation. Lynn Sweet and Bob Vrecenak of the University of Connecticut's Babbidge Library Interlibrary Loan Department have been resourceful in tracking down references and texts, magnificent in their perseverence, and generous in excusing my failings. Special, deeply felt thanks are given to John Elder for getting me started, to Ed Lueders for keeping me going, and to all the folks at the University of Utah Press for their help.

Every effort has been made to restore the photographs by Gene Stratton Porter which illustrate this volume to something approaching their original glory, using computer technology. My deepest thanks to Jim Egan, a professional photographer working in Providence, Rhode Island, who contributed his knowledge, energy, time, equipment, and—most importantly—his artistry, to the computer enhancement of these photographic reproductions. Jim was also patient enough to give me a rudimentary knowledge of Adobe Photoshop 3.0, and as I worked with her photographs, I was again in awe of the woman who worked in the swamp.

Sydney Landon Plum

Introduction

I N HER VARIOUS WRITINGS, Gene Stratton Porter often portrayed a wild-eyed child endowed with extraordinary patience and sensitivity, and intimate with the lives of birds, bees, or moths. This curious child is to a certain extent a self-portrait, and she is there to guide readers into the natural world. The child of nature who was born Geneva Stratton on August 17, 1863, took on many roles during her lifetime's work as advocate for nature's wonder: she was a gifted storyteller, observer, and photographic recorder. She was also a moralist and interpreter—self-schooled in the tradition of Emerson, Thoreau, and Whitman. Her success, her reliability as a teller of "tales you won't believe," depended in large part upon the steadfast projection of her image as someone with a passionate, open-eyed vision. Photographic self-portraits illustrate many of her non-fiction works. She is shown among her familiar flowers and vines, caring for them closely. Or she is the field worker, carrying the photographer's tripod and the naturalist's notebook, looking out of the page with fervent intensity.

Gene Stratton Porter's career as a writer and naturalist began with the telling of stories. This natural gift was probably as strong as her love for birds and her genius as an observer, and it was further developed and nurtured. She tells of crawling onto her father's lap to rest her head against his chest and feel the deep rumblings of his voice as he read the Bible and retold its stories for his twelve children. Gene boasted of her father's abilities as a raconteur, and although she tended to see her father through rose-colored glasses, Mark Stratton must have had a story-telling gift, for he was a lay preacher.

Geneva was the youngest child of Mark and Mary Stratton. While she was still quite young her mother became ill with typhoid. Mary Stratton was never completely well during Geneva's early years, and the young girl was left to wander around Hopewell Farm, along the banks of Indiana's Wabash River, under the loose supervision of her father and older siblings. She tells of napping under a fence post while the men worked in the fields. Despite her illness, Mary Stratton practiced a competent domesticity, in both the farmhouse and the farmyard, which taught Gene to care for hens and vegetable gardens, as well as wild birds and wildflowers.

By 1874, personal and financial hardships had forced the Strattons to move off their farm and into the town of Wabash. For the next thirteen years, Geneva Stratton lived in boarding houses and with a married sister. She did not have a garden, and her time in the natural world was limited to brief summer visits to the chautauquas on Sylvan Lake, northwest of Wabash. There, in 1884, she met Charles Dorwin Porter—then thirty-four years old and a successful druggist—with whom she began a sprightly correspondence. They were married in 1886, and a daughter, Jeannette, was born in 1887.

Although she would not duplicate the childhood idyll of Hopewell Farm, in her lifetime Gene Stratton Porter did build a series of increasingly elaborate rural nests for herself. She persuaded Charles to move to a house with a sizable garden in Geneva, Indiana; then, in 1894, after visiting the Chicago Exposition, she began the building of a "Queen Anne rustic" log home modeled after the Forestry Building at the Exposition. This is the famous "Limberlost Cabin," now an Indiana state historic site. It was built at the edge of the Limberlost Swamp, a natural refuge for many species of local and migratory birds. The interior of the cabin is graced with woodwork which is now all that remains of the magnificent hardwoods harvested from the swamp. The lace curtains of the parlor served as a backdrop for her photographs of moths, and as a resting place for moth cocoons.

Gene Stratton Porter's own story may be told, and her literary career traced, through the places she knew, and loved, and left behind. Her writing career began along the Wabash River, explored the Limberlost Swamp, gathered material from the banks of Sylvan Lake, and finally discovered new vistas in the sunshine and dry slopes of Southern California. She produced eleven novels, two works for children, seven nature studies, three book-length poems and several shorter poetic pieces, and an extraordinary number of magazine articles.

Her articles on birdlife began to be published in *Recreation* and *Outing* magazines in 1900. Her need for illustrations for these articles prompted her husband and daughter to give her a camera for Christmas. She was a self-taught photographer, and many of her early articles share her experience of photographing birds in the wild, described anecdotally. She makes much of her self-portrayal as a brown- or green-clad woman wading through a swamp or briar bushes, climbing trees or telegraph poles, rowing on the river or lying quite still in a drifting boat, sit-

ting quietly day and night out of doors in order to get the perfectly rep-
resentational photograph of her wildlife subject.

Gene Stratton Porter's first novel, *The Song of the Cardinal,* was published in 1903. The novel tells the story—from the cardinal's point of
view—of a young male cardinal establishing his territory along the
Wabash River, finding a mate, raising a family, and befriending an elderly
farmer and his wife. The cardinals' interior monologues and dialogues
with each other are neither stylistically nor thematically inappropriate,
since the writing does not rely primarily on the pathetic fallacy to engage
the reader and is imbued with a naturalism which could have come from
only a deep and immediate knowledge of the subject and surroundings.

In 1904 the novel *Freckles* was published by Doubleday. The story
grew in part out of the excitement Stratton Porter experienced finding
and photographing a rare black vulture chick. While it was not immediately a best seller, this tale of an orphaned boy finding livelihood, love,
and family through adventures and hardship in the wilderness, and at-
taining both a naturalist's and a businessman's knowledge in the process,
established the pattern for the successful novels which followed. Freckles, the boy, accepts a black feather falling through the trees one day as a
sign of the fitness of his new life. He nurtures the vulture chicks, and
other creatures of the swamp, as if to compensate for the nurturing he
has missed.

At the Foot of the Rainbow was published in 1907, and while many
critics preferred it to *Freckles,* it was soon overshadowed by the success of
the next novel, *A Girl of the Limberlost,* published by Doubleday in 1909.
When its popularity and commercial success were clear, Gene Stratton
Porter struck a deal with Nelson Doubleday. The company would publish one nature work for every novel. Eight novels, widely read and financially successful for publisher and author, came out of this collaboration:
The Harvester (1911), *Laddie: A True Blue Story* (1913), *Michael O'Halloran*
(1915), *A Daughter of the Land* (1918), *Her Father's Daughter* (1921), *The
White Flag* (1923), *The Keeper of the Bees* (1925), and *The Magic Garden*
(1927). The nature books did not keep pace: there were five published by
Doubleday, and two of these were reprintings of earlier works.

Gene Stratton Porter set all but one of her novels in rural areas, gardens, wilderness areas. She wanted her readers to experience some of the
wonder with which she beheld nature in all of its moods and seasons. Yet
there was more to her perception of a life out of doors than awe. Some of
the major characters in her books live through disease or live with dis-
abilities. Their time in the natural world often cures or relieves their
physical ailments. The protagonist of *The Bee Keeper* cures his war

wounds with vitamin C and daily ocean bathing; the major character of *The Harvester* is a herbalist whose cures bring him a national reputation. In an essay, "Why I Wrote *A Girl of the Limberlost*," which appeared in 1911 Stratton Porter wrote: "So I wrote *A Girl of the Limberlost* to carry to workers inside city walls, to hospital cots, to those behind prison bars, and to scholars in their libraries, my story of earth and sky."

Stratton Porter wrote to attempt to recreate in words the restorative powers of a life in the natural world. And it is not a physical cure alone which she intended: her characters are also cured of their mental anguish. When Stratton Porter wrote of sending her stories to those walled up in cities and otherwise imprisoned, she was putting forth her belief in nature's powers to restore man's social body as well as his physical body. It is interesting to note that she included scholars among the imprisoned and unhealthy, possibly the result of critical response to her first novels and of the common methods of bird study which she elsewhere condemned as barbaric.

She believed that the rhythms and ways of the natural world contained lessons for our lives. The figure of David Langston, the "Harvester," is perhaps the most shaped by her moralism. Langston says of the woods in which he harvests his beneficial plants:

> You not only discover miracles and marvels in them, you not only trace the evolution and origin of the species, but you get the greatest lessons taught in all the world ground into you early and alone—courage, caution, and patience.

In her article "Science, Sentiment, and Anxiety," which discusses the social and philosophical climate shaping the vision of early twentieth-century nature writers, Lisa Mighetto states that while scientists generally were determining the universe's indifference and novelists were exploring man's brutality, certain American nature writers were providing "through firsthand observation, evidence of dignity, beneficence and morality in the natural world." Though it is Stratton Porter's prose writings on birds that Mighetto primarily cites (she briefly mentions *Song of the Cardinal*) her description also fits the novels, which go further than the nature writing in presenting an identifiable figure in the landscape who takes moral lessons to heart and is made whole and good by them.

Jane S. Bakerman describes Freckles and Elnora Comstock, the "girl of the Limberlost," as inversions of Natty Bumppo and Huck Finn. Although one might have reservations about holding up Natty and Huck as paradigms of the human figure in balance with the natural world, Bakerman's point is that the characters in Gene Stratton Porter's novels measure themselves against the values of a civilized world, and measure the natural world in terms of its usefulness in helping them become more civilized.

The relationship Stratton Porter portrayed between her struggling but high-minded figures and the natural world in which they learn to overcome adversity is not without its problems. In response to *A Girl of the Limberlost,* Dr. Frank Lutz of the American Museum of Natural History bemoaned the implication in a novel of such wide appeal that someone could earn not just a living but a small fortune collecting moths. There are passages in the novels which explain the delicate balance of the natural world and the benefits of preserving that balance, and in her essays and articles Stratton Porter was vehement about conserving natural resources; however, the figures in the gardens of her novels for the most part live quite well from their exploitation of nature—an exploitation that if practiced on a larger scale would be devastating.

Kate Bates, the protagonist of *Her Father's Daughter,* struggles against the social obstacles to her having her own one-hundred-acre farm. She triumphs because of her perseverance and her obsession with the land, admirable qualities in a story of a woman denied what has been granted to her brothers. Yet such tenacity and obsessiveness in American farmers may not ultimately be good for the land, not for one hundred acres, and certainly not for the huge acreage of modern agribusiness—a tragedy depicted in Jane Smiley's *One Thousand Acres.* It is as if Kate Bates's desire sets in motion the forces which will lead to the physical and spiritual ravagement of Ginny, Smiley's protagonist.

Stratton Porter energetically espoused her ideal of wholesome human life flourishing in the natural world. The moralism and sentimentality which inform her ideal may work against contemporary acceptance of the novels. Still, these features, and the skillful depiction of specific settings, contributed to her popularity in her time and to her readers' commitment to the preservation of birds and bird habitats. Other writers who marshaled this support were Mabel Osgood Wright, Florence Merriam Bailey, Olive Miller, and Gene's friend Neltje Blanchan Doubleday. Gene Stratton Porter turned her storytelling talent to the service of awakening interest in the natural world. She also used her abilities as a photographer to further this cause. And photography helped shape her view of the world she wrote to preserve.

In a particularly dismissive treatment of Stratton Porter, Peter Schmitt refers to the author, in the space of one paragraph, as "a druggist's wife" and an "amateur nature photographer." The first epithet is chauvinistic; the second, inaccurate. Stratton Porter was an accomplished albeit self-taught professional photographer, a fact of which she was both quite self-conscious and proud. When a representative from Kodak came to see how she got such quality work from their papers and chemicals, she modestly declined to show him her darkroom/bathroom with its turkey-platter developing tray, and attributed her success to clean water. However, in early articles for various photographic periodicals, passages in essays, and in *What I Have Done With Birds* Stratton Porter proudly discussed her methods and their results.

In a series of articles for the *American Annual of Photography and Photographic Times-Bulletin Almanacs,* written between 1901 and 1905, Gene Stratton Porter explained her reasons for taking up photography and her purposes in devoting so much time and energy to photographic studies of birds. First, the camera offered the possibility of accurate representation, which available drawings of birds did not. She was particularly outraged by drawings of cardinals which showed a crest all out of proportion to the body's length. She often drew attention to the indisputable accuracy and objectivity of the camera lens in order to prove a point on which she disagreed with another authority.

She also made the point more than once that photography makes possible a new kind of "collecting," accomplished without injury to the species. She was adamant that no further bird studies need be illustrated with drawings done from several to even hundreds of dead individuals. In "Under My Vine and Fig Tree" she reported that her series of photographs of the black vultures in the Limberlost "has been pronounced by the experts of our country, as well as England, France, and Germany, to be almost, if not quite, the finest bird study ever made with a camera."

At the time of her interest in birds, the subject of contemporary studies was shifting from identification of species to description of behavior. The camera was the perfect tool for focusing on the aspect of bird life which had always held the greatest fascination for Gene: domesticity. She took uncounted numbers of photographs of birds nesting, feeding, and caring for their young, as well as other photographs of the nests themselves. Viewing birdlife from the perspective of the camera lens did not necessarily make Gene Stratton Porter's vision or writing more objective; often the photographs give an objective veneer to what is essentially a moralistic and sentimentalizing commentary. On the other hand, the hard work of the photography and the intimacy with her subject matter that her photographic projects required could not help but influence anyone as sensitive as Stratton Porter.

What I Have Done With Birds contains chapters on the rail, wood thrush, owl, killdeer, black vulture, loggerhead shrike, purple martin, catbird, belted kingfisher, yellow-bellied cuckoo, blue heron, mourning dove, cowbird, cardinal, robin, blue jay, hummingbird, and quail. When it was reissued ten years later as *Friends in Feathers,* the book included additional chapters on the tanager, indigo finch, goldfinch, wren, and kingbird. Primarily a documentation of the difficulties of photographing these birds in the wild, without violating her "mute contract between woman and bird"—which was not to disturb their lives—this work also contains a good deal of information about the lives of the birds.

Stratton Porter wrote often of the trials and tribulations of the field worker, and portrayed herself as an intrepid individual flying in the face of danger in pursuit of intimate knowledge of the nature world. In *Homing With the Birds* she wrote:

> Sometimes I have worked in deep, dark woods . . . again I have worked on embankments in the scorching suns of June and July without a trace of shelter. I have waded in swamps and braved the quicksands of lake shores, at times having mired until it was utterly impossible for me to extricate myself. I vividly recall one day at a lake near Silver Lake, in northern Indiana, when I entered the water shortly before nine o'clock in the morning and did not leave it until half past four in the afternoon.

Field work provided her a way into the woods and a way out of her role as a Midwestern wife and mother, although her work was always to some extent influenced by a sentimental view of nature seen through the lace curtains of a drawing-room window.

Many of her photographs, particularly in *Music of the Wild,* are of dirt roads winding into the woods. Sometimes Stratton Porter was able to transport the reader with words, as in the opening of "The Barn Owl" (from *What I Have Done With Birds* and *Friends in Feathers*):

> Did you ever traverse the Michigan Inland Route, before fire annihilated and lumbermen despoiled its great beauty? There was charm in every foot of that dark, marshy old Northern forest, in the narrow river flowing swiftly over its bed of golden sand, in the rushy, moss-covered swamps which bordered it, and in the clear, cool air perfumed with dank odours and the resin of pines.

This passage and what follows are comparable in structure and purpose to the opening passage of Mary Austin's *The Land of Little Rain* and the words approach Austin's in their ability to move the reader to a new vision of nature.

Photographic work makes certain demands upon the naturalist. Searching for a subject, waiting for the desired shot and for the appropriate lighting, dealing with the mechanics of photographic plates and cameras combined to educate the photographer of nature in the rewards of patience, leading to that incomparable experience of relinquishing one's own sense of human time to the quite different rhythms and expectations of the natural world.

Stratton Porter's study of moths was a supreme exercise in patience. She was anxious to produce illustrations for her study without destroying the moths, for their own sake and because she was convinced that the moths' colors faded and changed after death and exposure to chemicals. She made her photographic paper very sensitive, so that it recorded only the merest image of the moth, then she painstakingly hand-painted this photographic "ghost" from the live sample. Most of the work had to be done in the few hours it took for the moth to emerge from its cocoon and dry its wings. The unique quality of the individual chapters on different species of moths is a result of the writer's immersion in the lives of her subjects. "No one can comprehend the story of wings unless they have seen them develop," she wrote in "The King of the Poets: *Citheronia Regalis,*" *Moths of the Limberlost:*

> At twelve o'clock and five minutes, they measured two thirds of an inch from the base of the costa to the tip. At twelve fifteen they were two inches. At twelve forty-five they were two and a half, and at one o'clock they were three inches. At complete expansion this moth measured six and a half inches strong, and this full sweep was developed in one hour and ten minutes. To see these large, brilliantly coloured wings droop, widen and develop their markings, seemed little short of a miracle.

Many of the essays of *Moths of the Limberlost* have as their point of departure a personal recollection of the difficulty of acquiring an example of the species; however, the bulk of the writing is focused on presenting her empirical knowledge. An early chapter talks about eggs and caterpillars and winter quarters. Various taxonomic questions still unanswered at the time of her writing are reviewed. She reported that she had been told moths have served as examples of color combinations for the weaving of rugs; she detailed the relationship between moths and the environment. Her writing does such justice to her powers of observation that this book might be a nature writer's primer.

In moths Gene Stratton Porter had subjects little susceptible to the imposition of human values.

One can admire to fullest extent the complicated organism, wondrous colouring, and miraculous life processes in the evolution of the moth, but that is all. Their faces express nothing, their attitudes tell no story. . . . There is no part of their lives that makes such pictures of mother-love as birds and animals afford. The male finds its mate and disappears. The female places her eggs and goes out before her caterpillars break their shells. The caterpillar transforms to the moth without its consent. . . . The entire process is utterly devoid of sentiment, attachment or volition on the part of the creatures involved. They work out a law as inevitable as that which swings suns, moons, and planets in their courses. They are the most fragile and beautiful result of natural law with which I am acquainted.

Yet her writing is imbued with feeling by the awareness of the transient nature of this beauty. Photographs and words are reflections and interpretations of what was once immediate experience. Not only that; some of the poignant awareness of loss that colors our readings of the works of a naturalist such as Gene Stratton Porter comes from our knowledge of the losses which have been sustained since the time of the writing.

As part of her description of the Yellow Emperor moth she wrote:

When a child, I used to gather cowslips in a bed of lush swale, beside a little creek at the foot of a big hill on our farm. At the summit was an old orchard, and in a brush-heap a brown thrush nested. From a red winter pearmain the singer poured out his own heart in song, and then reproduced the love ecstasy of every other bird in the orchard. That moth's wings were so exactly the warm though delicate yellow of the flowers I loved, that as I looked at it I could feel my bare feet sinking in the damp ooze, smell the fragrance of the buttercups, and hear again the ripple of the water and the mating exaltation of the brown thrush.

Here, as in the finest portions of *Music of the Wild*, it is as if that barefoot child might lead us back into the orchard of her childhood, to the sights and sounds of a place which already by the time of the publication of the book had been disfigured by industry. Particularly in the middle essay, "Songs of the Fields," the writing and exquisite photographs grant the reader almost a primacy of experience.

Music of the Wild is Gene Stratton Porter's most ambitious work. In it she strove to recreate the Limberlost and surrounding areas without benefit of fictional narrative or an interpreting naturalist figure. In three essays—"The Chorus of the Forest," "The Songs of the Fields," and "The Music of the Marsh"—she described a myriad of wildlife and vegetation, from dragonflies to dusky falcons, foxgloves to wild rice, weaving together her observations through the recurrent device of a description of the sounds of these different areas.

Music of the Wild is replete with quotations from ancient and modern writers, including Anacreon, Bryant, Byron, Cowper, Emerson, Fosdick, Holmes, Lanier, Longfellow, Lowell, Riley, Shakespeare, Taylor, Whitman, and Whittier. There are also a good number of unattributed poetic captions—some of them quite possibly by Stratton Porter. Although there are a few quotations used as captions to photographs in *Moths,* nowhere else did she make such use of literary references. In other studies, she referred to, and often disputed, scientific sources, but in *Music of the Wild* she was trying her hand at a studied, literary nonfictional work and at a statement of her metaphysics.

Some of the language of this work is grandiloquent—not as grounded in observation or as direct as elsewhere. This is particularly true in the first essay, "The Chorus of the Forest," where Stratton Porter established what might be considered the controlling metaphor for this work: "The forest always has been compared rightly with a place of worship." She identified the aroma of the forest with incense, the shafts of sunlight with candlelight, the lichen and flowers with embroidery on liturgical vestments. The sounds of the wind and the birds and insects are the chorus.

> I doubt if any one can enter a temple of worship and not be touched with its import. Neither can one go to primal forests and not feel closer the spirit and essence of the Almighty than anywhere else in nature. In fact, God is in every form of creation; but in the fields and marshes the work of man so has effaced original conditions that he seems to dominate. The forest alone raises a chorus of praise under natural conditions. Here you can meet the Creator face to face, if anywhere on earth.

Yet, as this work continues, references to divinity and worship fairly vanish. It seems to be the case that this initial simile was introduced less to place the natural world in service to the worship of a supreme being than to validate the feelings which Stratton Porter would have us experience in the natural world.

> The only way to love the forest is to live in it until you have learned its pathless travel, growth, and inhabitants as you know

the fields. You must begin at the gate and find your road slowly, else you will not hear the Great Secret and see the Compelling Vision. There are trees you never before have seen; flowers and vines the botanists fail to mention; such music as your ears can not hear elsewhere; and never-ending pictures no artist can reproduce with pencil or brush.

As Stratton Porter places her foot on the road and immediately becomes completely absorbed in the natural wonders around her—prevailing upon all of her senses—her attention to causes (primal and otherwise) is distracted. The more specific "Creator" becomes the abstraction of "the Great Secret" and "the Compelling Vision." Her goal was not to attach her enthusiasm for the natural world to any religious purpose, but rather to underscore the importance of understanding and preserving nature.

Included in the essay "The Music of the Marsh" is a first version of an environmental warning Stratton Porter repeated in "The Search for 'Three Birds'" in *Tales*. She rails against "cutting down the clouds," which is what she called the process by which the Limberlost Swamp was being drained. Like Mary Austin confronting the Owens River project, Gene Stratton Porter saw the "reclamation" work in Noble County and was horrified.

> Drying up the springs, drying up the streams, and lowering the lake meant to exterminate the growth by running water, meant to kill the great trees that had flourished since the beginning of time around the borders of the lakes, meant to kill the vines and shrubs and bushes, the ferns and the iris and the water hyacinths, the arrowhead lilies and the rosemary and the orchids, and it meant, too, that men were madly and recklessly doing an insane thing without really understanding what they were doing. They had forgotten that where there is not moisture to arise to mass in rain clouds and fall back upon the earth, to be scattered in rain, no rain comes. They had forgotten that draining the water from all these acres of swamp land would dry and heat the air they were to breathe to an almost unendurable degree during summer. They had not studied the question scientifically and figured out for themselves how much rainfall they would take from their crops. *Not one of them had taken a spadeful of soil, water soaked for ages, and had its properties examined for humus and growing qualities. They did not know as I did that*

the soil they were so eagerly proposing to drain would take centu-
ries to become fit for growing crops because for centuries it had been
water soaked until there was not an element in it that would make
anything grow unless it were accustomed to growing in water.

Music of the Wild is a fine collection of renderings of a closely ob-
served and dearly loved natural habitat, and the purpose of the study is
not strictly a recording. In the end, Stratton Porter returned to a version
of her originally stated purpose by reminding the reader of what the natural world has to say on the subject of the spiritual:

> Dead as any death appears the marsh during winter's long
> sleep; no other place so abundant with life in summer. Most
> people dread the thought of annihilation. That marsh, that can
> die and yet return to life at the first breath of spring, seems each
> year to repeat anew to its lovers, "Though a man die, yet shall he
> live again." All men are cheered by that message, whether it
> comes by precept or impression.

She did not end on this rather easy benediction: the next few pages reca-
pitulate the messages of the bounty of the plumes of wild rice; the lily
pads "that shade off into black, unfathomable water"; "the stiff-legged
waders"; and "the killdeer's call trailing across the silver night," among
others. The ultimate message which cheers Stratton Porter is definitely
that which is transmuted to the senses by firsthand impressions gained
over a long period of intimacy with forests, fields, and marshes.

In *Ring of Bright Water*, Gavin Maxwell writes that the places the nature writer recreates are "symbols of freedom, whether it be from the
prison of over-dense communities and the close confines of human relationships, from the less complex incarceration of office walls and hours,
or simply freedom from the prison of adult life and an escape into the
forgotten world of childhood, of the individual or the race." There are
striking echoes in Maxwell's words of the purpose which Stratton Porter
espoused in her writing. Both Maxwell and Stratton Porter allude to a
theme common to much nature writing: the re-discovery of Eden. Stratton Porter's writing often aims at an Edenic vision. She wrote of childhood and, in her later writing, of "primitive" societies (a late, book-
length poem, *The Fire Bird*, tells the story of a Native American love triangle). Her last, posthumously published (*McCall's*, December 1927),
magazine article was entitled "The Healing Influence Of Gardens."

She had the ability to recreate the "slow time" of childhood in which
one could wander through the day:

Then came the planting, when barefeet loved the cool earth, and trotted over other untold miles, while little fingers carefully counted out seven grains from the store carried in my apron skirt. . . .

Then father covered them to the right depth, and stamped each hill with the flat of the hoe, while we talked of golden corn bread, and slices of mush, fried to a crisp brown that cook would make in the fall. We had to plant enough more to feed all the horses, cattle, pigs, turkeys, geese, and chickens, during the long winter, even if the sun grew uncomfortably warm, and the dinner bell was slow about ringing. *(Moths of the Limberlost)*

The writing of Gene Stratton Porter looks back at her childhood, and at a passing agrarian society, when time was measured in the seasons of the natural world.

The reader often is brought into that world through the eyes or sense of wonder of a young girl in the two essay collections *Homing With the Birds* (1919) and *Tales You Won't Believe* (1925). The essays in *Homing* are variously anecdotal and scientific. The essays tell of a red-winged blackbird eaten by a bass, and of the evolution of birds. They describe different bird songs and discuss theories of bird intelligence. One offers a recipe for helping birds that have been immersed in crude oil—a method the author developed during her years adjacent to the oil wells in the Limberlost. Her method of gently scrubbing oil-covered birds with hot water and a cleansing compound such as "Dutch Cleanser, Snow Boy, or Gold Dust," followed by her invalid's diet of mashed egg yolk, boiled potato, and rolled hemp seed, saved many birds and is similar to the modern method of treatment. An essay on the place of birds in the ecological balance—"Shall We Pay Our Debt?"—concludes the collection.

In the essay that begins *Homing* the child Geneva wanders through a landscape Edenic in its abundance:

All of the trees and most of the bushes surrounding the house were filled with bird nests. A privet bush in one corner of the garden always had at least one nest, while the grape arbour and berry bushes sheltered many. There were little cups of hair even among the currant and gooseberry bushes. Every bird that ever homed in an orchard in the Central States was to be found in the apple trees, in a big heap of trimmings at the back of the orchard, in the hollow rails of the fence, or in the grassy corners of our orchard. I think too that every bird of the fields was to be found in our meadow, our clover fields, and in the fence corners.

By the time of the writing of *Tales,* the author realized the true value of fence corners:

> The point is that from the time I could toddle around alone I began the work of transplanting wild flowers. They grew in such profusion and were so ruthlessly plowed under and spaded up in those days that . . . very speedily I began to see that culti-vation was going to wipe out the rarest and the most exquisite of the growing things in our land; so I began leaving the flowers in the fence corners and sheltered locations where they were, and gathering the ones I moved from the places where sugar camps were going to be set up in the woods, where roads were going to be made, where log heaps were stacked to be burned.

Fence lines are the repository and haven of survivors of a too greatly har-vested abundance. Similarly, Stratton Porter's words and photographs are like the fences: a line of defense against irreparable loss.

Gene Stratton Porter lost the Limberlost Swamp. She then built "Wildflower Woods" as a refuge for the birds and native plants of north-eastern Indiana, and as a retreat for herself. Then the grounds at Sylvan Lake were overrun by visitors who destroyed her flower beds and her se-renity. Even the cabin was not a safe haven from those who really wanted to see where she lived. Gene could not turn away anyone who came with a sick or injured animal; but these callers interrupted her work, left with her pens and books, and then wrote fantastic descriptions of her life and home. After the First World War, she looked to Southern California for new territory to learn from and be comforted by.

Members of her family were already living in Los Angeles County, and growing interest in filming her novels provided an artistic and fi-nancial reason for the move. Her deep-seated desire to reach a larger au-dience with her message of the "courage, caution and patience" to be learned from the natural world was her greater incentive in becoming involved in the film industry. In 1921 she formed a film company with Thomas Ince, who owned the film rights to *Michael O'Halloran* and had options on five of her other novels. They selected James Leo Meehan, an actor and journalist whom Gene already knew and trusted, to direct these projects. Stratton Porter's daughter, Jeannette, was also involved in this work. Eventually, Jeannette married Meehan and bore a son, who is now the executor of Gene Stratton Porter's estate. Gene had a vacation home and cottage built on Catalina Island, and was overseeing the finishing work on "Floraves," her hillside home in Bel-Air, when she was killed in an automobile accident in Los Angeles on December 6, 1924.

In Los Angeles, Stratton Porter belonged to an artistic community for the first time in her life. Among her friends were Edward Sherriff Curtis, the famous photographer of Native Americans; Dr. Charles Lummis, founder of the Southwest Museum; and the artist Jack Wilkinson Smith. *The Fire Bird* was inspired by Curtis's photographs. At this time Gene also began writing monthly columns for *McCall's* magazine on the practice of and moral values found in good homemaking, at the specific request of editor Harry Burton. Many of these essays attempt to translate the spiritual benefits of community with the natural world into a domestic moral code.

Gene Stratton Porter's writing never followed a prescribed philosophy or metaphysical stance. In her writing there is often evidence of the limitations of her formal education, and of the fact that she was for so long isolated from any community such as she found in Los Angeles after the war. Although she quoted often from the writings of Emerson and Thoreau, the writings of Walt Whitman come closer to being the model for her writings about nature.

During her early married life and Jeannette's childhood, Gene Stratton Porter belonged to a women's literary club in Geneva. For this club she once delivered a song of praise for Walt Whitman. Although it never was published during her lifetime, Jeannette included it in her remembrance of her mother, *The Lady of the Limberlost*. One can only wonder at the effect on her audience of Gene's adulation of such a colorful character, for she did not go about her remarks delicately. She applied herself with a gusto appropriate both to the subject and to her personality, not even shrinking at his "Children of Adam."

He liked to stretch his body on the greensward in the sun with the winds of heaven to fan him, and to be of the earth, earthy. He simply would not be confined; the world was his stage; he would travel it. . . . He was the most democratic man that ever lived; his life stands to prove it. Of Nature in her varying moods he feasted and feasted and was never filled. . . .

In this we find a manly salutation and the frankest confessions of pure passion to legitimate ends ever put in print. . . . Whitman believes in letting in sunlight, in opening up dark places, in equalising forces, in making every organ of the human body as common as the hand or foot with as common functions to perform. . . . If it brings a blush, it must not be for the author or what he has written, but for ourselves that the God-given power of pro-creation which it was meant we use, naturally, fully, freely as he describes, for the peopling of the earth with greater statesmen, poets, warriors, sailors, citizens, we have prostituted into a function exercised for our pleasure without creative intent or desire.

In her praise of Whitman's life and writings are intimations of the plots of her novels as well as hints of the burden of her moral essays in women's magazines. Stratton Porter's admiration for Whitman is rooted in his ability to express the freedom which can be found if one can achieve a unity with the natural. It is difficult to see the depth of this yearning in Gene Stratton Porter unless we see her work in its entirety. Unfortunately, it is her novels which have been more available to audiences in the second half of this century, and even the two which most often are reprinted, *Freckles* and *Girl of the Limberlost,* are commonly treated as fictions for young adults. The strongest writing in the novels is that which depicts the natural world and lives in contact with nature. The five works of nature writing—*What I Have Done With Birds (Friends in Feathers), Music of the Wild, Moths of the Limberlost, Homing with the Birds,* and *Tales You Won't Believe*—at the very least all contain sections which could be primers for those who wish to more deeply understand the natural world. In addition, they now are recollections of a time and world that no longer exist and cannot be reclaimed; a world Gene Stratton Porter enthusiastically, yet tenderly, embraced.

Visions of Eden are shaped by our sense of loss, and Stratton Porter's nature writing from the end of her life has the still sadness of an old photograph album. The earlier tone of childlike enthusiasm and wonder which marks the recollections of *Homing With the Birds* is harmonized in *Tales You Won't Believe* with the sense of loss inherent in remembered beauty. The tales she collected are of strange happenings, rare appearances in nature, idiosyncrasies of people and wildlife. She worked to recreate the wonder which is her particular gift; and the stories are autobiographical in the sense that they reveal inner qualities of her life. Which included anger. If there may be said to be evil in the gardens created and recollected by Gene Stratton Porter, it is not shaped like a snake but like a gun. The evil she depicted was the threat from outside the natural world. The hunter and the lumberjack, the cruel farmer and the obtuse visitor are all to some degree representative of a humanity blind to the basic morality and wonder of the natural world. In their blindness, they authorize or allow destruction. In the novels, someone always re-forms these figures or tricks them out of their possession of a piece of land or of an animal that needs protection. In the essays, this was also sometimes the case—but not always. In *Tales* she describes how for eight years her nearest neighbor on Sylvan Lake put out poisoned chickens at night to get rid of the Great Horned Owls nesting on his property. For eight years Gene trespassed their common boundary at night to retrieve the poisoned meat and save the owls.

Sometimes her stories pair a loss with a serendipitous find, as in "The Search for 'Three Birds,'" where attending the funeral of a child led Gene to discover a bed of rare flowers for which she had been searching. Many of the tales have at their center a loss which cannot be staved off: "The Bride of Red Wing Lake," "The Last Passenger Pigeon." In the con-cluding essay of the collection she rails at some young people for their inability to closely observe a threatened field of grass.

In winding up her remarks about Whitman and *Leaves of Grass* for the local women's literary society, Gene extolled: "if you love the green grass, flowers, and trees; if you know what the leaves whisper and the wa-ters murmur and the birds sing; if you love God's creation above man's manufacturing—read the book."

The same thing might be said in recommendation of her own writ-ings about the natural world. Whitman's vision is very like her own:

> All this world seems beautiful to me. I am larger and better than I thought. The East and West are mine; the North and South. I inhale great draughts of space. All seems beautiful to me.

As readers follow Gene Stratton Porter through the swamps to photo-graph a black vulture, row with her to find a blue heron, or bump along in the horse-drawn carriage in search of a wood thrush, we can only be astonished—just as she was—at the great number of wonderful things there are to be experienced. We can admire the dedication and generos-ity of spirit and light touch with which she recorded so much of the world she experienced. She left us an image, as if flashed upon a photo-graphic plate, of a cabin on a summer's evening, with a woman in a nightgown covered with moths.

"A Wonder Tale"

from *Tales You Won't Believe*

PRIMARILY I WENT AFIELD to make scientific and character studies of the birds. I intended to write of them on a basis of scientific truth, and to make a more intimate study than had as yet been made concerning their characteristics and habits. I wished to reproduce them exactly as they lived and carried out their home lives; I had no thought of undertaking any branch of field work beyond this.

But I soon learned that the fields, the swamps, and the woods were filled with rare and exquisite flowers, that here and there compelling landscapes were confronting me, while early in bird work afield I found clinging in deep, dark places, to branches, to bark, to the under sides of leaves, in hollow trees, huge creatures akin to butterflies, having wings ranging from three to over seven inches in sweep, gorgeously feathered with colours as bright as the brightest of the flowers, exquisitely marked, some of them having tiny moons and half moons like isinglass set in their wings through which the finest print could be read.

I was afield with a wagon load of cameras and paraphernalia for the purpose of picturing any pose or characteristic of the birds that I could materialize photographically. Naturally, my first thought was to secure reproductions of these wonderful big night moths also.

With only short experience, I found the forests and fields of May and June were flocking with moths; that night was made splendid by the colours of their softly fanning, jewelled velvet wings. I found these creatures everywhere—creeping up from the brown leaves of earth with wet wings in some cases not larger than my thumb nail and great pursy bodies striped with yellow, gray, and red. In enchanted amazement I watched the tiny wings droop and widen and spread until in a short time before my eyes they had developed to a sweep of four and a half, five, or even six inches. I found that the moths were unable to fly or to lift the weight of their bodies until these wings had dried and hardened.

I began making a collection of every work of note that ever had been published on the subject of moths. Back to the days of Linnæus and Pliny and Aristotle I went, searching for every record I could find pertaining to moths. I began making pictorial records of each moth I found in the open on a suitable location. Then, as I learned their habits and characteristics, I began carrying home the cocoons the caterpillars spun for winter quarters and making a collection of pupa cases which the burrowers in earth provide for their dormant period while the winds rave and the rain and snow fall.

At first I was bewildered by their life processes; then slowly, through experience, through research, I learned one of the most wonderful stories that Nature has to unfold to any of her lovers. The story of the life processes of our big native moths of May and June reads like the wildest fairy tale. We find them in the swamps and forests, fluttering around the lights in city parks where there is much foliage, but we do not realize that the present form of these fragile and exquisitely coloured creatures, so delicate and fine that the lightest touch of a finger tip brushes the feathers of velvet down from their wings, is the shortest link in the chain of their existence.

Like delicate fern fronds their antennæ quiver before them. Like silk and velvet of every colour of the rainbow their jewelled wings softly bear them through the night. Their eyes are so rudimentary that they only distinguish brilliant lights. Science has not discovered in what manner they seek and find each their own. They have no digestive organs. They take no food. From five to ten days accomplish the period of their lives and they creep away to a dark spot, their mission performed, their nights of glory in the orchards of May and June spent lavishly.

The first step the bewildered person who finds one of these beautiful creatures must take in learning moth history is to realize that it passed the winter, the ice, the snow, the storm, the alternate heat and cold, in a cocoon woven against the bark of a tree, under the roof of a building, in a hollow tree, or dangling by threads of silk from a branch, or a few inches underground in a brown shell-like case so thin that the antennæ and the sex of the moth may be distinguished through its covering.

The warmth and the fragrance of May bring moths from these winter quarters into the world in a beauty of birth not exceeded by any created thing. Their gorgeous wings are filled with little pneumatic tubes which harden and make flight possible for them. They are covered with millions of exquisite little feathers so lined and placed as to mark them into patterns of indescribable delicacy and beauty. The wing bases of the female are reinforced with stiff bristles that help to sustain their heavy, egg-laden abdomens in flight while in search of the right trees upon which each species deposits its eggs. Because of the necessity for longer flight, and greater activity in finding and courting the female, the males have an extra support to the lower wing which so strengthens it that male moths are enabled to fly even with wing edges badly tattered from being entangled in vines or attacked by birds, mice, and squirrels.

Usually the moths emerge about ten o'clock in the forenoon. Toward evening the tubes in their wings have hardened and been filled with air from the respiratory organs so that they are truly pneumatic; the wings have been raised and lowered in exercise to start circulation until they are so strong that the moths attempt flight.

The male is usually smaller than the female, brighter coloured in his markings, more agile on wing. The female, in some instances from a third to a fourth larger than the male, emerges for her mission having a wing sweep of perhaps an inch more than the male, her markings quite as elaborate but not so deep in colour, and having larger antennæ and a big, pursy abdomen which carries, by actual count, from two to over six hundred eggs, varying in number with the species. The weight of these eggs is so great that she usually remains where she emerges or attempts only very short flights to find her own particular tree, shrub, or vine. It is the mission of the male to find his mate and fertilize her eggs.

By morning she is ready to begin depositing them, and it is one of the miracles of a world teeming with natural history miracles how these creatures, so poorly endowed with sight, so uncertain and weighted in their flight, always find exactly the right shrub, tree, or vine upon which to deposit their eggs so that the tiny caterpillars, which soon emerge from the eggs, each shall be upon the right food for it to begin eating when it appears.

These little fellows, not much thicker than a thread, are about a quarter of an inch in length. In from six to fifteen days, varying with the species, they break from their shells and immediately begin eating them. Having finished this first meal, which probably acts as a laxative and a stimulant to the digestive organism, they advance to the edge of the leaf upon which they have hatched and start feeding. They eat so voraciously and continuously that in a short time they grow too big for their skins, literally bursting them and emerging in a new skin, large and wrinkly, which has been forming inside for exactly this contingency. This in turn becomes too small with a few days more of feeding and so the process is repeated, differing slightly with different species, until a caterpillar as thick as one's thumb and from four to six inches has developed. These change in colouring during their different moults, but in the fully matured specimens they are exquisitely coloured—some of them delicate greens, blues, or yellows indescribable in their beauty, having faint markings of pink and lavender or of black or blue. Some of them appear forbidding with heavy horns on their heads and threatening spines outlining the segments of their bodies.

When they are matured, each acts according to its kind. Some burrow in earth, forming an opening as large as a good-sized hen egg in which they burst their skins for the last time and lie encased in a delicate shell of pale tan colour which gradually grows darker until, in most instances, it becomes a rich mahogany or buck-eye brown.

In the case of the spinners the caterpillar ceases feeding, selects the bark or twig upon which it proposes to winter and begins the work of weaving its quarters. A distinctive pattern is used by each species; sometimes the cocoons are slightly different in size and shape, but all are made in practically the same way. When the spinning and weaving is finished, a liquid is ejected which oozes through the spinning and spreads in a complete coat over the outside of the weaving, making it water proof. The long threads at the top are cut off and interwoven so that no moisture or no small insect can penetrate. In the case of Polyphemus the water-proof covering extends all over the cocoon and the emerging moth must bite and tear its way and eject a liquid which will soften the case so that it can emerge safely. The spinning finished, these caterpillars also burst their skin and crowd the discarded garment to the bottom of the little leathery inner enclosure in which they lie and there await the coming of May.

After a number of years of work among the birds it became part of my daily business to watch for these cocoons and pupa cases, to carry them home, and at time of emergence, begin to record their life histories. I became so interested that I made a practice of copying every emerging moth in water colours so that I would have a perfect record of colour. I found that different specimens varied greatly; notably Eacles Imperiales, especially among males. These moths have a ground-work of delicate celandine yellow feathers with drifts of heliotrope markings. Sometimes these markings deepened almost to purple and sometimes they were a delicate lavender. Sometimes the markings drifted in faint lines across the wings, and sometimes they changed the colour of the entire moth so that the painting of each of these specimens became a work of reproducing individualities and also a delicate task of deciding exactly how much deeper the water colour should be in the original, in order that when it dried it would match the exact shade of the moth. Much practice was required for work so delicate that often I have cut a brush to three hairs in order to obtain a point sufficiently fine to pepper over the wing feathering the delicate drift of markings. This was always the case with Cecropia where the soft grays of the wings had a drift of fine black markings across them so delicate that more than three hairs would not reproduce them exactly.

It was a great day for me when I found that I had collected reproductions of the moths and caterpillars, the pupa cases and the eggs of every big night moth of the Limberlost. There had been thrilling adventures. There had been heart-breaks. There had been one real miracle.

When all of this work had resolved itself into a book which I had entitled "Moths of the Limberlost" and in the making of which I had known such joy as I never had known even in bird work because of the exquisite beauty of the creatures, because of the breathless care, the heart-throbbing pains necessary in handling my subjects to photograph them, and then to release them to the processes of their lives without the moths having been damaged by my work with them, I came to the place where I was almost ready to publish my book.

There came one night—and this was the night that I started to describe—a night late in May when May was at its supreme moment. My bedroom was on the first floor on the northeast corner of the Cabin. Owing to a slope in the land, my room opened on a small porch from which five or six steps led down to an orchard containing eight or ten apple trees in full bloom. Never had May a more perfect night. My room contained dozens of pupa cases and cocoons. The collecting of a year was yielding results. The book I had hoped for over a long period was rapidly coming to fulfillment.

This was a month during which I scarcely slept. Each night when I went to bed, I looked over my collection and listened with cocoons held to my ear as one would hold a watch. If I heard struggling and efforts of emergence going on inside the cocoon I laid it on a tray beside my pillow in order that I might be awake and ready to make my records when the moths appeared.

This night it was perhaps twelve before I lay down. The last act I had performed was to hang under the latch to the screen door leading to the veranda a twig from which, judging from its antennæ a big female Cecropia was emerging. I had such full and complete records of this moth that I meant to lie down and sleep soundly, but about two o'clock in the morning I was awakened by sounds that I did not understand. There was a faint vibration in the air, a soft bumping against the screen on the outside, a metallic sound as if the feet of dozens of moths were walking over the copper screen.

I threw back the sheet and went to the door. In the beneficence of the May moonlight streaming down so whitely that I could have read fine newspaper print in it, over the tops of the apple trees, over the branches reaching across the steps, beating themselves in useless flight against the screen door, there were uncountable numbers of Cecropia moths.

The moth on the inside proved to be a big female, one of the very largest I ever have seen. I was sure she was too recently emerged to fly, but I had in mind the thought that I would move her to some other location so that I might step out on the veranda and try to gain some accurate idea of the number of moths that were flocking above the orchard and sweeping through the veranda. I slipped my fingers under her abdomen and began gently working her feet loose from the wire to which she clung. I had forgotten for the instant what would happen if I disturbed her. Again science is baffled on a point concerning moths. Some time between emergence and finding their mates every moth exudes from the abdomen a quantity of pinkish, creamy liquid. It has not been determined whether this liquid wets the down and assists in emergence from the cocoon or pupa case, whether the eggs of the female lie in this liquid which keeps them segregated until near time for each to be fertilized and deposited, or whether the spray is intended by nature to carry a perfume on the air by which males and females shall be attracted. Evidently some of these purposes are served; very probably all. At any rate, any moth disturbed soon after emergence throws this fine spray. If not disturbed it is not ejected until time to fly, so that it may possibly be a means of defense also.

As I lifted this moth from the screen, she showered me, over my shoulders, over my night-dress, even to my bare feet. I knew by experience when I had her on my fingers that flight was impossible to her owing to her weight and the lack of exercise of her new wings. First I placed her on a window beside the door; then feeling sure, I took her on my fingers, swung open the door, and advanced to the steps. Standing there, between the bloom-whitened apple trees on either side, in the full radiance of the moonlight, I had an experience that probably never has fallen to the lot of any other human being.

With the big female moth on my fingers, with my shoulders and nightgown wet with spray, I became the best moth bait that the world knows and the night became a vibrant thing, a thing of velvet wings, of velvet sound and brilliant colour, a thing so exquisite that God Himself must have enjoyed the excellence of His handiwork. I had no way of numbering the moths that came fluttering around me. They alighted on my head, on my shoulders, on my hands; they clung to my night robe; they walked over my feet; they flocked over the apple trees; they fluttered through the moonlight, and there was no one to see or to know the poignant beauty of that perfect May hour.

I backed inside the door, carrying my moth and five others with me, so that I would have material for a group study in the morning. Then I went back to the veranda and sat on the steps until dawn. Once I followed the biggest male I ever saw across the grass until I coaxed him from a refuge he had taken under a grape leaf in deep foliage. I had the thought of mating him with my big female, in the hope of raising a moth having the greatest Cecropia wing sweep I had ever measured. Seven inches was my highest record, six and three quarters being a large female. Anything over six is large. I carried my big male in triumph to the female, but in spite of every device I could work, she chose for her mate a frowsy little ragged-winged male, sturdy and insistent—sure proof that her sight was very dim.

I have no way of numbering the moths that were in my orchard that night. In the first place, Cecropia is the commonest moth in America. In the second place, it was the height of the season. And lastly, in my own person I furnished them a lure such as they probably never had encountered before. Repeatedly I segregated and counted very close to one hundred; then more would sweep in, those I had numbered would circle back, and I would lose my count. Taken together, the triple lure of the May night, bloom time, and the moths, made the most exquisite sight I ever have seen.

"Earning a Title"
"A Gift of the Birds"

from *Homing with the Birds*

Homing with the Birds is at once a record of the intimate knowledge that Gene Stratton Porter acquired in her years of bird study, a story of her life, and a depiction of her photographic methods. The following, the opening chapters of *Homing*, give evidence of the young Geneva's patience, gentleness, keen eye, and good ear. Gene Stratton Porter rarely wrote of her family; when she did, they were idealized. She always idolized her father, Mark Stratton, referring to his noble lineage, for which there is no proof, and to his talents as a preacher. While there is support for her claim that her father was an impressive orator, he was a lay preacher, not an ordained minister.

"Peter," the brown thrasher in the book, was young Gene's favorite bird. The "most interesting bird" was probably the parrot she had during the years she lived in her Limberlost cabin. That bird would sing in accompaniment to her sewing machine.

"Earning a Title"

ALMOST MY FIRST DISTINCT MEMORY is connected with a bird. I found a woodpecker lying on the grass beneath a cherry tree. I could not understand why he did not fly with the birds flocking over the fruit; I spread his wings and tossed him through the air, but he only fell to the ground. Then I noticed that his kind were all flying from the tree tops and high places, so I carried him upstairs and launched him from a window. He fell as before. Then I thought perhaps he was hungry; I took him to the garden, pried open his beak, and stuffed him with green gooseberries, but still he would not fly. In complete discouragement, I sat on the front steps with the bird in my lap, wondering what I could do to help him. My father passed, so I began asking questions. That morning I learned a new word; I had not known "dead" before. Father very carefully explained that he never permitted robins, orioles, or any song bird to be killed, but that woodpeckers made no music, while they carried away distressingly large quantities of fruit. It was then that I made my first business proposition: "If you will make the boys stop shooting woodpeckers, I will not eat another cherry. The birds may have all of mine."

My father said that was a bargain. I never before noticed that cherries were so big, so red, so tempting, while it seemed that all of our family, helpers, and friends spent most of their time offering them to me. Our cook almost broke my heart by baking a little cherry pie in a scalloped tart-pan for me. I could not say a word, but I put my hands behind me and backed away from that awful temptation with tears in my eyes. At that point my mother intervened. She said she had decided that we had cherries enough for all of our needs and for the birds as well, so she gave me the pie.

It is probable that this small sacrifice on my part set me to watching and thinking about the birds, which every day flashed their bright colours and sang their unceasing songs all over and around us. For years one pair of wrens homed over the kitchen door, the entrance to their dwelling being a knot hole in the upper casing. While the mother bird brooded the father frequently spent an hour at a time, often in the rain, on a wooden acorn ornamenting the top of the pump on our back porch, becoming so tame that he frequently brushed us with his wings in going back and forth to his door, sometimes alighting on our heads. In his behalf I spent much time sweeping up the débris dropped by the pair on the back porch while building their nest, because my mother threatened to nail shut the opening; but as she never did, I strongly suspect that she had no real intention of so doing.

She was a great friend of a pair of hummingbirds that almost always nested in a honeysuckle over her bedroom window. One day, the front door having been left open, the male bird flew into the room and did not seem able to find his way out again. When he had circled the ceiling, striking his head until the feathers were worn away and tiny touches of red began to show on the paper, my mother could endure no more; so she summoned help and finally succeeded in capturing the bird, which she allowed me to hold in my hands while she showed me how small its body was, how tiny its feet, how fine its bill.

She had much trouble with the swifts that built in the chimney to a huge fireplace in our living room. A number of these birds would build their nests near the top of this chimney every season, beginning a rau-cous chatter very early in the morning, constantly dropping twigs and clay over the andirons and into the fireplace; while, either from imperfect construction or through heavy rains loosening the fastenings, there never was a season that one or more nests did not fall into the fireplace, frequently carrying young birds almost ready for flight with them. They were very seldom killed in the fall, but they swept down soot, and flopped around in the ashes to the vexation of Mother's housewifely soul. The old birds often fell with the nests or followed down the chimney and escaped into the room; so they, too, decorated the ceiling with their blood, if they fell when we chanced to be away from home and they were not released immediately. Often, if the nest were not completely shattered, I gathered up the pieces, wired them back into shape to the best of my ability, climbed from an upstairs window to the roof of the back part of the house, which was only one story, and from there to the roof of the second story. By using pieces of shingle and bits of wire, I replaced the nests inside the chimney, then put the little birds back into them. It was a frequent prophecy with the family that I should break my neck in this undertaking.

My experience with birds began as soon as I could walk, at my home, Hopewell Farm, in Wabash County, Indiana. As I recall our farm at that time, it was of unusual beauty, a perfect inland location for birds. The public highway ran north and south through the middle of the land. On the west of the road were a number of cultivated fields and one large tract of native timber. On the east of the road lay the residence, sur-rounded by a large, tree-filled dooryard, south of which was a garden, bright with flowers and shrubs. Behind the dooryard spread a very large orchard filled with apple trees and bordered with peach trees on three sides, with rare peach, plum, and pear trees on the fourth. A lane ran from the barnyard to a woods pasture where much of the heavy timber had been cut away leaving only a few large trees interspersed with berry bushes and thickets of wild rose and elder. Three streams of running wa-ter crossed the place, one flowing through the woods and rounding the foot of a steep hill south of the residence. A smaller one flowed in a par-allel direction on the north, both emptying into a larger stream coming from the north through our meadow and joining the Wabash River sev-eral miles south of us.

The land was new, a large part of it having been cleared and put into cultivation by my father. All of the wild growth was much ranker and more luxuriant than at the present time, while this was true also of every-thing we cultivated. My mother used the natural fertilizer from the poultry house and stable in her garden; the cleanings from the barn were scattered over the fields; but no other fertilizer ever was talked of at that time.

The flowers and all growth were more luxuriant than now because the soil was young, the temperature more equable. Summer always brought heavy rains every few days; long periods of heat and drought and cyclones or high, raging winds were unknown. As I recall, there were small flocks of birds for every *one* that is seen at the present time. We were taught to love the song birds for their beauty, their music, and the likeness of their life processes to ours. We were told that we must not harm a bird's nest because it would break the little mother bird's heart; but no one ever particularly impressed it upon us to protect them because the berry and fruit crops would fail if we did not. My father was the only person I ever heard mention the subject in my childhood. The birds' work as insect exterminators was not generally realized or taught at that time, while the spraying of fruit trees was unknown. When the trees had been pruned and the trunks given a thorough coat of whitewash, everything that was known to do for their care had been done; and so bounteous and fine were the fruit crops in my father's orchard that the whitewash was not used there, but I did see it in neighbouring orchards and dooryards.

I distinctly remember the swarms of birds that flocked over the cherry trees when the fruit was ripe, and the Babel of song that went up from the orchard, while the field birds were so numerous that we were always allowed to take the eggs from any quail nest we found, provided we first used the precaution of raking one egg from the nest with a long stick to see to what stage of incubation it had progressed. If the quail had not finished laying or had brooded only a few hours, we carried the eggs to the house, put them in cold water, boiled them for twelve minutes, let them cool in the water, and divided them among the children, as one of the greatest treats possible. No other egg I ever have tasted was so fine in grain and delicate in flavour. Despite the destruction we must have wrought in a season, the quail were so numerous that it was the custom to build traps of long, fine pieces of wood, covered with leaves, and set with a trigger, baited with grain. A trail of grain led to these traps, where from half a dozen up to twelve and more of the birds frequently imprisoned themselves at one time. The advantage over shooting was that the birds were in perfect condition when taken. Now, this seems a dreadful thing to have done, but at that time quail were so plentiful we never could distinguish any diminution in their numbers, while rabbits and squirrels were pests, which we had to fight to protect our fruit trees and for our comfort. After the cold weather set in at Thanksgiving time, we always had a large supply of frozen quail and rabbits hanging in the smokehouse for a treat upon the arrival of unexpected guests.

The only game bird, the protection of which I ever heard mentioned in my childhood, was the wild pigeon. My father never would allow our boys to go to the pigeon roosts, baffle the birds with the light of lanterns, club them, and carry them away by bagfuls, as some of our neighbours did. He said that such proceedings would eventually end in the extermination of the birds; that God gave us these creatures to enjoy but not to destroy; so he always cautioned all of us, either in hunting or fishing, to be content with a "moderate share." The prophecy he then made concerning the wild pigeons has found its fulfillment in my day, for a heavy reward has been offered for a number of years past for even one specimen of this beautiful bird, the metallic lustre of whose plumage made a gleam of light when on wing, and whose whistling flight was familiar music in my childhood. These birds now seem to have joined the extinct starlings of *Ile de la Réunion.*

All of the trees and most of the bushes surrounding the house were filled with bird nests. A privet bush in one corner of the garden always had at least one nest, while the grape arbour and berry bushes sheltered many. There were little cups of hair even among the currant and gooseberry bushes. Every bird that ever homed in an orchard in the Central States was to be found in the apple trees, in a big heap of trimmings at the back of the orchard, in the hollow rails of the fence, or in the grassy corners of our orchard. I think too that every bird of the fields was to be found in our meadow, our clover fields, and in the fence corners, while the big trees of the woods pasture and of the deep woods had their share of crows, hawks, owls; while twenty years after we moved away, a pair of golden eagles nested in the woods pasture, and were shot because they were carrying off small pigs and lambs. The female of this pair is my only mounted bird.

From my earliest recollection I was the friend and devoted champion of every bird that nested in the garden, on the fences, on the ground, in the bushes, in the dooryard, or in the orchard trees. From breakfast until dinner and from dinner until supper, almost my entire day was spent in making the rounds of these nests, watching the birds while they built, brooded, or fed their young, championing their cause against other children, cats, snakes, red squirrels, or larger animals such as skunks and foxes, which were so numerous that we held organized fox-chases for their extermination.

I was always on terms of the greatest intimacy with a pewee that built on a rafter supporting the roof of a log pig-pen. It was very easy to climb from a rail fence to the roof, then by working loose a clapboard near the nest I could watch the birds' daily life and make friends with them.

I do not recall one instance during my childhood when I ever intruded myself into the affairs of any bird in such a manner as to cause it to desert its nest location. I always approached by slow degrees, remained motionless a long time, and did the birds no harm whatever; so they very soon accepted me as a part of their daily life.

One of the heartbreaks of my childhood occurred when one of our hired men forgot his instructions and put up the third bar of an opening in one of the west field fences, which I had asked Father to have him leave down, because in the opening chiselled out to hold the bar was the nest of a chippy having four exquisite, speckled eggs. When I found this bar in place and could not remove it, I hurried to my father in a tumult of grief and anger which very nearly resulted in the dismissal of the man; but it was too late to save the bird and her nest.

I can not recall how many robin nests I located in a season, but there were two locations in which the robins built where access to them was especially convenient. One was a catalpa tree in the northwest corner of our dooryard, to the branches of which I could easily step from the front picket fence. In my morning rounds I always climbed to visit this robin, sitting on a branch talking to the brooding mother bird, almost always carrying her a worm or a berry in my apron pocket as a friendship offering. The other location was the early harvest apple tree of our orchard. This tree was especially designed by nature for the convenience of children in climbing. In the first place the tree grew at an angle, and in the second it had a growth as large as a good-sized butter bowl on the top side which was in the proper position to make a first step in the ascent of the tree. We used to start a few rods away on the run, take this first step, which brought us in reach of the nearest branch, and from there we went up the tree almost as swiftly as we ran along the path. I can not recall one spring of my childhood in which the robins did not have at least one nest in this tree.

Coming from it early one summer morning I heard the crack of my father's rifle in the dooryard, then I saw a big bird whirling to earth in the milk yard, which adjoined the garden on one side, the orchard on the other. I saw my father start toward the bird, so as fast as possible I sped after him, my bare feet making no sound on the hard, worn path. A large chicken hawk was sitting back on his tail, one wing stiffly extended, the tip hanging broken and bleeding, while in the bird's eyes there was a look of commingled pain, fear, and regal defiance that drove me out of my senses. My father grasped his rifle by the barrel. As the butt came whirling around, I sprang before him and sheltered the hawk with my body, the gun whizzing past my head so close that the rush of air fanned my face. My father dragged me away.

"Are you mad?" he cried. "I barely missed braining you!"

"I'd rather you did hit me," I answered, "than to have you strike a bird when its eyes are like that! Oh, Father, please don't kill him! He never can fly again. Give him to me! Do please give him to me!"

"Keep back!" cried my father. "He will tear your face!"

Father was an ordained minister, better versed in Biblical history than any other man I ever have known intimately. To him, "hawk" meant "Ayit." This old Hebrew word, literally translated, means "to tear and scratch the face." That is exactly what a hawk meant to my father; the word and bird were synonymous. To me, it meant something very different, because I had watched this pair of kingly birds carry heavy sticks and limbs, with which they had built a nest in a big oak tree overhanging a bank of the brook that ran through our meadow. The structure was bigger than a bushel basket, but no one else of our family knew about it, because it was well screened by the leaves of the tree. It was part of my self-imposed, daily task to gather up from the bank skeletons of any wild bird, rabbit, or domestic fowl, which the hawks had dropped there, and consign them to the current so that the telltale evidence of their location was quickly carried down stream. I envied these birds their power to soar in the face of the wind, to ride with the stiff gale of a beating storm, or to hang motionless as if frozen in air, according to their will, as I envied nothing else on earth. I had haunted the region of this nest so long that I knew it contained a mother bird and a pair of young big enough to look down at me over the edge of the nest, while I was quite sure that the birds were as well acquainted with me as I was with them.

So, for the first time in my life, I contradicted my father.

"He won't!" I cried. "This bird knows me. He knows I would not hurt him. Oh, do please give him to me!"

To prove my assertion, I twisted from my father's grasp and laid my hands on the bird. The hawk huddled against me for protection. In a choice between a towering man who threatened with a rifle and the familiar figure of a child who offered protection, is it any wonder that the bird preferred the child? My father gazed at us in amazement.

"God knows I do not understand you," he said in all reverence. "Keep the bird, if you think you can!"

After my father had gone, the hawk began to revive from the shock. He was not so friendly as I had hoped he would be. In fact, he showed decided signs of wanting to scratch and bite. I did not know how to begin caring for him. My first thought was that he should be in a shady place, where he could have something to perch upon. I hunted a long stick and by patient manœuvering drove him to the woodhouse, where he climbed to the highest part of the corded wood. There he sat in sullen suffering for the remainder of the day. The next morning I went to him very early. I thought that after a day and a night with a broken wing and without food or drink he would surely allow me to care for him. I cautiously approached him with a basin of water. He drew back as far as he could crowd into a corner. I had always heard that wounded soldiers were frantic for water, so I patiently held the basin before the bird, dabbling and splashing to show him that it contained water. Suddenly, he thrust in his beak and drank like a famished creature. Then I offered him some scraped meat, which he finally took from the end of a stick. The flies began to cluster over the broken wing, and I knew that that must be stopped; so with one clip of the sheep shears I cut through the skin and muscle that held the dangling tip. The bird uttered a shrill scream, but he did not attack me. Then I poured cold water over the hurt wing, which was kept stiffly extended, until it was washed clean. From the time I put the cold water on, the bird ceased even to threaten me. He seemed to realize that his pain was relieved. Then I went into the house to ask my mother if there was not something in her medicine chest that would help heal the wound and keep away the flies. She thought that there was, and as she measured out a white powder for me, she smiled and said: "What a little bird woman you are!"

In two weeks, the hawk was as well as he ever could be. By that time he would take food from my fingers and allow me to do anything I chose for him. Inside of a month he followed me through the dooryard, woodyard, and garden much like a dog, although he was a very awkward walker, probably having had less use for his feet in walking than in carrying and holding prey. There were times when birds of his kind, often his mate without doubt, swept low above us. Then he would beat his wings and try frantically to fly. Sometimes he followed them with his despairing eyes as they sailed from sight, and sent after them a scream that never failed to set my heart aching. At such times I could scarcely forgive my father for having deprived such a royal bird of his high estate. Although he never said so, I believe from after events that my father had the same feeling.

By this time I had become known in the family as the unfailing friend of the birds. Every unfortunate bird caught in a reaper, wounded by having been stepped on by stock, or that had escaped from the attack of a cat, a red squirrel, or a snake, was brought to me for treatment. No one told me how to care for them. I was so intimate with each different kind that when a member of any bird family was brought to me I tried to do for it what seemed to be the right thing for a bird of its species. I think that in doctoring them I copied very closely the methods of my mother in treating our hurts.

"A Gift of the Birds"

THE FOLLOWING YEAR, one morning in early spring, my father called me to him to ask whether I should like to have as a gift the most beautiful thing ever made by man. Of course I eagerly assured him that I should like it very much indeed. Then he told me that he had something for me even finer and more precious than anything man ever had made or ever could make: a gift straight from the hands of the Creator. He then proceeded formally to present me with the personal and indisputable ownership of each bird of every description that made its home on his land. Undoubtedly the completeness of this gift was influenced by his experience with the hawk. Before that time if he had been making such a gift I think he undoubtedly would have reserved the right to exterminate the hawks that preyed on the fields and poultry, the owls that infested the barns and chicken houses, and very probably, too, the woodpeckers, which seemed to take even more of the cherries than did the robins, orioles, or tanagers. That he made the gift complete, with no reservations, proved that he had learned to regard my regard for the laws of nature, which, even when very young, I seemed dimly to realize and stoutly to maintain; for the worst hawk or owl was quite as dear to me and fully as interesting as the most exquisitely coloured and ecstatic singer. He must have realized that the gift would not be perfect to me if there were exemptions, so he gave me for my very own not only the birds of free, wild flight with flaming colour and thrilling song, with nests of wonder, jewels of eggs, and queer little babies, but also the high flying, wide winged denizens of the big woods, which homed in hollow trees and on large branches, far removed from any personal contact I might ever hope to have with them.

Such is the natural greed of human nature that even while he was talking to me I was making a flashing mental inventory of *my property,* for now I owned the hummingbirds, dressed in green satin with ruby jewels on their throats; the plucky little brown wren that sang by the hour to his mate from the top of the pump, even in a hard rain; the green warbler, nesting in a magnificent specimen of wild sweetbriar beside the back porch; and the song sparrow in the ground cedar beside the fence. The bluebirds, with their breasts of earth's brown and their backs of Heaven's deepest blue; the robin, the rain song of which my father loved more than the notes of any other bird, belonged to me. The flaming cardinal and his Quaker mate, keeping house on a flat limb within ten feet of our front door, were mine; and every bird of the black silk throng that lived in the top branches of four big evergreens in front of our home was mine. The oriole, spilling notes of molten sweetness, as it shot like a ray of detached sunshine to its nest in the chestnut tree across the road was mine; while down beside the north creek, on a top branch of a willow sheltering an immense bed of blue calamus, nested a blood-red tanager, with black velvet wings. Every person visiting our family was taken to see him. With what pride I contemplated my next personally conducted trip to that tree to show the bird of blood-red! Now I owned the pewees in their marvellous little nest under the pig-pen roof, the song sparrow and the indigo finches of the privet bush at the foot of the garden, the swifts of our living room chimney, the swallows on the barn rafters, and the martins under the eaves. When it came to the orchard with its fruit trees and its shrub-filled snake fence corners of bloom and berries, I could not even begin to enumerate the vireos and bluebirds, the catbirds, robins, jays, and thrushes. Mine, too, was the friendly, delicately coloured cuckoo, slipping through the shrub-filled fence corners and bushes of the woods pasture, with his never failing prediction of rain. I remember that in the first moment of tumultuous joy, one thought was to hope that a storm would come soon so that I might remark in careless, proprietary tones: "Hear my cuckoo calling for rain!"

In my enumeration, I included the queer little stilt-legged killdeer that had a nest on the creek bank of the meadow. I was on terms of such intimacy with her during the last few days of her brooding that she would take food from my fingers and even allow me to stroke her wing. There was another pair of hawks nesting in the big oak overhanging the brook a short distance farther in its course to the south; while I was as proud to possess the owls, from every little brown screecher in a hollow apple tree of the orchard to the great horned hooter of the big woods, as I was the finest song and game birds. In the greed of my small soul I saw myself ordering my brothers and sisters never again to take the eggs from any quail nest of the fence corners. I do not recall that I made a virtuous resolve at that minute not to take any more myself, but I do remember that the next time I found a nest of eggs it occurred to me that if I left them to hatch I should have that many more birds, so I never robbed another nest. In that hour I was almost dazed with the wonder and the marvel of my gift, and to-day, after a lifetime of experience among the birds, this gift seems even more wonderful than it did then.

That same day the search began for new treasures. No queen on her throne, I am sure, ever felt so rich or so proud as the little girl who owned every bird on her father's land. Ever since I could remember I had loved, to the best of my ability, protected, and doctored the birds, but I never before had realized that they were quite so wonderful. From that hour in which they became my personal property every bird of them took on new beauty of colouring, new grace in flight, and previously unnoted sweetness of song. So with the natural acquisitiveness of human nature I began a systematic search to increase my possessions. I climbed every tree in the dooryard and looked over the branches carefully. Not a sweet scented shrub, a honeysuckle, a lilac, a syringa, a rose bush, or a savin escaped my exploring eyes. Then I proceeded to the garden, and one by one I searched the currant, gooseberry, blackberry, and raspberry bushes, the grape arbour, the vines clambering over the fence, and the trees and shrubs of its corners. Then I went over each vine-covered section of the fence enclosing the dooryard, hunting for nests set flat on the cross-pieces. I almost tore the hair from my head, while I did tear my apron to pieces and scratched my face, hands, and feet to bleeding in my minute exploration of the big berry patch east of the dooryard, where the Lawton blackberries grew high above my head. Then I extended my search to every corner of the fence enclosing the orchard and took its dozens of trees one at a time, climbing those that I could and standing motionless under those that I could not, intently watching until I am sure that few, if any, nests were overlooked. After that I gave the buggy-shed, the corn cribs, the pig-pens, and the barn a careful examination and then followed the lane fences to the woods pasture in one direction and to the woods in the other. Lastly, I went with my brothers to the fields, and while they cultivated the crops, I searched the enclosing snake fences, with their corner triangles of green, filled with bushes and trees. It is my firm conviction that at that time there were, at the most conservative estimate, fifteen birds to every one that can be located in an equally propitious place and the same amount of territory to-day. Before I had finished my inventory I had so many nests that it was manifestly impossible for me to visit all of them in a day; so I selected sixty of those, which were most conveniently located and belonged to the rarest and most beautiful birds, giving them undivided attention and contenting myself with being able to point out, describe, and boast about the remainder.

As always ownership brought its cares. At once an unusual sense of watchfulness developed. No landholder was ever more eager to add to his acres than I was to increase my flock of birds. My first act was to beg my mother for an old teaspoon that I might have to keep. A green warbler in the gooseberry bushes, when stepping into her nest, had pierced the shell of an egg with the sharp nail of one of her toes. If the broken egg began to leak, it would stick to and soil the others and the nest. I was afraid to put my fingers into the small hair-lined cup, so I secured the spoon for this purpose and afterward always carried it in my apron pocket.

Life became one round of battles with cats, snakes, and red squirrels, while crows and jays were not to be trusted near the nests and the young of other birds. It was a long, tedious task to make friends with the builders of each of the chosen nests, for I was forced to approach very slowly and with extreme caution, imitating the call note of the bird the best I could; and when I had gone so near a nest that the brooding mother began to plaster her feathers flat to her body, to draw up her wings, the light of fear began to shine in her beady eyes, and she started to rise to her feet, it was time for me to pause until she regained her confidence and again settled to brooding. Almost always at this point a few more steps could be taken. I usually contented myself with leaving a little of the food that the bird being approached liked best to eat. On going back the following day, it would be possible to advance with confidence as far as I had gone the day before; from there on I would be forced again to work my way slowly and cautiously toward the nest. In this manner gradually the confidence of the mothers could be won so completely that it was permissible to touch them while they brooded. Some of the friendliest would look at me steadily for a long time and then, with a dart so quick that I had to watch myself lest I shrink back and frighten them, they would snatch the worm or berry held before them.

At that time I sincerely thought that it was my work to help those birds feed their young. Half of my breakfast slipped into my apron pockets, while I worked like the proverbial beaver searching the bushes for bugs, hunting worms on the cabbages in the garden, digging them from the earth, and gathering berries and soft fruits. I carried with me grain from the bins in the barns, pounded fine with the hammer and soaked until it was soft for the young of the grain and seed eaters. Few mothers were so careful about the food they fed their children. I gave those nestlings only one bite at a time, and never a morsel of anything until I had watched what it was that the old birds were giving them. Before the nesting season was over they allowed me to take the most wonderful liberties with them. Warblers, Phoebes, sparrows, and finches swarmed all over me, perching indiscriminately on my head, shoulders, and hands, while I stood beside their nests, feeding their young.

When it was decided that I had reached a suitable age to attend a city school, I stoutly rebelled, capitulating only when Father said the most precious of my birds might go with me. These, of course, were unfortunates that had fallen from their nests in high trees, where I could not replace them, those orphaned by an accident or some prowling creature, while sometimes a nest of young birds was brought me by a neighbour who thought he was doing me a kindness; so I left the country in company with nine birds, none smaller than a grosbeak, that had been raised by hand. I had to arrange my school day so that there was a morning hour in which to clean the cages, change sand, scrape perches, scour bath-tubs, and cook food.

My especial favourite among my pets was a brown thrasher named Peter, because he had constantly called: "Pe-ter, Pe-ter" in the distressful days when he was missing his mother and growing accustomed to my longer intervals between feedings. One of my brothers had found him helpless and dying beside a country road and had picked him up and put him in his pocket for me. When he was given into my care, he was half-starved. After a few minutes, he opened his bill for food, and in a short time spent in getting acquainted we became the greatest friends. He grew to be a strong, fine, male bird, and in the spring of his second year developed a remarkably sweet voice, with which he imitated the song of every bird that could be heard around our house. He also made excursions into improvisations, which I could not recognize as familiar bird notes. One warm night of summer my father suggested that Peter would be more comfortable if left on the veranda. That was a mistake. Either a screech owl or a rat attacked him in the night and broke the tip of one wing. In the morning Peter hopped from his open door and showed me his wing. We did all we could to comfort each other. I doctored him as in childhood I had doctored the hawk. I never shall forget the fortitude with which he bore the amputation, not struggling nor making the slightest effort to get away from me, although he cried pitifully. The wing soon healed, but Peter had lost his equilibrium. He never again could fly. Always before, he had had the freedom of the premises. Now he was forced to ride on my shoulder when I went out into the yard, or to hop after me. There was one particular apple tree of our dooryard in which there was a perch where I could learn a lesson much more easily than in school. While I studied, Peter hopped from branch to branch through the tree. One day under pressure of an especially difficult Latin translation I forgot to take Peter with me to the apple tree. A maid in the house saw that he was fretting to be with me, so she put him outside the door. I heard his call, realized he was coming, and climbed down as speedily as possible, but before I could reach him a prowling cat darted from under a shed and caught him. Powerless to give him any aid, I listened to his last, pitiful calls. With one exception he was the most interesting bird I ever raised by hand.

I still had left in my family a splendid cardinal that I think must surely have belonged to the bigger, brighter red birds of the West, a pair of our common Indiana cardinals, and a pair of rose-breasted grosbeaks with their family of four youngsters. The rose-breasted grosbeaks had built a nest in a tall maple tree growing between our sidewalk and the street. A night of high wind and driving rain broke from the tree the branch on which they had located and dropped it in our yard. From an upstairs window I noticed it early in the morning, my attention having been attracted by the distressing calls of the old birds. There was scarcely a trace of the nest to be found as it had been torn to pieces in the parting of the branches, but I did find every one of the four babies. They were too small for my ministrations, so I repaired the nest, put it in a cage, and set it beside the branch. In a short time the mother bird entered to feed the young. The door was held open with a long piece of string and as soon as she entered it closed. Then she was removed to a larger cage in the house. Inside of half an hour the father bird was captured in the same way. Then the cage was put in a partially darkened room with plenty of food and the parents allowed to take care of their young, which they did with scarcely a sign of protest. I was not particularly attached to this family. I merely helped them out of their predicament the best I knew how and when the young ones were old enough to become self-supporting all of them were given their freedom. During my last two years in school the work became so rigorous that I could not care for my pets and make a grade that would pass me, so reluctantly and not without many tears all of them were trained to become self-supporting and given their freedom.

WHAT DOES HE SAY?
"I shall not ask Jean Jacques Rousseau
If birds confabulate or no.
'T is clear that they were always able
To hold discourse—at least in fable."
       —Cowper.

"What Birds Say and Sing"

from *Homing with the Birds*

Gene Stratton Porter's keen ear is evidenced throughout her writings. In this excerpt from *Homing* she highlights the bird songs she learned so well, using them as introductions to the portraits of birdlife which are her specialty. She refers to Ernest Thompson Seton (1860–1946), author of some fifty books of wildlife lore.

ANOTHER OF OUR FRIENDS is the jay bird, a beauty in plumage, friendly in disposition, a good husband and father, but dangerous to the nests and eggs of other birds. His call note is high, clear, and rather antagonistic: "D'jay, d'jay," certainly an obtrusive and self-satisfied note. He asks no favour, courts no bird but his mate. He may utter this cry once or a dozen times. I always get the impression from it that he would not avoid trouble if he met it, and usually he finds it. Perched on a conspicuous branch in early spring, when other birds are singing mating songs, the bluejay sings: "Ge-rul-lup" over and over, making rather an attractive song of it. The bluejay notes that really are pleasing to my ear are those uttered by a number of jays having a party after nesting affairs are over, when they gather in the top branches of a tree and in soft tones tell each other to "fill the kittle, fill the tea-kittle," and there are times, when Father Jay perching near his nest looks at his mate with an expression of extreme devotion, and in whispered, throaty utterances says to her something that sounds to me like "Chinkle-chee-tinkle, tankle, tunkle! Rinkle, rankle runkle! Tee chee, twee?" The jay can imitate perfectly the "Killy, killy" notes of the sparrow hawk or the "Ke-ah" cry of the red-shoulder. For this reason, he can cause undue commotion in the woods. As an interpretation of jaybird character and notes a poem by LeRoy T. Weeks, published in *The Century* in 1906, is equal to any attempt I ever have seen. I should like to quote the entire poem, but must content myself with a few lines of two verses:

"Saucy imp in white and blue,
What's your title? Tell me true.
Comes the answer, sharp, metallic:
'Smart
    Aleck!
      Smart
        Aleck!'
"In the leaves near by,
Crooning to his nesting mate
Songs beyond me to translate:
'Tear,
    Tee,
      Twink,
        Twee!
Room for two—just you and me!' "

On fences surrounding an old orchard and the horse pasture every season we have the bobolink at the Cabin, north. He is commonly called by his tribal note: "Bob o' link" twice repeated, to which he usually adds: "Spink, spank, spink!" We have few, if any, birds that sing a longer song from the vantage of any fence post or wood stump around our meadow. This veritable music-box pours out his song, the whole of which is an interrupted run, interspersed with his call note and ravishing variations which run high and drop again in a sort of fantasy of irrepressible, spontaneous clearness. Many writers on bird song have been able to follow him through the first two repetitions of his name and a choice assortment of "spink, wink, tink, link," only to be forced to give up when the outpouring reaches flood tide. The description of a bobolink in song which called him an "irrepressible music-box" is the best that I have seen.

There are birds which at times fail us, but I can remember no season during which we have not had goldfinches nesting in the bushes around the edges of the woods, in the woods pasture, and beside the field fences of the Cabin, north. These birds come late, nest but once in a season, and after nesting spend the greater part of their time in country gardens. They pass back and forth from these to the woods, singing on wing, so that they sow the air with warbled notes, impossible to syllabify because they are of such bubbling spontaneity. Our gardens seem to be full of lettuce, vegetable oyster, radish, and flower seeds on which these birds feed, and they flock over and claim possession of the long rows of Mr. Burbank's red and brown sunflowers, the small seeds of which are much more appreciated by them than those of the large variety, which have seeds the size of a grain of corn and are awkward for the small bills of these birds. Flocking over the sunflowers they constantly pass back and forth to each other their tribal call in the form of a question: "See me? See me?" Then they have a shorter, detached cry sometimes uttered in an exclamatory way, sometimes given in answer to the "See me?" call. The nearest anyone has arrived at this cry rendered in our speech, is: "P'tseet!" I have had considerable experience with these birds and I frequently have heard the male bird give the "See me?" call and the female, brooding or feeding her young the "P'tseet" cry in answer. It appeared to me that these cries were used much as human beings would when a man asks, "Where are you?" and his wife answers, "Here."

There are three sparrows that always home in Wildflower Woods, particularly beside a winding private road leading from the woods across the fields and out to the public highway. In the buckthorn bushes bordering one side of this road, in the grasses creeping to the wheel tracks, in the wild rose bushes, and even under rankly growing flowers, these sparrows are always with us. One is the white throat, with his cry of "Chip, chip," crisply and tersely uttered when about the business of life, changing to nervous and excited tones when a snake or squirrel approaches the nest location. His song, in pure, sweet tones, but of monotonous delivery, is the famous "Old Sam Peabody" so human in utterance that country folk call him the "Peabody bird." His cousin the chipping sparrow has a call note which is a sharper, more tensely inflected "Chip," and a song of scarcely more than a persistently reiterated note which is the least interesting music of the sparrow family. The field sparrow uses the same call note, very similar to the others, and has a song which he varies in a number of ways. These songs are difficult to put into words, while the musician's ending is almost invariably a roll of piping trills, sweet and melodious. In the length of the road from the woods to the highway, we had seven nests of these birds the season of 1918.

The chewink is a bird which comes to us at every spring migration, industriously scratching the earth among the leaves and roots and making himself extremely familiar all around the Cabin, north, especially in the thickets near the spring. The birds have a very distinctive dress, the male being conspicuous for a black head and coat touched with white on the sleeves and tail, white shirt, and a russet vest never closed in front, merely showing before the folded wings. The female has lovely shades of the same colour. Her russet is lighter and where the male is black she is a soft, warm, dust colour, a shade as effective as dove colour, but difficult to describe. In the business of rearing their young these birds seem to be extremely uneasy about each other. They find almost all of their food on the ground, much of the time scratching among the leaves for it, so that they are the prey of snakes and rodents. The male's call, frequent and distinct, is "Chee-wink?" from which these birds take their name. Sometimes the female answers him with a reproduction of the note in exclamatory form, where his call is interrogative. One pair I worked with more intimately and for a longer time than with any other I have known. The female's answer was always plainly given: "Chee-wee!"

The song of the male bird starts in clear, whistled tones, and is one of those previously referred to as extremely disappointing in its ending. The notes raised to twice eight va., begin on D, rise to A, on to E four or five times repeated. The best translation I ever have seen is that of Thompson Seton, who hears the chewink sing: "Chuck-burr, pill-a-will-a-will-a-will!" Sometimes the musician sings on low shrubbery near his nest, but when he is really giving a concert he selects the top branch of the tallest tree in hearing of his mate and sings the song described, with several variations.

Because of the same colouring, this bird calls to mind the rose-breasted grosbeak, with which I was intimately acquainted in childhood and during my residence in Limberlost Cabin, south. The rose-breasted bird has not appeared to any extent in my new location, nor do I hear his notes save very rarely while in field work. He is conspicuously black and white like the male chewink, but on his white breast there is a splash of purplish blood-red. His call note is a high "Chink!" which does not very well describe the sound. He makes this cry extremely emphatic when he is anxious about his mate and eggs. His song is lovely, of even tone, continuous, and of almost perfect rendition. These notes are as difficult for an amateur to catch in pitch as the song of any field bird I know. Experts agree as to the attractive character of his song, although they differ in its interpretation, several prominent writers insisting that the bird warbles the notes, a thing I never heard him do in a lifetime of closest intimacy. I know the male bird to be as tender and devoted to the female as is the mate of the brooding dove. It may be for this reason that I find his notes toned and inflected with sentiment; for in much work with set cameras before the nest of this bird it has been my experience that every morning about ten o'clock he enters his nest and patiently broods while his mate takes a bath and finds her breakfast, about which she does not in the least hurry herself, for very frequently she fails to return before twelve and sometimes not until one o'clock.

Always beside the road and through the fields we have "Bob White" calls, and on summer evenings while the female quail are nesting, the males, perched on fence riders, prolong this call into a real musical performance by repeating the first note once and quavering the last, making the song: "Bob, Bob White!" The beauty of this performance depends very largely on the age and experience of the singer; old birds content, fullfed, and having had much experience in life and making music, develop a mellow, pleasing tone.

Two birds of summer, seldom seen but very frequently heard, are the yellow-billed and black-billed cuckoo. These birds are sneakers, travelling through shrubbery with a serpentine motion equalled only by the brown thrasher. Their nests are crudely constructed, their eggs large and pale blue, the bird's plumage a delicate grey dust colour with touches of white on wings and tail, the body long and slender, the head almost hawklike in shape, with exquisitely cut, curved beak. The tribal call of the yellow-bill begins with two or three preparatory notes and ends with four clear and distinctly enunciated ones. He says: "Ur-r-r-coulp, coulp, oulp, olp!" The black-bill, very similar in shape and colour with the exception of his black bill, and almost identical in habits, probably named the species by his cry: "Cowk-coo, cowk-coo, cowk-cu-coo, cowk-cu-coo." This is repeated five or six times. In the scene beside the brook in "The Pastoral Symphony," Beethoven used the song of the nightingale, the call of the quail, and the notes of the cuckoo. If this bird can be said to have a song, it is merely a repetition of its call notes differently accented and inflected.

A bird which reminds me of the cuckoo in the handling of his notes is the whippoorwill, named from his cries singly uttered. These constitute a call note. In trouble, he hisses almost like a hawk. In giving a musical performance, he employs the "Whip-poor-will," cry. The notes are differently accented by different birds, but most of the time in a show performance they manage to quaver the "poor" and one can hear a sort of catch of breath before the falling note, when the quaver is unusually long.

A distinctive note, without which no summer at the Cabin, north, would be perfect, is the clearly intoned, incisive cry of the scarlet tanager. With the Cabin site, which included the song sparrow, there was a tanager thrown in for good measure. The bird does not truly belong to me. He does his courting and food hunting in Wildflower Woods, but he builds his nest every year in a maple tree about six inches on my neighbour's side of the line fence. His tribal call "Chip-bird, chip-bird!" sounds constantly around the garage and through the grounds as near to the Cabin as the woodshed. I never have seen him visit the lake front even once. If I wish to show him off to visitors in all the glory of his bloody coat and black silk wings, I must take them to his location, which he hugs very closely. He is one of the latest birds to arrive, nests but once with me, and although he comes late he immediately takes a cold, which persists throughout the season. The manner of his song suggests the robin, with nothing like the robin's cheerily inflected tones. The tanager is a serene, lazy bird alike in lovemaking, nesting, paternity, and above all in his song. He never voices his utterances with a touch of the joy of the song sparrow or the goldfinch, and as for the emphasis of the cardinal, there is no such vim in his system. I know no combination of syllables that will give an idea of his song, for to reproduce his notes a human being would be compelled to hum and whistle at the same time. Any syllabication that could be strung together would abound in r's and suggest Spanish rather than pure American.

In all my experience afield, no one bird, which I might have expected to meet frequently, has been so scarce with me as the cedar waxwing, which I have met only once while the bird was on a pokeberry debauch. His nest I never have found. I knew him well in my childhood. He was one of the most frequent feeders on our cherry trees, and I once had a living specimen, slightly winged, in my fingers, and had the privilege of minutely examining the soft, exquisitely shaded feathers of his back and breast—not grey, not brown, not olive, not yellow, but the daintiest shades that could be formed from delicate mingling of all of them. His crest was shaped much like the cardinal's but carried mostly in a line horizontal with the beak. There were bars of yellow on his tail and red touches like wax on his secondaries, from which he takes the name of waxwing. His cry is a queer, whistled complaint like a gust of steam escaping from a small pipe, and higher than the last note on a piano. If he has a song, I never have heard it.

A bird with which I am extremely familiar through much experience around his nest, is the red-eyed vireo. His call note: "Preach-er, preach-er!" is constantly used as a nickname for him. His song is so divided and intoned that he lends colour to this translation of his tribal call. Wilson Flagg's inimitable interpretation of his song is the best that I have seen. He imagines the little orator standing in his pulpit of leafy green, addressing a feathered audience, at whom he shouts: "You see it! You know it! Do you hear me? Do you believe it?" My enjoyment of this translation of the red-eye's song does not prevent my giving the ideas of another expert in bird music, who sees nothing clerical about the bird and thinks he says: "Tom Kelly, whip Tom Kelly!" How he ever heard or imagined that the bird made a note that could be so translated, is a mystery to me. More pleasing is the version of the third writer, who makes the vireo a gourmand and hears him sing:

"Fat worms—plenty to eat—
Gobble 'em up—they're sweet—
Come, dear—don't delay—
I'm here—fly this way."

All these experts do agree upon seems to be that there is a pronounced oratorical effect about the bird's delivery, and that his song is broken into distinct groupings of notes.

The chestnut-sided warbler warbles a strain of bubbling, rolling notes after the manner of his kind, but his call note is a clear "T'see, t'see." To him is attributed the famous rendition of his song: "I wish, I wish, to see Miss Beecher." These words he enunciates as clearly as any killdeer or Bob White I ever heard afield.

Every spring our woods are full of warblers. On a day of warm, drizzling rain interspersed with bright sunshine, in May, 1918, the tall trees, with grape vines and bittersweet climbing in tangled masses through the tops, were used as a landing place for a whole flock of warblers, most of them seeming to be males that had arrived in spring migration during the night or early morning. By slipping into the location and remaining motionless against a tree for a few minutes, I saw countless little painted creatures, gleaming in strong tints of yellow and green, black and grey, blue and rose, while they sang a rolling chorus full of "See-see, zip-zee, wee, wee, tu, tu, 'tswee-e, zillup, zip, zip." Which note belonged to which bird it was out of the question to say in the dense foliage so nearly the delicate yellowish green of many of the birds that it was impossible to distinguish the green and yellow ones until they moved.

I have had several experiences working around the nest of a Maryland yellow-throat, but I can describe his call note no better than to say that it is a sweep of sound, which I can not express in syllables of even the crudest form, but when it comes to a song in tones distinctly human and clearly defined, the yellow-throat sings: "Witchery, witchery, witchery" and again: "What a pity," two or three times repeated. Then, like a breath of grace notes, he warbles: "You, you" followed by a clear tide of pure, full song: "I beseech you, I beseech you, I beseech you!" These notes are so clearly uttered and so charmingly intoned that there is no question whatever that the little singer would have his demands granted if he only would go so far as to say what it is that he wants.

Another of our star performers is the catbird, named from his tribal call: "Me-ouw" sometimes cut short and sometimes long-drawn, always of such feline quality that it is easy to see how he gained his common name. As a singer, he is one of our choicest. He sings a mocking conglomeration of high notes of the robin, chat, vireo, several of our best thrush singers, song sparrow, and oriole, while he intersperses this charmingly melodious performance with stray cries of the whippoorwill, killdeer, and quail, and he imitates the whistle of the redbird to perfection. He sings from the bushes, doing his best work by no rule about ten o'clock in the morning. No catbird ever sings twice the same, since he is so purely an imitator that he reproduces not only the sounds of birds around him, but also the crowing of the barnyard cock, the cries of the guinea and peacock, the squeal of the pig, bawl of the calf, the whinny of the colt. I have heard him reproduce even the rattle of wheels on the loose floor of a bridge spanning the Wabash River, while he could imitate the rattle of loose spindles in a cart-wheel to perfection.

I can think of no combination of letters, and I have found none in the writings of any ornithologist, that will reproduce the tribal call of the brown thrasher. It is a weird, wailing, whistled note. Because his song is a medley, it is usually compared with that of the catbird. The thrasher is a larger bird, and his first difference from the catbird lies in the fact that the catbird sings solely to please himself, while in seclusion. The thrasher seems to demand an audience. For exhibiting his best art, he selects the highest perch he can find, where he is sure to attract the attention of every bird and human in sound of his voice. Then, as a rule, he sings out loudly and clearly, although he can drop to a faint whisper of sound when he chooses. His second difference from the catbird lies in the fact that, while he starts in to give a public recital he presently becomes so entranced with his own remarkable performance that he grasps the twig upon which he perches, presses his wings tight to his sides, ruffles the feathers of his breast and back until his wings are obscured, and tucks his tail until a line dropped from the point of his beak straight down would very nearly touch the tail tip. From a widely parted beak he pours out a rolling volume of song that even the most expert collector of birds' records never succeeds in truthfully reproducing. His is a more colourful and spectacular performance than the catbird's, but to me the little grey bird, hanging on an elder over the spring, doing all nature from the goldfinch coasting on waves of summer air above him to the soft gurgle of the running water below, is the more finished performer. To the brown thrasher has been attributed the following advice to farmers:

"Shuck it! Shuck it! Sow it! Sow it;
Plow it! Plow it! Hoe it! Hoe it!"

and by some this has been elaborated to include starting in a hurry, harrowing, seeding, covering, raking in, pushing in, weeding, pulling up, ending with, "Leave it alone!"

The choicest singer that belongs to my personal choir of birds at the Cabin, north, is the wood thrush, a bird which I love to call the "bell bird" on account of the exquisite bell-toned sweetness of his notes. His home is in a spice thicket over and surrounding a pool in the deepest woods behind the ice-house. I am very familiar with this bird, as a number of times I have set up my camera in front of his nest. The tribal call is a wispy whisper. The song, as nearly as it can be expressed, is: "A-e-o-lee." Each note is dropped into the dim green of our woods like a pearl slowly slipping from a thread of pure gold. No bird of field or forest can surpass him, with the exception of the hermit thrush. The hermit is his relative, not quite so highly coloured as the wood thrush, even shyer, and more timid, seeking deeper woods and more seclusion for his nest. Many people consider the hermit's song the purest, loveliest bird notes. A free translation of what he sings might be summed up: "Oh fear all! Oh holy! Oh holy! Oh Klêräh-wäh! Klêr-äh!" The wood thrushes sing in slightly faster time, with a touch of passion's more colourful note at nesting time, and I think this also is true of the hermits; but when they sing the latter part of August from four in the afternoon to six in the evening, their notes are pure, cool, high, and passionless so that no other bird's song surpasses them.

One of our earliest arrivals and one that remains with us until late in the fall is an ever-welcome signal of spring with me. I am quite sure that I am wide awake every spring at the sound of the first note of the killdeer over the lake. He always comes calling about half past three or four in the morning, crying in tones that one could imagine were plaintive, if it were not remembered that the bird is coming home and probably as happy to arrive as a human being after a time of exile. I feel bound to claim my location as the home of the killdeer, because he comes to me sometimes in late February, always in March, and stays until late November, and where a bird or human spends nine months out of twelve certainly is the location that could be justly called home for him. This bird has a plaintive tribal call, as it flashes around the lake shore, sweeping low on wing, trying to guard the flashing feet of its young too small to fly. At these times, the old bird cries: "Te-dit! te-dit!" and the youngsters take up this cry in the cunningest baby talk that it has been my experience to hear among any youngsters of birdland.

In commonly accepted interpretation of what the birds say, I once wrote the following for the children of Limberlost Cabin:

BOB WHITE AND PHOEBE BEECHER

Bob White tilled the acres of an Indiana farm,
Phoebe Beecher was his neighbour, full of youthful charm.
As Bob did his farming, Phoebe lingered near.
The birds all helped him woo her, with their notes of cheer.

"Spring o' year! Spring o' year!" larks cried overhead.
"Wet! Wet! Wet!" the gaudy flickers said.
"I'll never finish plowing!" cried the discouraged fellow.
"What a pity! What a pity!" wailed a bird with throat of yellow.

"Yankey! Yankey! Yank! Yank! Yank!" jeered a nuthatch grey.
"Hire old Sam Peabody! Old Sam Peabody!" Bob heard a sparrow say.
"T'check! T'check! T'check!" came the blackbird's pert refrain:
"Phoebe'll never have a man who's scared of a little rain."

"Cheer up! Cheer up! Cheer up, dearie!" the robins sang to Bob;
"Cheer up, dearie! Cheer up, dearie! we'll help you with the job."
"Shuck it! Shuck it! Sow it! Sow it!" advised a bird of brown;
"Plow it! Plow it! Hoe it! Hoe it! Go it! Hoe it down!"

"Bob, Bob White!" the unseen quail whistled from the clover.
"I'm plowing," answered Robert, to the saucy mocking rover.
"Phoebe! Phoebe! Phoebe!" sweet the pewee cried.
"She's coming down the lane," the happy Bob replied.

"Witchery! Witchery! Witchery!" sang a warbler gay.
"She has me worse bewitched," said Bob, "every blessed day."
"Come to me! Come to me!" intoned a woodland thrush.
"Come to me! Come to me!" Bob echoed with a blush.

"I beseech you! I beseech you!" sang a bird of golden throat.
"I beseech you! I beseech you!" Bob caught up the note.
"I love, I love, I love you!" the olive thrush repeated;
"I love, I love you, Phoebe," the joyful Bob entreated.

"Kiss her! Kiss her! Kiss her!" advised the bobolink.
Bob took his advice and kissed her quick as wink.
Chestnut Warbler warbled: "I wish, I wish to see Miss Beecher—"
"Preacher! Preacher!" cried the vireo. "Somebody bring a preacher!"

Song of the Cardinal

from *The Song of the Cardinal*

From her early investigations of the habits of the birds at Hopewell Farms, and inspired by finding on the roadway the body of a cardinal which had been shot, Gene Stratton Porter set out to write a book which would help others feel the reverence she felt for the natural world.

Abjuring a human story, she chose instead to write her first novel as the story of a cardinal. The male cardinal who is the protagonist of the novel begins life in the Limberlost Swamp, but as a juvenile he becomes discontented with the swamp climate and flies off in search of more open territory. He discovers the banks of the Wabash River; yet although he has set his heart on life along the river, he must still migrate to Florida for the winter. In Florida, his family attempts to replicate the swampy conditions up north by choosing the Everglades as a winter home. At this point, the cardinal makes his break from his family and finds a winter home in an orange grove, where a young girl becomes so beguiled by him she treats him to special foods and answers his calls. In the spring he returns to the north, and—back on the Wabash— begins the serious business of finding a mate. It is at this point that our selection from the novel begins, the descriptions of the riparian environment being among the finer touches.

H E WENT TO THE RIVER to bathe. After finding a spot where the water flowed crystal-clear over a bed of white limestone, he washed until he felt that he could be no cleaner. Then the Cardinal went to his favourite sun-parlour, and stretching on a limb, he stood his feathers on end, and sunned, fluffed and prinked until he was immaculate.

On the tip-top antler of the old stag sumac, he perched and strained until his jetty whiskers appeared stubby. He poured out a tumultuous cry vibrant with every passion raging in him. He caught up his own rolling echoes and changed and varied them. He improvised, and set the shining river ringing, "Wet year! Wet year!"

He whistled and whistled until all birdland and even mankind heard, for the farmer paused at his kitchen door, with his pails of foaming milk, and called to his wife:

"Hear that, Maria! Jest hear it! I swanny, if that bird doesn't stop predictin' wet weather, I'll get so scared I won't durst put in my corn afore June. They's some birds like killdeers an' bobwhites 'at can make things pretty plain, but I never heard a bird 'at could jest speak words out clear an' distinct like that fellow. Seems to come from the river bottom. B'lieve I'll jest step down that way an' see if the lower field is ready for the plow yet."

"Abram Johnson," said his wife, "bein's you set up for an honest man, if you want to trapes through slush an' drizzle a half-mile to see a bird, why say so, but don't for land's sake lay it on to plowin' 'at you know in all conscience won't be ready for a week yet 'thout pretendin' to look."

Abram grinned sheepishly. "I'm willin' to call it the bird if you are, Maria. I've been hearin' him from the barn all day, an' there's somethin' kind o' human in his notes 'at takes me jest a little diffrunt from any other bird I ever noticed. I'm really curious to set eyes on him. Seemed to me from his singin' out to the barn, it 'ud be mighty near like meetin' folks."

"Bosh!" exclaimed Maria. "I don't s'pose he sings a mite better 'an any other bird. It's jest the old Wabash rollin' up the echoes. A bird singin' beside the river always sounds twict as fine as one on the hills. I've knowed that for forty year. Chances are 'at he'll be gone 'fore you get there."

As Abram opened the door, "Wet year! Wet year!" pealed the flaming prophet.

He went out, closing the door softly, and with an utter disregard for the corn field, made a bee line for the musician.

"I don't know as this is the best for twinges o' rheumatiz," he muttered, as he turned up his collar and drew his old hat lower to keep the splashing drops from his face. "I don't jest rightly s'pose I should go; but I'm free to admit I'd as lief be dead as not to answer when I get a call, an' the fact is, I'm *called* down beside the river."

"Wet year! Wet year!" rolled the Cardinal's prediction.

"Thanky, old fellow! Glad to hear you! Didn't jest need the information, but I got my bearin's rightly from it! I can about pick out your bush, an' it's well along towards evenin', too, an' must be mighty near your bedtime. Looks as if you might be stayin' round these parts! I'd like it powerful well if you'd settle right here, say 'bout where you are. An' where are you, anyway?"

Abram went peering and dodging beside the fence, peeping into the bushes, searching for the bird. Suddenly there was a whir of wings and a streak of crimson.

"Scared you into the next county, I s'pose," he muttered.

But it came nearer being a scared man than a frightened bird, for the Cardinal flashed straight toward him until only a few yards away, and then, swaying on a bush, it chipped, cheered, peeked, whistled broken notes, and manifested perfect delight at the sight of the white-haired old man. Abram stared in astonishment.

"Lord A'mighty!" he gasped. "Big as a blackbird, red as a live coal, an' a-comin' right at me. You are somebody's pet, that's what you are! An' no, you ain't either. Settin' on a sawed stick in a little wire house takes all the ginger out of any bird, an' their feathers are always mussy. Inside o' a cage never saw you, for they ain't a feather out o' place on you. You are finer'n a piece o' red satin. An' you got that way o' swingin' an' dancin' an' high-steppin' right out in God A'mighty's big woods, a teeterin' in the wind, an' a dartin' 'crost the water. Cage never touched you! But you are somebody's pet jest the same. An' I look like the man, an' you are tryin' to tell me so, by gum!"

Leaning toward Abram, the Cardinal turned his head from side to side, and peered, "chipped," and waited for an answering "Chip" from a little golden-haired child, but there was no way for the man to know that.

"It's jest as sure as fate," he said. "You think you know me, an' you are tryin' to tell me somethin'. Wish to land I knowed what you want! Are you tryin' to tell me 'Howdy'? Well, I don't 'low nobody to be politer 'an I am, so far as I know."

Abram lifted his old hat, and the raindrops glistened on his white hair. He squared his shoulders and stood very erect.

"Howdy, Mr. Redbird! How d'ye find yerself this evenin'? I don't jest riccolict ever seein' you before, but I'll never meet you agin 'thout knowin' you. When d'you arrive? Come through by the special midnight flyer, did you? Well, you never was more welcome any place in your life. I'd give a right smart sum this minnit if you'd say you came to settle on this river bank. How do you like it? To my mind it's jest as near Paradise as you'll strike on earth.

"Old Wabash is a twister for curvin' and windin' round, an' it's lime-stone bed half the way, an' the water's as pretty an' clear as in Maria's springhouse. An' as for trimmin', why say, Mr. Redbird, I'll jest leave it to you if she ain't all trimmed up like a woman's spring bunnit. Look at the grass a-creepin' right down till it's a trailin' in the water! Did you ever see jest quite such fine fringy willers? An' you wait a little, an' the flowerin' mallows 'at grows long the shinin' old river are fine as garden holly-hocks. Maria says 'at they'd be purtier 'an hers if they were only double; but, Lord, Mr. Redbird, they are! See 'em once on the bank, an' agin in the water! An' back a little an' there's jest thickets of papaw, an' thorns, an' wild grape-vines, an' crab, an' red an' black haw, an' dogwood, an' su-mac, an' spicebush, an' trees! Lord! Mr. Redbird, the sycamores, an' ma-ples, an' tulip, an' ash, an' elm trees are so bustin' fine 'long the old Wabash they put 'em into poetry books an' sing songs about 'em. What do you think o' that? Jest back o' you a little there's a sycamore split into five trunks, any one o' them a famous big tree, tops up 'mong the clouds, an' roots diggin' under the old river; an' over a little farther's a maple 'at's eight big trees in one. Most anything you can name, you can find it 'long this ole Wabash, if you only know where to hunt for it.

"They's mighty few white men takes the trouble to look, but the In-dians used to know. They'd come canoein' an' fishin' down the river an' camp under these very trees, an' Ma 'ud git so mad at the old squaws. Settlers wasn't so thick then, an' you had to be mighty careful not to rile 'em, an' they'd come a-trapesin' with their wild berries. Woods full o' berries! Anybody could get 'em by the bushel for the pickin', an' we had-n't got on to raisin' much wheat, an' had to carry it on horses over into Ohio to get it milled. Took Pa five days to make the trip; an' then the blame old squaws 'ud come, an' Ma 'ud be compelled to hand over to 'em her big white loaves. Jest about set her plumb crazy. Used to get up in the night, an' fix her yeast, an' bake, an' let the oven cool, an' hide the bread out in the wheat bin, an' get the smell of it all out o' the house by good daylight, so's 'at she could say there wasn't a loaf in the cabin. Oh! if it's good pickin' you're after, they's berries for all creation 'long the river yet; an' jest wait a few days till old April gets done showerin' an' I plow this corn field!"

Abram set a foot on the third rail and leaned his elbows on the top. The Cardinal chipped delightedly and hopped and tilted closer.

"I hadn't jest 'lowed all winter I'd tackle this field again. I've turned it every spring for forty year. Bought it when I was a young fellow, jest married to Maria. Shouldered a big debt on it; but I always loved these slopin' fields, an' my share of this old Wabash hasn't been for sale nor tradin' any time this past forty year. I've hung on to it like grim death, for it's jest that much o' Paradise I'm plumb sure of. First time I plowed this field, Mr. Redbird, I only hit the high places. Jest married Maria, an' I didn't touch earth any too frequent all that summer. I've plowed it every year since, an' I've been 'lowin' all this winter, when the rheumatiz was gettin' in its work, 'at I'd give it up this spring an' turn it to medder; but I don't know. Once I got started, b'lieve I could go it all right an' not feel it so much, if you'd stay to cheer me up a little an' post me on the weather. Hate the doggondest to own I'm worsted, an' if you say it's stay, b'lieve I'll try it. Very sight o' you kinder warms the cockles o' my heart all up, an' every skip you take sets me a-wantin' to be jumpin', too.

"What on earth are you lookin' for? Man! I b'lieve it's grub! Somebody's been feedin' you! An' you want me to keep it up? Well, you struck it all right, Mr. Redbird. Feed you? You bet I will! You needn't even 'rastle for grubs if you don't want to. Like as not you're feelin' hungry right now, pickin' bein' so slim these airly days. Land's sake! I hope you don't feel you've come too soon. I'll fetch you everything on the place it's likely a redbird ever teched, airly in the mornin' if you'll say you'll stay an' wave your torch 'long my river bank this summer. I haven't a scrap about me now. Yes, I have, too! Here's a handful o' corn I was takin' to the banty rooster; but shucks! he's fat as a young shoat now. Corn's a leetle big an' hard for you. Mebby I can split it up a mite."

Abram took out his jack-knife, and dotting a row of grains along the top rail, he split and shaved them down as fine as possible; and as he reached one end of the rail, the Cardinal, with a spasmodic "Chip!" dashed down and snatched a particle from the other, and flashed back to the bush, tested, approved, and chipped his thanks.

"Pshaw now!" said Abram, staring wide-eyed. "Doesn't that beat you? So you really are a pet? Best kind of a pet in the whole world, too! Makin' everybody 'at sees you happy, an' havin' some chance to be happy yourself. An' I look like your friend? Well! Well! I'm monstrous willin' to adopt you if you'll take me; an', as for feedin', from to-morrow on I'll find time to set your little table 'long this same rail every day. I s'pose Maria 'ull say 'at I'm gone plumb crazy; but, for that matter, if I ever get her down to see you jest once, the trick's done with her, too, for you're the prettiest thing God ever made in the shape of a bird, 'at I ever saw. Look at that topknot a wavin' in the wind! Maybe praise to the face is open dis-grace; but I'll take your share an' mine, too, an' tell you right here an' now 'at you're the blamedest prettiest thing 'at I ever saw.

"But Lord! You ortn't be so careless! Don't you know you ain't noth-in' but jest a target? Why don't you keep out o' sight a little? You come a-shinneyin' up to nine out o' ten men 'long the river like this, an' your purty, coaxin', palaverin' way won't save a feather on you. You'll get the little red heart shot plumb outen your little red body, an' that's what you'll get. It's a dratted shame! An' there's law to protect you, too. They's a good big fine for killin' such as you, but nobody seems to push it. Every fool wants to test his aim, an' you're the brightest thing on the river bank for a mark.

"Well, if you'll stay right where you are, it 'ull be a sorry day for any cuss 'at teches you; 'at I'll promise you, Mr. Redbird. This land's mine, an' if you locate on it, you're mine till time to go back to that other old fellow 'at looks like me. Wonder if he's any willinger to feed you an' stand up for you 'an I am?"

"Here! Here! Here!" whistled the Cardinal.

"Well, I'm mighty glad if you're sayin' you'll stay! Guess it will be all right if you don't meet some o' them Limberlost hens an' tole off to the swamp. Lord! the Limberlost ain't to be compared with the river, Mr. Redbird. You're foolish if you go! Talkin' 'bout goin', I must be goin' myself, or Maria will be comin' down the line fence with the lantern; an', come to think of it, I'm a little moist, not to say downright damp. But then you *warned* me, didn't you, old fellow? Well, I told Maria seein' you 'ud be like meetin' folks, an' it has been. Good deal more'n I counted on, an' I've talked more'n I have in a whole year. Hardly think now 'at I've the reputation o' being a mighty quiet fellow, would you?"

Abram straightened and touched his hat brim in a trim half military salute. "Well, good-bye, Mr. Redbird. Never had more pleasure meetin' anybody in my life 'cept first time I met Maria. You think about the plowin', an', if you say 'stay', it's a go! Good-bye; an' do be a little more careful o' yourself. See you in the mornin', right after breakfast, no count taken o' the weather."

"Wet year! Wet year!" called the Cardinal after his retreating figure.

Abram turned and gravely saluted the second time. The Cardinal went to the top rail and feasted on the sweet grains of corn until his craw was full, and then nestled in the sumac and went to sleep. Early next morning he was abroad and in fine toilet, and with a full voice from the top of the sumac greeted the day—"Wet year! Wet year!"

Far down the river echoed his voice until it so closely resembled some member of his family replying that he followed, searching the banks mile after mile on either side, until finally he heard voices of his kind. He located them, but it was only several staid old couples, a long time mated, and busy with their nest-building. The Cardinal returned to the sumac, feeling a degree lonelier than ever.

He decided to prospect in the opposite direction, and taking wing, he started up the river. Following the channel, he winged his flight for miles over the cool sparkling water, between the tangle of foliage bordering the banks. When he came to the long cumbrous structures of wood with which men had bridged the river, where the shuffling feet of tired farm horses raised clouds of dust and set the echoes rolling with their thunderous hoof beats, he was afraid; and rising high, he sailed over them in short broken curves of flight. But where giant maple and ash, leaning, locked branches across the channel in one of old Mother Nature's bridges for the squirrels, he knew no fear, and dipped so low beneath them that his image trailed a wavering shadow on the silver path he followed.

He rounded curve after curve, and frequently stopping on a conspicuous perch, flung a ringing challenge in the face of the morning. With every mile the way he followed grew more beautiful. The river bed was limestone, and the swiftly flowing water, clear and limpid. The banks were precipitate in some places, gently sloping in others, and always crowded with a tangle of foliage.

At an abrupt curve in the river he mounted to the summit of a big ash and made boastful prophecy, "Wet year! Wet year!" and on all sides there sprang up the voices of his kind. Startled, the Cardinal took wing. He followed the river in a circling flight until he remembered that here might be the opportunity to win the coveted river mate, and going slower to select the highest branch on which to display his charms, he discovered that he was only a few yards from the ash from which he had made his prediction. The Cardinal flew over the narrow neck and sent another call, then without awaiting a reply, again he flashed up the river and circled Horseshoe Bend. When he came to the same ash for the third time, he understood.

The river circled in one great curve. The Cardinal mounted to the tip-top limb of the ash and looked around him. There was never a fairer sight for the eye of man or bird. The mist and shimmer of early spring were in the air. The Wabash rounded Horseshoe Bend in a silver circle, rimmed by a tangle of foliage bordering both its banks; and inside lay a low open space covered with waving marsh grass and the blue bloom of sweet calamus. Scattered around were mighty trees, but conspicuous above any, in the very center, was a giant sycamore, split at its base into three large trees, whose waving branches seemed to sweep the face of heaven, and whose roots, like miserly fingers, clutched deep into the black muck of Rainbow Bottom.

It was in this lovely spot that the rainbow at last materialized, and at its base, free to all humanity who cared to seek, the Great Alchemist had left His rarest treasures—the gold of sunshine, diamond water-drops, emerald foliage, and sapphire sky. For good measure, there were added seeds, berries, and insects for the birds; and wild flowers, fruit, and nuts for the children. Above all, the sycamore waved its majestic head.

It made a throne that seemed suitable for the son of the king; and mounting to its topmost branch, for miles the river carried his challenge: "Ho, cardinals! Look this way! Behold me! Have you seen any other of so great size? Have you any to equal my grace? Who can whistle so loud, so clear, so compelling a note? Who will fly to me for protection? Who will come and be my mate?"

He flared his crest high, swelled his throat with rolling notes, and appeared so big and brilliant that among the many cardinals that had gathered to hear, there was not one to compare with him.

Black envy filled their hearts. Who was this flaming dashing stranger, flaunting himself in the faces of their females? There were many unmated cardinals in Rainbow Bottom, and many jealous males. A second time the Cardinal, rocking and flashing, proclaimed himself; and there was a note of feminine approval so strong that he caught it. Tilting on a twig, his crest flared to full height, his throat swelled to bursting, his heart too big for his body, the Cardinal shouted his challenge for the third time; when clear and sharp arose a cry in answer, "Here! Here! Here!" It came from a female that had accepted the caresses of the brightest cardinal in Rainbow Bottom only the day before, and had spent the morning carrying twigs to a thicket of red haws.

The Cardinal, with a royal flourish, sprang in air to seek her; but her outraged mate was ahead of him, and with a scream she fled, leaving a tuft of feathers in her mate's beak. In turn the Cardinal struck him like a flashing rocket, and then red war waged in Rainbow Bottom. The females scattered for cover with all their might. The Cardinal worked in a kiss on one poor little bird, too frightened to escape him; then the males closed in, and serious business began. The Cardinal would have enjoyed a fight vastly with two or three opponents; but a half-dozen made discretion better than valour. He darted among them, scattering them right and left, and made for the sycamore. With all his remaining breath, he insolently repeated his challenge; and then headed down stream for the sumac with what grace he could command.

There was an hour of angry recrimination before sweet peace brooded again in Rainbow Bottom. The newly mated pair finally made up; the females speedily resumed their coquetting, and forgot the captivating stranger—all save the poor little one that had been kissed by accident. She never had been kissed before, and never had expected that she would be, for she was a creature of many misfortunes of every nature.

She had been hatched from a fifth egg to begin with; and every one knows the disadvantage of beginning life with four sturdy older birds on top of one. It was a meager egg, and a feeble baby that pipped its shell. The remainder of the family stood and took nearly all the food so that she almost starved in the nest, and she never really knew the luxury of a hearty meal until her elders had flown. That lasted only a few days; for the others went then, and their parents followed them so far afield that the poor little soul, clamouring alone in the nest, almost perished. Hunger-driven, she climbed to the edge and exercised her wings until she managed some sort of flight to a neighbouring bush. She missed the twig and fell to the ground, where she lay cold and shivering.

She cried pitifully, and was almost dead when a brown-faced, barefoot boy, with a fishing-pole on his shoulder, passed and heard her.

"Poor little thing, you are almost dead," he said. "I know what I'll do with you. I'll take you over and set you in the bushes where I heard those other redbirds, and then your mammy will feed you."

The boy turned back and carefully set her on a limb close to one of her brothers, and there she got just enough food to keep her alive.

So her troubles continued. Once a squirrel chased her, and she saved herself by crowding into a hole so small her pursuer could not follow. The only reason she escaped a big blue racer when she went to take her first bath, was that a hawk had his eye on the snake and snapped it up at just the proper moment to save the poor, quivering little bird. She was left so badly frightened that she could not move for a long time.

All the tribulations of birdland fell to her lot. She was so frail and weak she lost her family in migration, and followed with some strangers that were none too kind. Life in the South had been full of trouble. Once a bullet grazed her so closely she lost two of her wing quills, and that made her more timid than ever. Coming North, she had given out again and finally had wandered into Rainbow Bottom, lost and alone.

She was such a shy, fearsome little body, the females all flouted her; and the males never seemed to notice that there was material in her for a very fine mate. Every other female cardinal in Rainbow Bottom had several males courting her, but this poor, frightened, lonely one had never a suitor; and she needed love so badly! No one ever before had sought her; now she had been kissed by this magnificent stranger!

Of course, she knew it really was not her kiss. He had intended it for the bold creature that had answered his challenge, but since it came to her, it was hers, in a way, after all. She hid in the underbrush for the remainder of the day, and was never so frightened in all her life. She brooded over it constantly, and morning found her at the down curve of the horseshoe, straining her ears for the rarest note she ever had heard. All day she hid and waited, and the following days were filled with longing, but he never came again.

So one morning, possessed with courage she did not understand, and filled with longing that drove her against her will, she started down the river. For miles she sneaked through the underbrush, and watched and listened; until at last night came, and she returned to Rainbow Bottom. The next morning she set out early and flew to the spot from which she had turned back the night before. From there she glided through the bushes and underbrush, trembling and quaking, yet pushing stoutly onward, straining her ears for some note of the brilliant stranger's.

It was mid-forenoon when she reached the region of the sumac, and as she hopped warily along, only a short distance from her, full and splendid, there burst the voice of the singer for whom she was searching. She sprang into air, and fled a mile before she realized that she was flying. Then she stopped and listened, and rolling with the river, she heard those bold true tones. Close to earth, she went back again, to see if, unobserved, she could find a spot where she might watch the stranger that had kissed her. When at last she reached a place where she could see him plainly, his beauty was so bewildering, and his song so enticing that she gradually hopped closer and closer without knowing she was moving.

High in the sumac the Cardinal had sung until his throat was parched, and the fountain of hope was almost dry. There was nothing save defeat from overwhelming numbers in Rainbow Bottom. He had paraded, and made all the music he ever had been taught, and improvised much more. Yet no one had come to seek him. Was it of necessity to be the Limberlost then? This one day more he would retain his dignity and his location. He tipped, tilted, and flirted. He whistled, and sang, and trilled. Over the lowland and up and down the shining river, ringing in every change he could invent, he sent for the last time his prophetic message, "Wet year! Wet year!"

"The Blue Heron"

from *What I Have Done With Birds*

What I Have Done With Birds, a collection of photographs and brief essays which describe the photographs as much as they do the species of bird, was first published in 1907. A revised version, with six additional essays and photographs, was published in 1917 as *Friends in Feathers.* Both "The Blue Heron" and "Black Vulture" were included in the original volume.

"Molly-Cotton" was Gene Stratton Porter's affectionate nickname for her daughter, Jeannette, as "the Deacon" was for her husband. Jeannette accompanied her mother on many photographic excursions, and both daughter and father were aides to Stratton Porter's naturalistic studies, particularly during the years they lived near the Limberlost Swamp. Jeannette was married one year before *Girl of the Limberlost* was published and Gene built "Wildflower Woods" on Sylvan Lake. Jeannette assisted her mother's enterprises again after she divorced her first husband and married filmmaker James Leo Meehan. The "Deacon," who fished while Gene photographed or dug up moth cocoons for her studies, did not live at Wildflower Woods full time, needing to be closer to his business. He also did not make the move to California in 1920 (when he was 70), although he spent several months of each year there.

Note: A muskellunge, or muscalonge, is a large North American pike which may measure up to seven feet in length and weigh about seventy-five pounds.

I FOUND THIS BLUE HERON myself, hunted him to his favourite feeding grounds alone, then secured these studies of him, which may be the reason I am so especially fond of them. I was stopping at a little boarding-house on the Inland Route, and with my boat had access to half a dozen lakes and rivers which make up this chain. The small river nearest us opened shortly into a large lake. From my room Blue Herons could be seen sweeping above the water morning after morning, settling in one spot, which seemed easy to locate. The Deacon probably had good reason to be nervous about my entering those swamps and forests alone. But one day he was away trout-fishing; Molly-Cotton was trying, under the instruction of the landlady, to prepare a pair of deer horns for mounting, so I slipped away to search for the haunt of the Heron.

The row up the river was delightful. For once the veil of nature was lifted everywhere. I could see as far as my eyes could penetrate, while even the water hid no mysteries. The air was clear and cool, touched with the odour of balsam, and sweeping in light breezes. The sky was a great arch of blue, with lazy floating clouds; the sun not too ardent in his attentions. On either hand the marsh was teeming with life. There were tracks beside the water edge where deer and bear came down to drink, small water-rats and beaver lived in the banks, and in the rushes were Duck, Teal, Plover, Heron—every kind of northern water-bird you could mention. This river was the first of my experience to give up its secrets. The bed was white sand, washed of every impurity by a swift current, while the water was pure and clear. At a depth of twenty and even thirty feet I could see every detail of the bed.

I have not time to tell of its wonders and mysteries in mineral formation; its dainty growing vines and mosses. But the water folk! If you never saw such a spot you can not dream how beautiful it is. The flowers on the bank or the birds and butterflies of the air were not more gaily coloured than the fish of that little river. Every shade of silver was striped and mottled with green, yellow, blue and red. Pike that seemed half as long as the boat swam past or darted under it. Big black bass, the kind that wreck your tackle and keep it, swam lazily unless moved to a sudden dart after small fry. There were a few rainbow trout, innumerable speckled perch, shad, and the most beautiful big sunfish. Occasionally an eel, monster turtles, sometimes a muskrat and a few water-puppies came slowly into sight and as slowly vanished. Oh, I could not row very fast on that river! And it was no wonder Herons and Cranes stalked with slowly lifted feet beside those banks, no wonder Kingfishers poised above that water by day, or that raccoons flattened themselves and lay immovable while they fished for frogs by night, for all of them could see their prey plainly and know exactly how to capture it.

I pulled into the lake, took my bearings and started toward the point where the Herons seemed to congregate. On reaching it I found the remains of an old saw-mill. The shores of all these northern lakes and rivers were dotted with mills a few years ago. There was an oozy landing-place on sawdust foundation, while the old mill probably would collapse in the first wind-storm. I pulled the boat up on the landing and entered the mill which was a shed, the floor half covered with water. Many boards were lacking, but enough were left to shelter me, so quietly creeping to the back end where the mill had been built over the water on purpose to float in logs, I saw an interesting sight.

The rushes had grown through what formerly had been a bed of sawdust, until they almost reached the mill. In this rotten sawdust there seemed to be a big white worm, of which the Herons were fond, and how they did gobble frogs! Undoubtedly the old mill was the attraction for both frogs and birds. The story was told in nature's plainest writ. The sun shining on the water-soaked sawdust raised a sweetish, sappy odour. This odour attracted flies and other insects in myriads. The insects in turn lured the frogs. The frogs made a feast which called up the Herons, while the Herons furnished subjects for my cameras. Inside the old mill, so close I could almost reach out and touch the actors, I interpreted these "signs."

Surely I am qualified to tell how a Blue Heron catches frogs. There is no hunting; his prey comes to him. The big birds, some of them over three feet in height, came winging across the lake, selecting the spot from which they wished to fish, quietly alighting. After looking carefully around him, each bird would move several yards, stepping high and with great care, flattening his body and slipping between grasses often taller than he was. When he had selected a fine location he stood perfectly still, mostly on one foot, his long slender leg seeming so like the cattails and rushes as to be unnoticed; folded his wings tight; drew in his neck; pointed his bill at an angle of about twenty-three degrees before him, and went to sleep—apparently.

This was queer hunting. I wondered if it could be possible that those Herons left their nests in the tall timber across the lake, came over there behind that old mill and stood in the water among those rushes to sleep. The first pounce that was made straight in front of me startled me so that I almost cried out. After a lifetime of field work I cannot suppress a sort of breathless snap of an "Ow," when I am surprised. It is a cry to which a bird rises every time. I barely saved myself. The thing was so unexpected. There stood the Heron, a big fine fellow, the light striking to brilliancy the white of his throat, wet with dew from the rushes, the deep steel-blue of his back, and bringing out sharply the black on the flattened crest and the narrow line down the front of his throat.

I had not seen a frog climb to the sawdust in front of the bird, so intent was my watch on him; so tremblingly was I setting up my camera and focussing, in an effort to get everything just right and avoid his seeing me slide the camera before the opening beside me. I was wondering if he possibly could hear the shutter, or if the plate could be changed before he did something more interesting than sleep, when snap! like a machine, out darted the Heron's neck, clip went his shear-like beak, then it pointed skyward, crest flat, the frog was tossed around and caught head-first—one snap, two, it was half-way down the gullet of the bird, whose beak was drawn in, crest flared and chin raised, before I recovered from my surprise enough to remember that I held the bulb in my hand and must squeeze it to secure the picture.

Hurriedly I shoved in the slide, whirled over the holder, set the shutter and drew the slide again. The bird had turned and moved several feet toward me, coming more in the open. I set the focus by scale and snapped again. That time in my eagerness I moved out too far, he saw me and away he swept, several of his fellows nearest following. I put away the plates and tested my focus on the spot where he had been. It seemed sufficiently sharp for a fine picture. Developing the plate proved that it was almost as nice a piece of work as I could have done if blest with plenty of time.

Then I glanced over my background. For a Heron picture it scarcely could have been improved. The mill stood in a small bay. Behind it rushes grew in a tangled mass, the body of the lake crept close to them, out in the water a couple of runaway logs were bobbing in the sunlight, while in the distance a far shore showed faintly. There was only one thing to keep me from having fine natural-history pictures. The bird was dripping with the heavy dew of the swamp; but if I had reproduced his head sidewise, and his bill and one eye, and the frog going down, surely that would not hurt my picture. In fact, thinking it over, it seemed to add to the naturalness of it and help portray the damp, swampy atmosphere.

Then I heard voices, the splashing of water and remembered that I was alone. I caught up my tripod and carrying case, tumbled them into my boat, pushed off and jumped in, not a minute too soon. I pulled into the lake barely in time to miss a crew of half a dozen men coming around the shore driving a log float and gathering up stray timber. When far away from the logs I put away my paraphernalia, set a small hand-camera in reach on the seat before me and started down the river.

The day had grown slightly warmer, but that was made up for by rowing with the current, for after entering the river I need not pull; but by steering could travel quite as fast as I desired. On that return trip my first muscalonge showed himself. Really, in the water it appeared as long as my boat. The fish must have weighed fifty pounds. It was only a short way in the river mouth, bewildered, no doubt, by the clear water, for it turned almost beneath my boat and went back. A magnificent big fish it was. My attention was called to it by the commotion caused among small fish darting in all directions to escape it.

On my way back I had a shot with a small hand-camera at a Heron on wing, but it was so far away that developing the plate disclosed only a speck on the sky. I tried some Plover and a Duck with better results, but that is another story. This is of the Blue Heron, and is one of my best pieces of work, quite by myself.

"Black Vulture"

from *What I Have Done With Birds*

Although Gene Stratton Porter is known for her writings about the Limberlost Swamp, early in her career as a naturalist she wandered only the edges of this area, which she knew held many delights for her. She had promised her husband, Charles—"the Deacon"—that she would stay away from the dangerous, rattlesnake-infested swamp. In this piece we see how Gene circumvented his proscriptions. It is important to note that, worries aside, Charles Dorwin Porter's interest in and support of his wife's enthusiasms was crucial to her early success.

Stratton Porter was a pioneer in the photography of birds, and she wrote many articles discussing both her techniques and equipment. She ardently supported the use of photography for nature study as a substitute for the common practice of killing scores of the natural subjects in order to study them. Nevertheless, she had an enormous collection of butterflies and moths, still on view at Limberlost Cabin. And in the essay "Shall We Pay Our Debt to the Birds?" she advocated the extermination of the English sparrow in America in order to halt this intruder's displacement of native sparrows from their habitats.

The naming of the Black Vulture "Little Chicken" is less a comparison of this large bird to the domesticated barnyard fowl than it is a reference to a European name for the vulture: "Pharaoh's Chicken."

I AM INDEBTED to Otty Bolds, who owns that portion of the Limberlost selected as their happy home by the Black Vultures, for word of their location. Mr. Bolds sent a messenger to tell me that in a big hollow elm tree, of last year's felling, was a nest containing a bird baby as big as a Gosling, but white as snow, and beside it a pale blue egg heavily speckled with brown and shaped like a Hen's, but large as a Turkey's.

This was bewildering. I knew where for three years Turkey Buzzards had nested in a hollow tree on the Wabash River, on Dan Hawbaker's farm, but their eggs were cream-coloured. The blue eggs "sent me to sea." We had no native bird that laid the egg described. If the description were at all correct, it could only mean something unusual, and strays in ornithology are extremely interesting.

On hearing of a bird that is new to me I think of Pliny's classification of species; "those that have hooked tallons, as Hawkes; or long round claws, as Hennes; or else they be broad, flat and whole-footed, as Geese," wondering in which class the bird can be placed. I was all eagerness to see these birds, but hesitated, not because of doubts that I would go and make studies of them eventually, but because it required thinking as to how it could be accomplished. The Limberlost, at that time, was my one spot of forbidden territory. A rash promise had been made never to go there, but this sounded too alluring. I immediately sought the Deacon.

"I want to take back my promise not to go to the Limberlost," I said.

"Can't release you," he answered.

We do not live long with people in this world until we discover their weak spots. The Deacon's is relics, specimens and curios—first cousin to natural history.

"What a pity!" I murmured meditatively. "This is the only opportunity I ever have had to reproduce a white baby as large as a Gosling, with a big speckled blue egg beside it, and of course I'll never have another."

"What's that!" cried the Deacon.

"How do you expect me to tell what it is, if I must not go and see?" I countered.

"When did you want to go?" he questioned.

I thought of the old adage about striking the hot iron and answered promptly: "This minute!"

"But I can't go now," said the Deacon.

"Then the blue egg will hatch, so I won't get a picture of it beside the white baby. I am reliably informed that it has large dark speckles on it—the egg, not the baby. Mr. Bolds sent a man to tell me."

"Umph!" he muttered, starting toward the stable.

My soul was joyful as I went to pack my paraphernalia.

This was the beginning of a series of swamp-studies that is, in all probability, without an equal in natural history or photography. The Limberlost at that time was dangerous. It had not been shorn, branded and tamed. There were excellent reasons why I should not go there. Most of it was impenetrable. There had been one or two roads cut by expert lumbermen, who had located valuable trees; a very little timber had been taken out. No one knew when tree-hunters were there, while always it had been a rendezvous for outlaws and cutthroats in hiding. The swamp was named for a man who became lost in its fastnesses and wandered around, failing to find a way out until he died of starvation. In its physical aspect it was steaming, fetid, treacherous swamp and quagmire, filled with every danger common to the central states.

A few oil-wells had been drilled near the head of the swamp. It was over a road, cut to one of these, that we were to travel as far as a certain well. After that the way led north a quarter of a mile, then straight east, until we came to the prostrate trunk of a giant elm, with a hollow five feet in diameter. That sounds easy, but it was not. In the beginning I had to pay a tenant a dollar for the privilege of driving over the road the oil and lumbermen used. A rod inside the swamp the carriage wheels on one side mired to the hub. Another rod, I took the camera intended for use in my lap, shielding it with my arms. Every few yards, I expected the light carriage we drove to be twisted to pieces. We left it at the oil-well, starting on foot with an ax, hatchet and two revolvers, to find the tree.

The Deacon wore high, heavy leather boots, while I wore waist-high rubber waders. We had to cut our way before us, as the felled tree had been hollow, not worth taking out, so no road had been made to it. For two hours we searched for that log. The time was late June; there was not a breath of air stirring in the swamp; there were steaming, fetid pools everywhere, swarms of flies, gnats, mosquitoes, and poisonous insects, masses of poisonous vines, while at every step not only the ground, but the bushes, had to be watched for rattlesnakes. The muck was so spongy we sank ankle-deep, branches scratched or tore at us while logs we thought were solid let us down knee-deep.

An observer readily could have seen that the Deacon had his cognomen by contraries. His face was crimson, his wet clothing plastered to his shoulders. He smoked one cigar after another to drive the clouds of insects from his head and neck. The portion of my body covered by rubber was in a Turkish bath, while the remainder was bitten until I was lumpy as a beaded pincushion, but every breath was a prayer that the Deacon would not lost his patience or give up. And he did not! Of course we had to find it after a while, when we searched like that.

I was glad that it was the Deacon who first sighted the location. He would be more interested in it if he did. When we reached the tree, a big black bird was brooding. We held a council. I must have the baby while it was a tiny baby and the blue egg if possible. A camera was set up and focussed on the mouth of the log. The Deacon plunged into the swamp and started back beside the trunk, tapping it gently to drive out the bird. She was to be snapped as she emerged.

The light was bad, but the experiment was worth a plate. We did not dare risk frightening the bird by doing any clearing while she was brooding. These matters must be handled delicately and with common sense. To cut down a tree with her watching us, in all probability meant to frighten her into creeping to the farthermost recesses of the log, where she might refuse to come out for hours. Then for the Deacon to enter to bring out the baby while she was there would mean to give her a fright from which she would never recover; one that might result in her deserting the nest. She must be coaxed out, before any clearing to throw light on the opening was done. I was watching the log, my shaking fingers grasping the bulb. I had depended on her walking to the opening, then flying from there. She came out on wing, with a rush. My shutter was set too slow for flight. There was only an indistinct wave across my plate.

Then the Deacon entered the log, creeping its length, to carry out the baby and the egg in his hat, which we previously had lined with leaves. The odour was so unbearable we could work close the log only by dipping our handkerchiefs in disinfectant, then binding them over our mouths and nostrils. The Deacon said there was not a trace of nest. The baby and the egg were in a small hollow in the decayed, yellow elm fiber.

The baby was cunning as possible, white and soft as a powder-puff. He had a little, quaint, leathery, black old face. The unhatched egg was beautiful, but too light weight to contain a young bird ready to pip the shell. We at once named the baby "Little Chicken," after Pharaoh's Chickens of old. The Deacon placed him in the mouth of the log, exactly as he found him, while I cut away vines to make a footing. Then we cut down several trees and bushes to secure a good light on the mouth of the log. A study was made of the location, two of Little Chicken and the egg, finally one of the baby alone.

Then the Deacon crept back into the log to replace the baby and the egg, although we knew it would not hatch. The following morning the mother broke it and ate the contents.

The birds were Black Vultures, the pioneers of their kind in this part of the country. The female was a brilliant young bird, with fresh face and feet. The male was much larger than his mate, duller of colouring, with a wrinkled old face, while his feet and legs were encrusted with a lime-coloured growth at which he bit and worked.

When we left the swamp we were so overheated that we chilled until we were compelled to wrap ourselves in the side curtains and lap-robe of the carriage, lower the top so that we sat in the sun of a hot June day, and to drive at a slow walk. The Deacon turned to me with the first word he had uttered, save to ask what I wanted done next, and inquired: "Do you think that *paid?*"

Never in all my life had I been so uncomfortable, so unspeakably miserable. I was chilling until I shook under my leather covering, so pretended not to hear him. The following morning I produced my bunch of proofs.

"Do *you* think it paid?" I asked.

The Deacon examined the proofs several times, finally selecting the best one of Little Chicken and the egg.

"That more than pays," he said succinctly. "When are we going again?"

"I want to go every day to feed Little Chicken some liver or sweetbreads and become acquainted with his parents. I want to make a study of him every three days; as many as I can of the old ones," I answered.

"All right!" said the Deacon.

"But you can't spare all that time," I cried in astonishment.

"I must," said the Deacon. "No one less careful of you than I am ever shall take you to the Limberlost."

So for weeks, until October, in fact, we watched over that baby and courted his parents. We found in our woods a dead calf which we carried into the swamp, placing it conveniently for the old ones and for me to take pictures of them. When Little Chicken was a few weeks old, without our knowledge lumbermen removed the log for a watering-trough, but sent me word where they had placed the baby. His parents were very indifferent about feeding him in his new location so I had to visit him daily. Once when I was called from town for several days he was brought to the Cabin, in the carriage. A woman was hired to feed him until my return, when he was taken back to the swamp. There is no way of adequately describing what we endured for that series of pictures.

The birds were friendly, the male especially, and responded beautifully to our advances. From Little Chicken just before he stood to walk, I secured the study here given, which covers every natural history point possible to one photograph, even the tongue. The baby was obliging about posing, while in two weeks he answered to his name and took food from my hand as readily as from his mother. When he was almost full-grown with only a trace of down showing around his ears, he would follow me across the swamp with his queer rocking walk, humping his shoulders and ducking his head: looking so uncanny in that dark weird place, he made me think of witches and goblins.

The last time I saw him was late in October. He followed me to the edge of the Limberlost, so I turned and made this picture, used as a tail-piece, when his wings were raised for a sweep that carried him skyward to his parents. That season the Limberlost yielded me the only complete series of Vulture studies ever made, dozens of studies of other birds, material for the book "Freckles," more natural history stuff than could be put into several big volumes, many rare specimens and much priceless experience in swamp work, for all of which I acknowledge my indebtedness to Mr. Bolds, to Little Chicken, and to the Deacon.

The following season, having become familiar with the Swamp and therefore indifferent to its annoyances and dangers, I prepared myself suitably to meet them, and went as often as I chose. I hoped this pair of Vultures would return, and I am very sure they did; but finding the only favourable nesting location gone, they moved nearly a mile away, to our farm, where they were investigating a hollow log, when our farmer, not knowing what they were, mistook them for Hawks, and tried to shoot them.

They speedily left. The next I heard of them a man living five miles east of us sent me word there was a pair of big birds nesting in a hollow tree in his woods, so I went to pay them a visit. Having been unmolested, they had a fine pair of young, almost three weeks of age, when I arrived. The female was the same small, sleek bird; not so timid as she had been the previous summer. The male was the same big, old, scale-encrusted fellow; exactly as I remembered him, so that I am sure as I ever get of anything I cannot prove, that these were Freckles' Chickens of the Limberlost. I even enjoyed the hope that they knew me, the small black horse, and the load of cameras; but very probably that was a case where the "wish was father to the thought."

The best study, from a scientific natural history standpoint, it ever
has been my good luck to secure

"Wherein Freckles Proves His Mettle and Finds Friends"

from *Freckles*

Freckles walks into the Limberlost Swamp, into the camp of the Grand Rapids Lumber Company, on the opening page of Gene Stratton Porter's first novel. He is fresh from the orphanage where he has lived since he was a child, and his frankness appeals to the company "Boss," who gives him the job of "checking the lines." The company has leased the lumber rights on a new piece of land within the swamp but cannot set up camp to harvest the trees for a few months. It has set up a line of barbed wire around the lease to warn off trespassers and poachers. Freckles talks the Boss into hiring him, overcoming the man's reservations about hiring such a young man, and one who has only one hand. The circumstances surrounding the loss of his hand are made known to Freckles when the identity of his family is discovered, near the end of the novel. Freckles's *true* identity is revealed through his relationships with the birds, most notably the black vulture, and the people who frequent the pathways he guards in the Limberlost Swamp.

NEXT MORNING FOUND FRECKLES in clean, whole clothing, fed, and rested. Then McLean outfitted him and gave him careful instruction in the use of his weapon. The Boss showed him around the timber-line, and engaged him a place to board with the family of his head-teamster, Duncan, whom he had brought from Scotland with him, and who lived in a small clearing he was working out between the swamp and the corduroy. When the gang was started for the south camp, Freckles was left to guard a fortune in the Limberlost. That he was under guard himself those first weeks he never knew.

Each hour was torture to the boy. The restricted life of a great city orphanage was the other extreme of the world compared with the Limberlost. He was afraid for his life every minute. The heat was intense.

The heavy wading-boots rubbed his feet until they bled. He was sore and stiff from his long tramp and outdoor exposure. The seven miles of trail was agony at every step. He practised at night, under the direction of Duncan, until he grew sure in the use of his revolver. He cut a stout hickory cudgel, with a knot on the end as big as his fist; this never left his hand. What he thought in those first days he himself could not recall clearly afterward.

His heart stood still every time he saw the beautiful marsh-grass begin a sinuous waving *against* the play of the wind, as McLean had told him it would. He bolted half a mile with the first boom of the bittern, and his hat lifted with every yelp of the sheitpoke. Once he saw a lean, shadowy form following him, and fired his revolver. Then he was frightened worse than ever for fear it might have been Duncan's collie.

The first afternoon that he found his wires down, and he was compelled to plunge knee deep into the black swamp-muck to restring them, he became so ill from fear and nervousness that he scarcely could control his shaking hand to do the work. With every step, he felt that he would miss secure footing and be swallowed in that clinging sea of blackness. In dumb agony he plunged forward, clinging to the posts and trees until he had finished restringing and testing the wire. He had consumed much time. Night closed in. The Limberlost stirred gently, then shook herself, growled, and awoke around him.

There seemed to be a great owl hooting from every hollow tree, and a little one screeching from every knothole. The bellowing of big bullfrogs was not sufficiently deafening to shut out the wailing of whippoor-wills that seemed to come from every bush. Night-hawks swept past him with their shivering cry, and bats struck his face. A prowling wild cat missed its catch and screamed with rage. A straying fox bayed incessantly for its mate.

The hair on the back of Freckles' neck arose as bristles, and his knees wavered beneath him. He could not see whether the dreaded snakes were on the trail, or, in the pandemonium, hear the rattle for which McLean had cautioned him to listen. He stood motionless in an agony of fear. His breath whistled between his teeth. The perspiration ran down his face and body in little streams.

Something big, black, and heavy came crashing through the swamp close to him, and with a yell of utter panic Freckles ran—how far he did not know; but at last he gained control over himself and retraced his steps. His jaws set stiffly and the sweat dried on his body. When he reached the place from which he had started to run, he turned and with measured steps made his way down the line. After a time he realized that he was only walking, so he faced that sea of horrors again. When he came toward the corduroy, the cudgel fell to test the wire at each step.

Sounds that curdled his blood seemed to encompass him, and shapes of terror to draw closer and closer. Fear had so gained the mastery that he did not dare look behind him; and just when he felt that he would fall dead before he ever reached the clearing, came Duncan's rolling call: "Freckles! Freckles!" A shuddering sob burst in the boy's dry throat; but he only told Duncan that finding the wire down had caused the delay.

The next morning he started on time. Day after day, with his heart pounding, he ducked, dodged, ran when he could, and fought when he was brought to bay. If he ever had an idea of giving up, no one knew it; for he clung to his job without the shadow of wavering. All these things, in so far as he guessed them, Duncan, who had been set to watch the first weeks of Freckles' work, carried to the Boss at the south camp; but the innermost, exquisite torture of the thing the big Scotchman never guessed, and McLean, with his finer perceptions, came only a little closer.

After a few weeks, when Freckles learned that he was still living, that he had a home, and the very first money he ever had possessed was safe in his pockets, he began to grow proud. He yet side stepped, dodged, and hurried to avoid being late again, but he was gradually developing the fearlessness that men ever acquire of dangers to which they are hourly accustomed.

His heart seemed to be leaping when his first rattler disputed the trail with him, but he mustered courage to attack it with his club. After its head had been crushed, he mastered an Irishman's inborn repugnance for snakes sufficiently to cut off its rattles to show Duncan. With this victory, his greatest fear of them was gone.

Then he began to realize that with the abundance of food in the swamp, flesh-hunters would not come on the trail and attack him, and he had his revolver for defence if they did. He soon learned to laugh at the big, floppy birds that made horrible noises. One day, watching behind a tree, he saw a crane solemnly performing a few measures of a belated nuptial song-and-dance with his mate. Realizing that it was intended in tenderness, no matter how it appeared, the lonely, starved heart of the boy sympathized with them.

Before the first month passed, he was fairly easy about his job; by the next he rather liked it. Nature can be trusted to work her own miracle in the heart of any man whose daily task keeps him alone among her sights, sounds, and silences.

When day after day the only thing that relieved his utter loneliness was the companionship of the birds and beasts of the swamp, it was the most natural thing in the world that Freckles should turn to them for friendship. He began by instinctively protecting the weak and helpless. He was astonished at the quickness with which they became accustomed to him and the disregard they showed for his movements, when they learned that he was not a hunter, while the club he carried was used more frequently for their benefit than his own. He scarcely could believe what he saw.

From the effort to protect the birds and animals, it was only a short step to the possessive feeling, and with that sprang the impulse to caress and provide. Through fall, when brooding was finished and the upland birds sought the swamp in swarms to feast on its seeds and berries, Freckles was content with watching them and speculating about them. Outside of half a dozen of the very commonest they were strangers to him. The likeness of their actions to humanity was an hourly surprise.

When black frost began stripping the Limberlost, cutting the ferns, shearing the vines from the trees, mowing the succulent green things of the swale, and setting the leaves swirling down, he watched the departing troops of his friends with dismay. He began to realize that he would be left alone. He made especial efforts toward friendliness with the hope that he could induce some of them to stay. It was then that he conceived the idea of carrying food to the birds; for he saw that they were leaving for lack of it; but he could not stop them. Day after day, flocks gathered and departed: by the time the first snow whitened his trail around the Limberlost, there were left only the little black-and-white juncos, the sapsuckers, yellowhammers, a few patriarchs among the flaming cardinals, the blue jays, the crows, and the quail.

Then Freckles began his wizard work. He cleared a space of swale, and twice a day he spread a birds' banquet. By the middle of December the strong winds of winter had beaten most of the seed from the grass and bushes. The snow fell, covering the swamp, and food was very scarce and difficult to find. The birds scarcely waited until Freckles' back was turned to attack his provisions. In a few weeks they flew toward the clearing to meet him. During the bitter weather of January they came half-way to the cabin every morning, and fluttered around him as doves all the way to the feeding-ground. Before February they were so accustomed to him, and so hunger-driven, that they would perch on his head and shoulders, and the saucy jays would try to pry into his pockets.

Then Freckles added to wheat and crumbs, every scrap of refuse food he could find at the cabin. He carried to his pets the parings of apples, turnips, potatoes, stray cabbage-leaves, and carrots, and tied to the bushes meat-bones having scraps of fat and gristle. One morning, coming to his feeding-ground unusually early, he found a gorgeous cardinal and a rabbit side by side sociably nibbling a cabbage-leaf, and that instantly gave to him the idea of cracking nuts, from the store he had gathered for Duncan's children, for the squirrels, in the effort to add them to his family. Soon he had them coming—red, gray, and black; then he became filled with a vast impatience that he did not know their names or habits.

So the winter passed. Every week McLean rode to the Limberlost; never on the same day or at the same hour. Always he found Freckles at his work, faithful and brave, no matter how severe the weather.

The boy's earnings constituted his first money; and when the Boss explained to him that he could leave them safe at a bank and carry away a scrap of paper that represented the amount, he went straight on every pay-day and made his deposit, keeping out barely what was necessary for his board and clothing. What he wanted to do with his money he did not know, but it gave to him a sense of freedom and power to feel that it was there—it was his and he could have it when he chose. In imitation of McLean, he bought a small pocket account-book, in which he carefully set down every dollar he earned and every penny he spent. As his expenses were small and the Boss paid him generously, it was astonishing how his little hoard grew.

That winter held the first hours of real happiness in Freckles' life. He was free. He was doing a man's work faithfully, through every rigour of rain, snow, and blizzard. He was gathering a wonderful strength of body, paying his way, and saving money. Every man of the gang and of that locality knew that he was under the protection of McLean, who was a power; this had the effect of smoothing Freckles' path in many directions.

Mrs. Duncan showed him that individual kindness for which his hungry heart was longing. She had a hot drink ready for him when he came from a freezing day on the trail. She knit him a heavy mitten for his left hand, and devised a way to sew and pad the right sleeve that protected the maimed arm in bitter weather. She patched his clothing—frequently torn by the wire—and saved kitchen-scraps for his birds, not because she either knew or cared anything about them, but because she herself was close enough to the swamp to be touched by its utter loneliness. When Duncan laughed at her for this, she retorted: "My God, mannie, if Freckles hadna the birds and the beasts he would be always alone. It was never meant for a human being to be so solitary. He'd get touched in the head if he hadna them to think for and to talk to."

"How much answer do ye think he gets to his talkin', lass?" laughed Duncan.

"He gets the answer that keeps the eye bricht, the heart happy, and the feet walking faithful the rough path he's set them in," answered Mrs. Duncan earnestly.

Duncan walked away appearing very thoughtful. The next morning he gave an ear from the corn he was shelling for his chickens to Freckles, and told him to carry it to his wild chickens in the Limberlost. Freckles laughed delightedly.

"Me chickens!" he said. "Why didn't I ever think of that before? Of course they are! They are just little, brightly coloured cocks and hens! But 'wild' is no good. What would you say to me 'wild chickens' being a good deal tamer than yours here in your yard?"

"Hoot, lad!" cried Duncan.

"Make yours light on your head and eat out of your hands and pockets," challenged Freckles.

"Go and tell your fairy tales to the wee people! They're juist brash on believin' things," said Duncan. "Ye canna invent any story too big to stop them from callin' for a bigger."

"I dare you to come see!" retorted Freckles.

"Take ye!" said Duncan. "If ye make juist ane bird licht on your heid or eat frae your hand, ye are free to help yoursel' to my corn-crib and wheat-bin the rest of the winter."

Freckles sprang in air and howled in glee.

"Oh, Duncan! You're too aisy," he cried. "When will you come?"

"I'll come next Sabbath," said Duncan. "And I'll believe the birds of the Limberlost are tame as barnyard-fowl when I see it, and no sooner!"

After that Freckles always spoke of the birds as his chickens, and the Duncans followed his example. The very next Sabbath, Duncan, with his wife and children, followed Freckles to the swamp. They saw a sight so wonderful it will keep them talking all the remainder of their lives, and make them unfailing friends of all the birds.

Freckles' chickens were awaiting him at the edge of the clearing. They cut the frosty air around his head into curves and circles of crimson, blue, and black. They chased each other from Freckles, and swept so closely themselves that they brushed him with their outspread wings.

At their feeding-ground Freckles set down his old pail of scraps and swept the snow from a small level space with a broom improvised of twigs. As soon as his back was turned, the birds clustered over the food, snatching scraps to carry to the nearest bushes. Several of the boldest, a big crow and a couple of jays, settled on the rim and feasted at leisure, while a cardinal, that hesitated to venture, fumed and scolded from a twig overhead.

Then Freckles scattered his store. At once the ground resembled the spread mantle of Montezuma, except that this mass of gaily coloured feathers was on the backs of living birds. While they feasted, Duncan gripped his wife's arm and stared in astonishment; for from the bushes and dry grass, with gentle cheeping and queer, throaty chatter, as if to encourage each other, came flocks of quail. Before any one saw it arrive, a big gray rabbit sat in the midst of the feast, contentedly gnawing a cabbage-leaf.

"Weel, I be drawed on!" came Mrs. Duncan's tense whisper.

"Shu-shu," cautioned Duncan.

Lastly Freckles removed his cap. He began filling it with handfuls of wheat from his pockets. In a swarm the grain-eaters arose around him as a flock of tame pigeons. They perched on his arms and the cap, and in the stress of hunger, forgetting all caution, a brilliant cock cardinal and an equally gaudy jay fought for a perching-place on his head.

"Weel, I'm beat," muttered Duncan, forgetting the silence imposed on his wife. "I'll hae to give in. 'Seein'' is believin'.' A man wad hae to see that to believe it. We mauna let the Boss miss that sight, for it's a chance will no likely come twice in a life. Everything is snowed under and thae craturs near starved, but trustin' Freckles that complete they are tamer than our chickens. Look hard, bairns!" he whispered. "We winna see the like o' yon again, while God lets ye live. Notice their colour against the ice and snow, and the pretty skippin' ways of them! And spunky! Weel, I'm beat fair!"

Freckles emptied his cap, turned his pockets and scattered his last grain. Then he waved his watching friends good-bye and started down the timber-line.

A week later, Duncan and Freckles arose from breakfast to face the bitterest morning of the winter. When Freckles, warmly capped and gloved, stepped to the corner of the kitchen for his scrap-pail, he found a big pan of steaming boiled wheat on the top of it. He wheeled to Mrs. Duncan with a shining face.

"Were you fixing this warm food for me chickens or yours?" he asked.

"It's for yours, Freckles," she said. "I was afeared this cold weather they wadna lay good without a warm bite now and then."

Duncan laughed as he stepped to the other room for his pipe; but Freckles faced Mrs. Duncan with a trace of every pang of starved mother-hunger he ever had suffered written large on his homely, splotched, narrow features.

"Oh, how I wish you were my mother!" he cried.

Mrs. Duncan attempted an echo of her husband's laugh.

"Lord love the lad!" she exclaimed. "Why, Freckles, are ye no bricht enough to learn without being taught by a woman that I am your mither? If a great man like yoursel' dinna ken that, learn it now and ne'er forget it. Ance a woman is the wife of any man, she becomes wife to all men for having had the wifely experience she kens! Ance a man-child has beaten his way to life under the heart of a woman, she is mither to all men, for the hearts of mithers are everywhere the same. Bless ye, laddie, I am your mither!"

She tucked the coarse scarf she had knit for him closer over his chest and pulled his cap lower over his ears, but Freckles, whipping it off and holding it under his arm, caught her rough, reddened hand and pressed it to his lips in a long kiss. Then he hurried away to hide the happy, embarrassing tears that were coming straight from his swelling heart.

Mrs. Duncan, sobbing unrestrainedly, swept into the adjoining room and threw herself into Duncan's arms.

"Oh, the puir lad!" she wailed. "Oh, the puir mither-hungry lad! He breaks my heart!"

Duncan's arms closed convulsively around his wife. With a big, brown hand he lovingly stroked her rough, sorrel hair.

"Sarah, you're a guid woman!" he said. "You're a michty guid woman! Ye hae a way o' speakin' out at times that's like the inspired prophets of the Lord. If that had been put to me, now, I'd 'a' felt all I kent how to and been keen enough to say the richt thing; but dang it, I'd 'a' stuttered and stammered and got naething out that would ha' done onybody a mite o' good. But ye, Sarah! Did ye see his face, woman? Ye sent him off lookin' leke a white light of holiness had passed ower and settled on him. Ye sent the lad away too happy for mortal words, Sarah. And ye made me that proud o' ye! I wouldna trade ye an' my share o' the Limberlost with ony king ye could mention."

He relaxed his clasp, and setting a heavy hand on each shoulder, he looked straight into her eyes.

"Ye're prime, Sarah! Juist prime!" he said.

Sarah Duncan stood alone in the middle of her two-roomed log-cabin and lifted a bony, claw-like pair of hands, reddened by frequent immersion in hot water, cracked and chafed by exposure to cold, black-lined by constant battle with swamp-loam, calloused with burns, and stared at them wonderingly.

"Pretty lookin' things ye are!" she whispered. "But ye hae juist been kissed. And by such a man! Fine as God ever made at His verra best. Duncan wouldna trade wi' a king! Na! Nor I wadna trade with a queen wi' a palace, an' velvet gowns, an' diamonds big as hazel-nuts, an' a hundred visitors a day into the bargain. Ye've been that honoured I'm blest if I can bear to souse ye in dish-water. Still, that kiss winna come off! Naething can take it from me, for it's mine till I dee. Lord, if I amna proud! Kisses on these old claws! Weel, I be drawed on!"

"Wherein Margaret Sinton Reveals a Secret . . ."

from *A Girl of the Limberlost*

In this novel, Gene Stratton Porter again creates characters whose lives and identities are interwoven with their natural surroundings: Elnora Comstock and her mother, Katharine. Robert Comstock, father and husband, died in the swamp the night Elnora was born. Childbirth prevented Katharine from going after him—something for which she has never forgiven her daughter. Deprived of her mother's affection, Elnora turned all the more readily to acquiring an intimacy with the swamp, in particular the moths which were so plentiful there. Elnora has inherited the cases which hold the moths collected by Freckles from the earlier novel, and her own collecting has helped her raise the money needed to attend school in town. She has plans to go to college, but she needs to complete a collection by finding a Yellow Emperor moth.

ELNORA, BRING ME THE TOWEL, quick!" cried Mrs. Comstock.

"In a minute, mother," mumbled Elnora.

She was standing before the kitchen mirror, tying the back part of her hair, while the front turned over her face.

"Hurry! There's a varmint of some kind!"

Elnora ran into the sitting room and thrust the heavy kitchen towel into her mother's hand. Mrs. Comstock swung open the screen door and struck at some object. Elnora tossed the hair from her face so that she could see past her mother. The girl screamed wildly.

"Don't! Mother, don't!"

Mrs. Comstock struck again. Elnora caught her arm.

"It's the one I want! It's worth a lot of money! Don't! Oh, you shall not!"

"Shan't, missy?" blazed Mrs. Comstock. "When did you get to bossing me?"

The hand that held the screen swept a half-circle and stopped at Elnora's cheek. She staggered with the blow, and across her face, paled with excitement, a red mark rose rapidly. The screen slammed shut, throwing the creature on the floor before them. Instantly Mrs. Comstock's foot crushed it. Elnora stepped back. Excepting the red mark, her face was very white.

"That was the last moth I needed," she said, "to complete a collection worth three hundred dollars. You've ruined it before my eyes!"

"Moth!" cried Mrs. Comstock. "You say that because you are mad. Moths have big wings. I know a moth!"

"I've kept things from you," said Elnora, "because I didn't dare confide in you. You had no sympathy with me. But you know I never told you untruths in all my life."

"It's no moth!" reiterated Mrs. Comstock.

"It is!" cried Elnora. "It's just out of a case in the ground. Its wings take two or three hours to expand and harden."

"If I had known it was a moth—" Mrs. Comstock wavered.

"You did know! I told you! I begged you to stop! It meant just three hundred dollars to me."

"Bah! Three hundred fiddlesticks!" sneered Mrs. Comstock.

"They are what have paid for books, tuition, and clothes for the last four years. They are what I could have started on to college. You've crushed the last one I needed before my face. You never have made any pretence of loving me. At last I'll be equally frank with you. I hate you! You are a selfish, wicked woman! I hate you!"

Elnora turned, went through the kitchen and out the back door. She followed the garden path to the gate and walked toward the swamp a short distance when reaction overtook her. She dropped on the ground and leaned against a big log. When a little child, desperate as now, she had tried to die by holding her breath. She had thought in that way to make her mother sorry, but she had learned that life was a thing thrust upon her and death would not come at her wish.

She was so crushed over the loss of that moth, which she had childishly named the yellow Emperor, that she scarcely remembered the blow. She had thought no luck in all the world would be so rare as to complete her collection, and she just had been forced to see a splendid Imperialis crushed to a mass before her. There was a possibility that she could find another, but now she was facing the certainty that the one she might have had and with which she undoubtedly could have attracted others, was ruined—by her mother. How long she sat there Elnora did not know or care. She simply suffered in dumb, abject misery, an occasional dry sob shaking her. Aunt Margaret was right. Elnora felt that morning that her mother never would be any different. The girl had reached the place where she realized that she could bear it no longer.

As Elnora left the room, Mrs. Comstock took one step after her.

"You little huzzy!" she gasped.

But Elnora was gone. Her mother stood staring.

"She never did lie to me," she muttered. "I guess it was a moth. And the only one she needed to get three hundred dollars, she said. I wish I hadn't been so fast! I never saw anything like it. I thought it was some deadly, stinging, biting thing. A body does have to be mighty careful here. But likely I've spilt the milk now. Pshaw! She can find another! There's no use to be foolish. Maybe moths are like snakes, where there's one, there's two."

Mrs. Comstock took the broom and swept the moth out of the door. Then she got down on her knees and carefully examined the steps, logs and the earth of the flower beds at each side. She found the place where the creature had emerged from the ground, and the hard, dark brown case which had enclosed it, still wet inside. Then she knew Elnora had been right. It was a moth. Its wings had been damp and not expanded. Mrs. Comstock never before had seen one in that state, and she did not know how they originated. She had thought all of them came from cases spun on trees or against walls or boards. She only had seen enough to know that there were such things, just as a flash of white told her that an ermine was on her premises, or a sharp "buzzzzz" warned her of a rattler.

So it was from creatures like that Elnora had gotten her school money. In one sickening sweep there rushed into the heart of the woman a full realization of the width of the gulf which separated her from her child. Lately many things had pointed toward it, none more plainly than when Elnora, like a reincarnation of her father, had stood fearlessly before a large city audience and played with even greater skill than he, on what Mrs. Comstock felt very certain, was his violin. But that little crawling creature of earth, crushed by her before its splendid yellow and lavender wings could spread and carry it into the mystery of night, had brought a realizing sense.

"We are nearer strangers with each other than we are with any of the neighbours," she muttered.

So one of the Almighty's most delicate and beautiful creations was sacrificed without fulfilling the law, yet none of its species ever served so glorious a cause, for at last Mrs. Comstock's inner vision had cleared. She went through the cabin mechanically. Every few minutes she glanced toward the back walk to see if Elnora was coming. She knew arrangements had been made with Margaret to go to the city some time that day, so she grew more nervous and uneasy every moment. She was haunted by the fear that the blow might discolour Elnora's cheek, and that she would tell Margaret. She went down the back walk, looking intently in all directions, left the garden and took the swamp path. Her step was noiseless on the soft, black earth, and soon she came near enough to see Elnora. Mrs. Comstock stood looking at the girl in troubled uncertainty. Not knowing what to say, at last she turned and went back to the cabin.

Noon came and she prepared dinner, calling, as she always did, when Elnora was in the garden, but she got no response, and the girl did not come. A little after one o'clock Margaret stopped at the gate.

"Elnora has changed her mind. She is not going," called Mrs. Comstock.

She felt that she hated Margaret as she hitched her horse and came up the walk instead of driving on.

"You must be mistaken," said Margaret. "I was going on purpose for her. She asked me to take her. I had no errand. Where is she?"

"I will call her," said Mrs. Comstock.

She followed the path again, and this time found Elnora sitting on the log. Her face was swollen and discoloured, and her eyes red with crying. She paid no attention to her mother.

"Mag Sinton is here," said Mrs. Comstock harshly. "I told her you had changed your mind, but she said you asked her to go with you, and she had nothing to go for herself."

Elnora arose, recklessly took a short cut through the deep swamp grasses and so reached the path ahead of her mother. Mrs. Comstock followed as far as the garden, but she could not enter the cabin. She busied herself among the vegetables, barely looking up when the back door screen slammed noisily. Margaret Sinton approached colourless, and with such flaming eyes that Mrs. Comstock shrank back.

"What's the matter with Elnora's face?" demanded Margaret.

Mrs. Comstock made no reply.

"You struck her, did you?"

"I thought you wasn't blind!"

"I have been, for twenty long years now, Kate Comstock," said Margaret Sinton, "but my eyes are open at last. What I see is that I've done you no good and Elnora a big wrong. I had an idea that it would kill you to know, but I guess you are tough enough to stand anything. Kill or cure, you get it now!"

"What are you frothing about?" coolly asked Mrs. Comstock.

"You!" cried Margaret. "You! The woman who don't pretend to love her only child. Who lets her grow to a woman, as you have let Elnora, and can't be satisfied with every sort of neglect, but must add abuse yet; and all for a fool idea about a man who wasn't worth his salt!"

Mrs. Comstock picked up a hoe.

"Go right on!" she said. "Empty yourself. It's the last thing you'll ever do!"

"Then I'll make a tidy job of it," said Margaret. "You'll not touch me. You'll stand there and hear the truth at last, and because I dare face you and tell it, you will know in your soul it is truth. When Robert Comstock shaved that quagmire out there so close he went in, he wanted to keep you from seeing where he was coming from. He'd been to see Elvira Carney. They had plans to go to a dance that night—"

"Close your lips!" said Mrs. Comstock in a voice of deadly quiet.

"You know I wouldn't dare open them if I was not telling you the truth. I can prove what I say. I was coming from Reeds. It was hot in the woods and I stopped at Carney's as I passed for a drink. Elvira's bedridden old mother heard me, and she was so crazy for some one to talk with, I stepped in a minute. I saw Robert come down the path. Elvira saw him, too, and she ran out of the house to head him off. It looked funny, and I just deliberately moved where I could see and hear. He brought her his violin, and told her to get ready and meet him in the woods with it that night, and they would go to a dance. She took it and hid it in the little loft to the well-house and promised she'd go."

"Are you done?" demanded Mrs. Comstock.

"No. I am going to tell you the whole story. You don't spare Elnora anything. I shan't spare you. I hadn't been here that day, but I can tell you just how he was dressed, which way he went and every word they said, though they thought I was busy with her mother and wouldn't notice them. Put down your hoe, Kate. I went to Elvira, told her what I knew and made her give me Comstock's violin for Elnora over three years ago. She's been playing it ever since. I won't see her slighted and abused another day on account of a man who would have broken your heart if he had lived. Six months more would have showed you what everybody else knew. He was one of those men who couldn't trust himself, and so no woman was safe with him. Now, will you drop grieving over him, and do Elnora justice?"

Mrs. Comstock gripped the hoe tighter and turning she went down the walk, and started across the woods to the home of Elvira Carney. With averted head she passed the pool, steadily pursuing her way. Elvira Carney, hanging towels across the back fence, saw her coming and went toward the gate to meet her. Twenty years she had dreaded that visit. Since Margaret Sinton had compelled her to produce the violin she had hidden so long, because she was afraid to destroy it, she had come more near expectation than dread. The wages of sin are the hardest debts on earth to pay, and they are always collected at inconvenient times and unexpected places. Mrs. Comstock's face and hair were so white, that her dark eyes seemed burned into their setting. Silently she stared at the woman before her a long time.

"I might have saved myself the trouble of coming," she said at last, "I see you are guilty as sin!"

"What has Mag Sinton been telling you?" panted the miserable woman, gripping the fence.

"The truth!" answered Mrs. Comstock succinctly. "Guilt is in every line of your face, in your eyes, all over your wretched body. If I'd taken a good look at you any time in all these past years, no doubt I could have seen it just as plain as I can now. No woman or man can do what you've done, and not get a mark set on them for everyone to read."

"Mercy!" gasped weak little Elvira Carney. "Have mercy!"

"Mercy?" scoffed Mrs. Comstock. "Mercy! That's a nice word from you! How much mercy did you have on me? Where's the mercy that sent Comstock to the slime of the bottomless quagmire, and left me to see it, and then struggle on in agony all these years? How about the mercy of letting me allow my baby to be neglected all the days of her life? Mercy! Do you really dare use the word to me?"

"If you knew what I've suffered!"

"Suffered?" jeered Mrs. Comstock. "That's interesting. And pray, what have you suffered?"

"All the neighbours have suspected and been down on me. I ain't had a friend. I've always felt guilty of his death! I've seen him go down a thousand times, plain as ever you did. Many's the night I've stood on the other bank of that pool and listened to you, and I tried to throw myself in to keep from hearing you, but I didn't dare. I knew God would send me to burn forever, but I'd better done it; for now, He has set the burning on my body, and every hour it is slowly eating the life out of me. The doctor says it's a cancer—"

Mrs. Comstock exhaled a long breath. Her grip on the hoe relaxed and her stature lifted to towering height.

"I didn't know, or care, when I came here, just what I did," she said. "But my way is beginning to clear. If the guilt of your soul has come to a head, in a cancer on your body, it looks as if the Almighty didn't need any of my help in meting out His punishments. I really couldn't fix up anything to come anywhere near that. If you are going to burn until your life goes out with that sort of fire, you don't owe me anything!"

"Oh, Katharine Comstock!" groaned Elvira Carney, clinging to the fence for support.

"Looks as if the Bible is right when it says, 'The wages of sin is death,' don't it?" asked Mrs. Comstock. "Instead of doing a woman's work in life, you chose the smile of invitation, and the dress of unearned cloth. Now you tell me you are marked to burn to death with the unquenchable fire. And him! It was shorter with him, but let me tell you he got his share! He left me with an untruth on his lips, for he told me he was going to take his violin to Onabasha for a new key, when he carried it to you. Every vow of love and constancy he ever made me was a lie, after he touched your lips, so when he tried the wrong side of the quagmire, to hide from me the direction in which he was coming, it reached out for him, and it got him. It didn't hurry, either! It just sucked him down, slow and deliberate."

"Mercy!" groaned Elvira Carney. "Mercy!"

"I don't know the word," said Mrs. Comstock. "You took all that out of me long ago. The last twenty years haven't been of the sort that taught mercy. I've never had any on myself and none on my child. Why, in the name of justice, should I have mercy on you, or on him? You were both older than me, both strong, sane people, you deliberately chose your course when you lured him, and he, when he was unfaithful to me. When a Loose Man and a Light Woman face the death the Almighty ordained for them, why should they shout at me for mercy? What did I have to do with it?"

Elvira Carney sobbed in panting gasps.

"You've got tears, have you?" marvelled Mrs. Comstock. "Mine all dried long ago. I've none left to shed over my wasted life, my disfigured face and hair, my years of struggle with a man's work, my wreck of land among the tilled fields of my neighbours, or the final knowledge that the man I so gladly would have died to save, wasn't worth the sacrifice of a rattlesnake. If anything yet could wring a tear from me, it would be the thought of the awful injustice I always have done my girl. If I'd lay hand on you for anything, it would be for that."

"Kill me if you want to," sobbed Elvira Carney. "I know that I deserve it, and I don't care."

"You are getting your killing fast enough to suit me," said Mrs. Comstock. "I wouldn't touch you, any more than I would him, if I could. Once is all any man or woman deceives me about the holiest things of life. I wouldn't touch you any more than I would the black plague. I am going back to my girl."

Mrs. Comstock turned and started swiftly through the woods, but she had gone only a few rods when she stopped, and leaning on the hoe, she stood thinking deeply. Then she turned back. Elvira still clung to the fence, sobbing bitterly.

"I don't know," said Mrs. Comstock, "but I left a wrong impression with you. I don't want you to think that I believe the Almighty set a cancer to burning you as a punishment for your sins. I don't! I think a lot more of the Almighty. With a whole sky-full of worlds on His hands to manage, I'm not believing that He has time to look down on ours, and pick you out of all the millions of we sinners, and set a special kind of torture to eating you. It wouldn't be a gentlemanly thing to do, and, first of all, the Almighty is bound to be a gentleman. I think likely a bruise and bad blood is what caused your trouble. Anyway, I've got to tell you that the cleanest housekeeper I ever knew, and one of the noblest Christian women, was slowly eaten up by a cancer. She got hers from the careless work of a poor doctor. The Almighty is to forgive sin and heal disease, not to invent and spread it."

She had gone only a few steps when she again turned back.

"If you will gather a lot of red clover bloom, make a tea strong as lye of it, and drink quarts, I think likely it will help you, if you are not too far gone. Anyway, it will cool your blood and make the burning easier to bear."

Then she swiftly walked home. Enter the lonely cabin she could not, neither could she sit outside and think. She attacked a bed of beets and hoed until the perspiration ran from her face and body, then she began on the potatoes. When she was too tired to take another stroke she bathed and put on dry clothing. In securing her dress she noticed her husband's carefully preserved clothing lining one wall. She gathered it in a great armload and carried it out to the swamp. Piece by piece she pitched into the green maw of the quagmire all those articles she had dusted carefully and fought moths from for years, and stood watching as it slowly sucked them down. She went back to her room and gathered every scrap that had in any way belonged to Robert Comstock, excepting his gun and revolver, and threw it into the swamp. Then for the first time she set her door wide open.

She was too weary now to do more, but an urging unrest drove her. She wanted Elnora. It seemed to her she never could wait until the girl came and delivered her judgment. At last in an effort to get nearer to her, Mrs. Comstock climbed the stairs and stood looking around Elnora's room. It was very unfamiliar. The pictures were strange to her. Commencement had filled it with packages and bundles. The walls were covered with cocoons; moths and dragon flies were pinned about. Under the bed she could see a half-dozen large white boxes. She did not know what they contained. She pulled out one and lifted the lid. The bottom was covered with a sheet of thin cork, and on long pins sticking in it were dozens of great, velvet-winged moths. Each one was labelled, always there were two of a kind, in many cases four, showing under and upper wings of both male and female. They were of every colour and shape.

Mrs. Comstock caught her breath sharply. When and where had Elnora gotten all of them? They were the most exquisite sight the woman ever had seen, so she opened all the boxes to feast on their beautiful contents. As she did so there came more fully a sense of the distance between her and her child. She could not understand how Elnora had gone to school, and performed all this work secretly. When it was finished, up to the very last moth, she, the mother who should have been the first confidant and helper, had been the one to bring disappointment. Small wonder Elnora had come to hate her.

Mrs. Comstock carefully closed and replaced the boxes, and again stood looking around the room. This time her eyes rested on some books she did not remember having seen before, so she picked up one and found that it was a moth book. She glanced over the first pages and was soon eagerly reading. When the text reached the classification of species, she laid it down, took up another and read its introductory chapters. Then she found some papers and studied them. By that time her brain was in a confused jumble of ideas about capturing moths with differing baits and bright lights.

She went downstairs thinking deeply. Being unable to sit still and having nothing else to do she glanced at the clock and began preparing supper. The work dragged. A chicken was snatched up and dressed hurriedly. A spice cake sprang into being in short order. Strawberries that had been intended for preserves went into shortcake. Delicious odours crept from the cabin. She put many extra touches on the table and then commenced watching the road. Everything was ready, but Elnora did not come. Then began the anxious process of trying to keep cooked food warm and not spoil it. The birds went to bed and dusk came. Mrs. Comstock gave up the fire and set the supper on the table. Then she went out and sat on the front door step watching night creep all around her. She started eagerly as the gate creaked, but it was only Wesley Sinton coming down the walk.

"Katharine, Margaret and Elnora passed where I was working this afternoon, and Margaret got out of the carriage and called me to the fence. She told me what she had done. I've come to say to you that I am sorry. She has heard me threaten to do it a good many times, but I never would have got it done. I'd give a good deal if I could undo it, but I can't, so I've come to tell you how sorry I am."

"You've got something to be sorry for," said Mrs. Comstock, "but likely we ain't thinking of the same thing. It hurts me less to know the truth, than to live in ignorance. If Mag had the sense of a pewee, she'd told me long ago. That's what hurts me, to think that both of you knew Robert was not worth an hour of honest grief, yet you'd let me mourn him all these years and neglect Elnora while I did it. If I have anything to forgive you, that is what it is."

Sinton took off his hat and sat on a bench.

"Katharine," he said solemnly, "nobody ever knows how to take you."

"Would it be asking too much to take me for having a few grains of plain common sense?" she inquired. "You've known all this time that Comstock got what he deserved, when he undertook to sneak in an unused way across a swamp, with which he was none too familiar. Now I should have thought that you'd figure that knowing the same thing would be the best method to cure me of pining for him, and slighting my child."

"Heaven only knows we have thought of that, and talked of it often, but we were both too big cowards. We didn't dare tell you."

"So you have gone on year after year, watching me show indifference to Elnora, and yet a little horse-sense would have pointed out to you that she was my salvation. Why, look at it! Not married quite a year. All his vows of love and fidelity made to me before the Almighty forgotten in a few months, and a dance and a Light Woman so alluring he had to lie and sneak for them. What kind of a prospect is that for a life? I know men and women. An honourable man is an honourable man, and a liar is a liar; both are born and not made. One cannot change to the other any more than that some old leopard can change its spots. After a man tells a woman the first untruth of that sort, the others come piling thick, fast, and mountain high. The desolation they bring in their wake overshadows anything I have suffered completely. If he had lived six months more I should have known him for what he was born to be. It was in the blood of him. His father and grandfather before him were fiddling, dancing people; but I was certain of him. I thought we could leave Ohio and come out here alone, and I could so love him and interest him in his work, that he would be a man. Of all the fool, fruitless jobs, making anything of a creature that begins by deceiving her, is the foolest a sane woman ever undertook. I am more than sorry you and Margaret didn't see your way clear to tell me long ago. I'd have found it out in a few more months if he had lived, and I wouldn't have borne it a day. The man who breaks his vows to me once, don't get the second chance. I give truth and honour. I have a right to ask it in return. I am glad I understand at last. Now, if Elnora will forgive me, we will take a new start and see what we can make out of what is left of life. If she won't, then it will be my time to learn what suffering really means."

"But she will," said Sinton. "She must! She can't help it when things are explained. Don't you worry over her."

"I notice she isn't hurrying any about coming home. Do you know where she is or what she is doing?"

"I do not. But likely she will be along soon. I must go help Billy with the night work. Good-bye, Katharine. Thank the Lord you have come to yourself at last!"

They shook hands and Sinton went down the road while Mrs. Comstock entered the cabin. She went to the supper table, but she could not swallow food. She stood in the back door watching the sky for moths, but they did not seem to be very numerous. Her spirits sank and she breathed unevenly. Then she heard the front screen. She reached the middle door as Elnora touched the foot of the stairs.

"Hurry, and get ready, Elnora," she said. "Your supper is almost spoiled now."

Elnora closed the stair door behind her, and for the first time in her life, threw the heavy lever which barred out anyone from downstairs. Mrs. Comstock heard the thud, and knew what it meant. She reeled slightly and caught the doorpost for support. For a few minutes she clung there, then sank to the nearest chair. After a long time she arose and stumbling half blindly, she put the food in the cupboard and covered the table. She took the lamp in one hand, the butter in the other, and started for the spring house. Something brushed close by her face, and she looked just in time to see a winged creature rise above the cabin and sail away.

"That was a night bird," she muttered. As she stooped to set the butter in the water, came another thought. "Perhaps it was a moth!" Mrs. Comstock dropped the butter and hurried out with the lamp; she held it high above her head and waited until her arms ached. Small insects of night gathered, and at last a little dusty miller, but nothing came of any size.

"I got to go where they are, if I get them," muttered Mrs. Comstock.

She hurried into the cabin, set the lamp on the table, and stood thinking deeply. She went to the barn for the pair of stout high boots she used in feeding stock in deep snow. Throwing the boots by the back door she climbed to the loft over the spring house, and hunted an old lard oil lantern and one of first manufacture for oil. Both these she cleaned and filled. She listened until everything upstairs had been still for over a half-hour. By that time if was after eleven o'clock. Then she took the good lantern from the kitchen, the two old ones, a handful of matches, a ball of twine, and went from the cabin, softly closing the door.

Sitting on the back steps, she put on the boots, and then stood gazing into the sweet June night, first in the direction of the woods on her land, then toward the Limberlost. Its outline looked so dark and forbidding she shuddered and went down the garden, taking the path toward the woods, but as she neared the pool her knees wavered and her courage fled. The knowledge that in her soul she was now glad Robert Comstock was at the bottom of it made a coward of her, who fearlessly had mourned him there, nights untold. She could not go on. She skirted the back of the garden, crossed a field, and came out on the road. Soon she reached the Limberlost. She hunted until she found the old trail, then followed it stumbling over logs and through clinging vines and grasses. The heavy boots clumped on her feet, overhanging branches whipped her face and pulled her hair. But her eyes were on the sky as she went straining into the night, hoping to find signs of a living creature on wing.

By and by she began to see the wavering flight of something she thought near the right size. She had no idea where she was, but she stopped, lighted a lantern and hung it as high as she could reach. A little distance away she placed the second and then the third. The objects came nearer and sick with disappointment she saw that they were bats. Crouching in the damp swamp grasses, without a thought of snakes or venomous insects, she waited, her eyes roving from lantern to lantern. Once she thought a creature of high flight dropped near the lard oil light, so she arose breathlessly waiting, but either it passed or it was an illusion. She glanced at the old lantern, then at the new, and was on her feet in an instant creeping close. Something large as a small bird was fluttering around. Mrs. Comstock began to perspire, while her hand shook wildly. Closer she crept and just as she reached for it, something similar swept by and both flew away together.

Mrs. Comstock set her teeth and stood shivering. For a long time the locusts rasped, the whip-poor-wills cried and a steady hum of night life throbbed in her ears. Away in the sky she saw something coming when it was no larger than a falling leaf. Straight on toward the light it came. Without in the least realizing what she was doing, Mrs. Comstock began to pray aloud.

"This way, O Lord! Make it come this way! Please! You know how I need it! O Lord, send it lower!"

The moth hesitated at the first light, then slowly, easily it came toward the second, as if following a path of air. It touched a leaf near the lantern and settled. As Mrs. Comstock reached for it a thin yellow spray wet her hand and the surrounding leaves. When its wings raised above its back, her fingers came together. She held the moth to the light. It was nearer brown than yellow, and she remembered having seen some like it in the boxes that afternoon. It was not the one needed to complete the collection, but Elnora might want it, so Mrs. Comstock held on. Just there the Almighty was kind, or nature was sufficient, as you look at it, for following the law of its being when disturbed, the moth again threw the spray by which some suppose it attracts its kind, and liberally sprinkled Mrs. Comstock's dress front and arms. From that instant, she became the best moth bait ever invented. Every Polyphemus in range hastened to her, and other fluttering creatures of night followed. The influx came her way. She snatched wildly here and there until she had one in each hand and no place to put them. She could see more coming, and her aching heart, swollen with the strain of long excitement hurt pitifully. She prayed in broken exclamations that not always sounded reverent, but never was human soul in more deadly earnest.

Moths were coming. She had one in each hand. They were not yellow, and she did not know what to do. She glanced around to try to discover some way to keep what she had, and her throbbing heart stopped and every muscle stiffened. There was the dim outline of a crouching figure not two yards away, and a pair of eyes their owner thought hidden, caught the light in a cold stream. Her first impulse was to scream and fly for life. Before her lips could open a big moth alighted on her breast while she felt another walking over her hair. All sense of caution deserted her. She did not care to live if she could not replace the yellow moth she had killed. She set her eyes on those among the leaves.

"Here, you!" she cried hoarsely. "I need you! Get yourself out here, and help me. These critters are going to get away from me, and I've got to have them. Hustle!"

Pete Corson parted the bushes and stepped into the light.

"Oh, it's you!" said Mrs. Comstock. "I might have known! But you gave me a start. Here, hold this until I make some sort of bag for them. Go easy! If you break them I don't guarantee what will happen to you!"

"Pretty fierce, ain't you!" laughed Pete, but he advanced and held out his hands. "For Elnora, I s'pose?"

"Yes," said Mrs. Comstock. "In a mad fit, I trampled one this morning, and by the luck of the old boy himself it was the last moth she needed to complete a collection. I got to get another one or die."

"Then I guess it's your funeral," said Pete. "There ain't a chance in a dozen the right one will come. What colour was it?"

"Yellow, and big as a bird."

"The Emperor, likely," said Pete. "You dig for that kind, and they are not numerous, so's 'at you can smash 'em for fun."

"Well, I can try to get one, anyway," said Mrs. Comstock. "I forgot all about bringing anything to put them in. You take a pinch on their wings until I make a poke."

Mrs. Comstock removed her apron, tearing off the strings. She unfastened and stepped from the skirt of her calico dress. With one apron string she tied shut the band and placket. She pulled a wire pin from her hair, stuck it through the other string, and using it as a bodkin ran it around the hem of her skirt. Her fingers flew, and shortly she had a large bag. She put several branches inside to which the moths could cling, closed the mouth partially and held it toward Pete.

"Put your hand well down and let the things go!" she ordered. "But be careful, man! Don't run into the twigs! Easy! That's one. Now the other. Is the one on my head gone? There was one on my dress, but I guess it flew. Here comes a kind of a gray looking one."

Pete slipped several more moths into the bag.

"Now, that's five, Mrs. Comstock," he said. "I'm sorry, but you'll have to make that do. You must get out of here lively. Your lights will be taken for hurry calls, and inside the next hour a couple of men will ride here like fury. They won't be nice Sunday school men, and they won't hold bags and catch moths for you. You must go quick!"

Mrs. Comstock laid down the bag and pulled one of the lanterns lower.

"I won't budge a step," she said. "This land don't belong to you. You have no right to order me off it. Here I stay until I get a yellow Emperor, and no little petering thieves of this neighbourhood can scare me away."

"You don't understand," said Pete. "I'm willing to help Elnora, and I'd take care of you, if I could, but there will be too many for me, and they will be mad at being called out for nothing."

"Well, who's calling them out?" demanded Mrs. Comstock. "I'm catching moths. If a lot of good-for-nothings get fooled into losing some sleep, why, let them, they can't hurt me, or stop my work."

"They can, and they'll do both."

"Well, I'll see them do it!" said Mrs. Comstock. "I've got Robert's revolver in my dress, and I can shoot as straight as any man, if I'm mad enough. Anyone that interferes with me to-night will find me mad aplenty. There goes another!"

She stepped into the light and waited until a big brown moth settled on her and was easily taken. Then in light, airy flight came a delicate pale green thing, and Mrs. Comstock started in pursuit. But the scent was not right. The moth fluttered high, then dropped lower, still lower, and sailed away. With outstretched hands Mrs. Comstock pursued it. She hurried one way and another, then ran over an object which tripped her and she fell. She regained her feet in an instant, but she had lost sight of the moth. With livid face she turned on the crouching man.

"You nasty, sneaking son of Satan!" she cried. "Why are you hiding there? You made me lose the one I wanted most of any I've had a chance at yet. Get out of here! Go this minute, or I'll fill your worthless carcass so full of holes you'll do to sift cornmeal. Go, I say! I'm using the Limberlost to-night, and I won't be stopped by the devil himself! Cut like fury, and tell the rest of them they can just go home. Pete is going to help me, and he is all of you I need. Now go!"

The man turned and went. Pete leaned against a tree, held his mouth shut and shook inwardly. Mrs. Comstock came back panting.

"The old scoundrel made me lose that!" she said. "If anyone else comes snooping around here I'll just blow them up to start with. I haven't time to talk. Suppose that had been yellow! I'd have killed that man, sure! The Limberlost isn't safe to-night, sooner those whelps find it out, the better it will be for them."

Pete stopped laughing to look at her. He saw that she was speaking the truth. She was quite past reason, sense, or fear. The soft night air stirred the wet hair around her temples, the flickering lanterns made her face a ghastly green. She would stop at nothing, that was evident. Pete suddenly began catching moths with exemplary industry. In putting one into the bag, another escaped.

"We must not try that again," said Mrs. Comstock. "Now, what will we do?"

"We are close to the old case," said Pete. "I think I can get into it. Maybe we could slip the rest in there."

"That's a fine idea!" said Mrs. Comstock. "They'll have so much room there they won't be likely to hurt themselves, and the books say they don't fly in daytime unless they are disturbed, so they will settle when it's light, and I can come with Elnora to get them."

They captured two more, and then Pete carried them to the case.

"Here comes a big one!" he cried as he returned.

Mrs. Comstock looked up and stepped out with a prayer on her lips. She could not tell the colour at that distance, but the moth appeared different from the others. On it came, dropping lower and darting from light to light. As it swept near her, "O Heavenly Father!" exulted Mrs. Comstock, "it's yellow! Careful, Pete! Your hat, maybe!"

Pete made a long sweep. The moth wavered above the hat and sailed away. Mrs. Comstock leaned against a tree and covered her face with her shaking hands.

"That is my punishment!" she cried. "Oh, Lord, if you will give a moth like that into my possession, I'll always be a better woman!"

The Emperor again came in sight. Pete stood tense and ready. Mrs. Comstock stepped into the light and watched the moth's course. Then a second appeared in pursuit of the first. The larger one wavered into the radius of light once more. The perspiration rolled down the man's tense face. He half lifted the hat.

"Pray, woman! Pray now!" he panted.

"I guess I best get over by that lard oil light and go to work," breathed Mrs. Comstock. "The Lord knows this is all in prayer, but it's no time for words just now. Ready, Pete! You are going to get a chance first!"

Pete made another long, steady sweep, but the moth darted beneath the hat. In its flight it came straight toward Mrs. Comstock. She snatched off the remnant of apron she had tucked into her petticoat band and held the calico before her. The moth struck full against it and clung to the goods. Pete crept up stealthily. The second moth followed the first, and the spray showered the apron.

"Wait!" gasped Mrs. Comstock. "I think they have settled. The books say they won't leave now."

The big pale yellow creature clung firmly, lowering and raising its wings. The other came nearer. Mrs. Comstock held the cloth with rigid hands, while Pete could hear her breathing in short gusts.

"Shall I try now?" he implored.

"Wait!" whispered the woman. "Something seems to say wait!"

The night breeze stiffened and gently waved the apron. Locusts rasped, mosquitoes hummed and frogs sang uninterruptedly. A musky odour slowly filled the air.

"Now shall I?" questioned Pete.

"No. Leave them alone. They are safe now. They are mine. They are my salvation. God and the Limberlost gave them to me! They won't move for hours. The books all say so. O Heavenly Father, I am thankful to You, and you, too, Pete Corson! You are a good man to help me. Now, I can go home and face my girl."

Instead, Mrs. Comstock dropped suddenly. She spread the apron across her knees. The moths were undisturbed. Then her tired white head dropped, the tears she had thought forever dried gushed forth, and she sobbed for pure joy.

"Oh, I wouldn't do that now, you know!" comforted Pete. "Think of getting two! That's more than you ever could have expected. A body would think you would cry, if you hadn't got any. Come on, now. It's almost morning. Let me help you home."

Pete took the big and the two old lanterns. Mrs. Comstock carried her moths and the best lantern and went ahead to light the way.

Elnora had sat by her window far into the night. At last she undressed and went to bed, but sleep would not come. She had gone to the city to talk with members of the School Board about a room in the grades. There was a possibility that she might secure the moth, and so be able to start to college that fall, but if she did not, then she wanted the school. She had been given some encouragement, but she was so unhappy that nothing mattered. She could not see the way open to anything in life, while she remained with her mother, save a long series of disappointments. Yet Margaret Sinton had advised her to go home and try once more. Margaret had seemed so sure there would be a change for the better, that Elnora had consented, although she had no hope herself. So strong is the bond of blood, she could not make up her mind to seek a home elsewhere, even after the day which had passed. Unable to sleep she arose at last, and the room being warm, she sat on the floor by the window. The lights in the swamp caught her eye. She was very uneasy, for quite a hundred of her best moths were in the case. However, there was no money, and no one ever had touched a book or any of her apparatus. Watching the lights set her thinking, and before she realized it, she was in a panic of fear.

She hurried down the stairway softly calling her mother. There was no answer. She lightly stepped across the sitting room and looked in at the open door. There was no one, and the bed had not been used. Her first thought was that her mother had gone to the pool; and the Limberlost was alive with signals. Pity and fear mingled in the heart of the girl. She opened the kitchen door, crossed the garden and ran back to the swamp. As she neared it she listened, but she could hear only the usual voices of night.

"Mother!" she called softly. Then louder, "Mother!"

There was not a sound. Chilled with fright she hurried back to the cabin. She did not know what to do. She understood what the lights in the Limberlost meant. Where was her mother? She was afraid to enter, while she was growing very cold and still more fearful about remaining outside. At last she went to her mother's room, picked up the gun, carried it into the kitchen, and crowding in a little corner behind the stove, she waited in trembling anxiety. The time was dreadfully long before she heard her mother's voice. Then she decided that someone had been ill and sent for her, so she took courage, and stepping swiftly across the kitchen she unbarred the door and drew back out of sight by the table.

Mrs. Comstock entered dragging her heavy feet. Her dress skirt was gone, her petticoat wet and drabbled, and the waist of her dress was almost torn from her body. Her hair hung in damp strings; her eyes were red with crying. In one hand she held the lantern, and in the other stiffly extended before her, on a wad of calico reposed a magnificent pair of yellow Emperors. Elnora stared, her lips parted.

"Shall I put these others in the kitchen?" inquired a man's voice.

The girl shrank back to the shadows.

"Yes, anywhere inside the door," replies Mrs. Comstock as she moved a few steps to make way for him. Pete's head appeared. He set down the moths and was gone.

"Thank you, Pete, more than ever woman thanked you before!" said Mrs. Comstock.

She placed the lantern on the table and barred the door. As she turned Elnora came into view. Mrs. Comstock leaned toward her, and held out the moths. In a voice vibrant with tones never before heard she said, "Elnora, my girl, mother's found you another moth!"

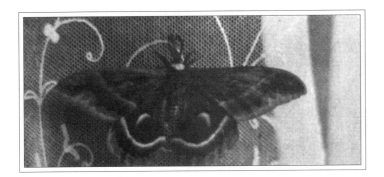

"The Robin Moth," "The Yellow Emperor," "Hera of the Corn"

from *Moths of the Limberlost*

At the beginning of the chapter on the *Cecropia,* or "Robin Moth," Stratton Porter relates two anecdotes of her early days of moth collecting. Her first *Cecropia* escaped from the house because she left it on the parlor curtains rather than down in the cellar as she had been told.

These three chapters are from *Moths of the Limberlost,* the best known of Stratton Porter's nature books, although still unfortunately all too little known. They illustrate both her abilities and the value of her writing as a record of the natural world and the human community it supported in the rural areas of the American midwest at the beginning of the twentieth century.

"The Robin Moth"

SO I LOST MY FIRST Cecropia, and from that day until a woman grown and much of this material secured, in all my field work among the birds, flowers, and animals, I never had seen another. They had taunted me in museums, and been my envy in private collections, but find one, I could not. When in my field work among the birds, so many moths of other families almost had thrust themselves upon me that I began a collection of reproductions of them, I found little difficulty in securing almost anything else. I could picture Sphinx Moths in any position I chose, and Lunas seemed eager to pose for me. A friend carried to me a beautiful tan-coloured Polyphemus with transparent moons like isinglass set in its wings of softest velvet down, and as for butterflies, it was not necessary to go afield for them; they came to me. I could pick a Papilio Ajax, that some of my friends were years in securing, from the pinks in my garden. A pair of Antiopas spent a night, and waited to be pictured in the morning, among the leaves of my passion vine. Painted Beauties swayed along my flowered walks, and in September a Viceroy reigned in state on every chrysanthemum, and a Monarch was enthroned on every sunbeam. No luck was too good for me, no butterfly or moth too rare, except forever and always the coveted Cecropia, and by this time I had learned to my disgust that it was one of the commonest of all.

Then one summer, late in June, a small boy, having an earnest, eager little face, came to me tugging a large box. He said he had something for me. He said "they called it a butterfly, but he was sure it never was." He was eminently correct. He had a splendid big Cecropia. I was delighted. Of course to have found one myself would have filled my cup to overflowing, but to secure a perfect, living specimen was good enough. For the first time my childish loss seemed in a measure compensated. Then, I only could study a moth to my satisfaction and set it free; now, I could make reproductions so perfect that every antler of its antennæ could be counted with the naked eye, and copy its colours accurately, before giving back its liberty.

I asked him whether he wanted money or a picture of it, and as I expected, he said "money," so he was paid. An hour later he came back and said he wanted the picture. On being questioned as to his change of heart, he said "mamma told him to say he wanted the picture, and she would give him the money." My sympathy was with her. I wanted the studies I intended to make of that Cecropia myself, and I wanted them very badly.

I opened the box to examine the moth, and found it so numb with the cold over night, and so worn and helpless, that it could not cling to a leaf or twig. I tried repeatedly, and fearing that it had been subjected to rough treatment, and soon would be lifeless, for these moths live only a short time, I hastily set up a camera focusing on a branch. Then I tried posing my specimen. Until the third time it fell, but the fourth it clung, and crept down a twig, settling at last in a position that far surpassed any posing that I could do. I was very pleased, and yet it made a complication. It had gone so far that it might be off the plate and from focus. It seemed so stupid and helpless that I decided to risk a peep at the glass, and hastily removing the plate and changing the shutter, a slight but most essential alteration was made, everything replaced, and the bulb caught up. There was only a breath of sound as I turned, and then I stood horrified, for my Cecropia was sailing over a large elm tree in a corner of the orchard, and for a block my gaze followed it skyward, flying like a bird before it vanished in the distance, so quickly had it recovered in fresh air and sunshine.

I have undertaken to describe some very difficult things, but I would not attempt to portray my feelings, and three days later there was no change. It was in the height of my season of field work, and I had several extremely interesting series of bird studies on hand, and many miscellaneous subjects. In those days some pictures were secured that I then thought, and yet feel, will live, but nothing mattered to me. There was a standing joke among my friends that I never would be satisfied with my field work until I had made a study of a "Ha-ha bird," but I doubt if even that specimen would have lifted the gloom of those days. Everything was a drag, and frequently I would think over it all in detail, and roundly bless myself for taking a prize so rare, to me at least, into the open.

The third day stands lurid in my memory. It was the hottest, most difficult day of all my years of experience afield. The temperature ranged from 104 to 108 in the village, and in quarries open to the east, flat fields, and steaming swamps it certainly could have been no cooler. With set cameras I was working for a shot of a hawk that was feeding on all the young birds and rabbits in the vicinity of its nest. I also wanted a number of studies to fill a commission that was pressing me. Subjects for several pictures had been found, and exposures made on them when the weather was so hot that the rubber slide of a plate holder would curl like a horseshoe if not laid on a case, and held flat by a camera while I worked. Perspiration dried, and the landscape took on a sombre black velvet hue, with a liberal sprinkling of gold stars. I sank into a stupor going home, and an old farmer aroused me, and disentangled my horse from a thicket of wild briers into which it had strayed. He said most emphatically that if I did not know enough to remain indoors weather like that, my friends should appoint me a "guardeen."

I reached the village more worn in body and spirit than I ever had been. I felt that I could not endure another degree of heat on the back of my head, and I was much discouraged concerning my work. Why not drop it all, and go where there were cool forests and breezes sighing? Perhaps my studies were not half so good as I thought! Perhaps people would not care for them! For that matter, perhaps the editors and publishers never would give the public an opportunity to see my work at all!

I dragged a heavy load up the steps and swung it to the veranda, and there stood almost paralyzed. On the top step, where I could not reach the Cabin door without seeing it, newly emerged, and slowly exercising a pair of big wings, with every gaudy marking fresh with new life, was the finest Cecropia I ever had seen anywhere. Recovering myself with a start, I had it under my net—that had waited twenty years to cover it! Inside the door I dropped the net, and the moth crept on my fingers. What luck! What extra golden luck! I almost felt that God had been sorry for me, and sent it there to encourage me to keep on picturing the beauties and wonders of His creations for people who could not go afield to see for themselves, and to teach those who could to protect helpless, harmless things for their use and beauty.

I walked down the hall, and vaguely scanned the solid rows of books and specimens lining the library walls. I scarcely realized the thought that was in my mind, but what I was looking for was not there. The dining-room then, with panelled walls and curtains of tapestry? It was not there! Straight to the white and gold music room I went. Then a realizing sense came to me. It was *Brussels lace* for which I was searching! On the most delicate, snowiest place possible, on the finest curtain there, I placed my Cecropia, and then stepped back and gazed at it with a sort of "Touch it over my dead body" sentiment in my heart. An effort was required to arouse myself, to realize that I was not dreaming. To search the fields and woods for twenty years, and then find the specimen I had sought awaiting me at my own door! Well might it have been a dream, but that the Cecropia, clinging to the meshes of the lace, slowly opening and closing its wings to strengthen them for flight, could be nothing but a delightful reality.

A few days later, in the valley of the Wood Robin, while searching for its nest I found a large cocoon. It was above my head, but afterward I secured it by means of a ladder, and carried it home. Shortly there emerged a yet larger Cecropia, and luck seemed with me. I could find them everywhere through June, the time of their emergence, later their eggs, and the tiny caterpillars that hatched from them. During the summer I found these caterpillars, in different stages of growth, until fall, when after their last moult and casting of skin, they reached the final period of feeding; some were over four inches in length, a beautiful shade of greenish blue, with red and yellow warty projections—tubercles, according to scientific works.

It is easy to find the cocoons these caterpillars spin, because they are the largest woven by any moth, and placed in such a variety of accessible spots. They can be found in orchards, high on branches, and on water sprouts at the base of trees. Frequently they are spun on swamp willows, box-elder, maple, or wild cherry. Mr. Black once found for me the largest cocoon I ever have seen; a pale tan colour with silvery lights, woven against the inside of a hollow log. Perhaps the most beautiful of all, a dull red, was found under the flooring of an old bridge crossing a stream in the heart of the swamp, by a girl not unknown to fiction, who brought it to me. In a deserted orchard close the Wabash, Raymond once found a pair of empty cocoons at the foot of a big apple tree, fastened to the same twigs, and within two inches of each other.

But the most wonderful thing of all occurred when Wallace Hardison, a faithful friend to my work, sawed a board from the roof of his chicken house and carried to me twin Cecropia cocoons, spun so closely together they were touching, and slightly interwoven. By the closest examination I could discover slight difference between them. The one on the right was a trifle fuller in the body, wider at the top, a shade lighter in colour and the inner case seemed heavier.

All winter those cocoons occupied the place of state in my collection. Every few days I tried them to see if they gave the solid thump indicating healthy pupæ, and listened to learn if they were moving. By May they were under constant surveillance. On the fourteenth I was called from home a few hours to attend the funeral of a friend. I think nothing short of a funeral would have taken me, for the moth from a single cocoon had emerged on the eleventh. I hurried home near noon, only to find that I was late, for one was out, and the top of the other cocoon heaving with the movements of the second.

The moth that had escaped was a male. It clung to the side of the board, wings limp, its abdomen damp. The opening from which it came was so covered with terra cotta coloured down that I thought at first it must have disfigured itself; but full development proved it could spare that much and yet appear all right.

In the fall I had driven a nail through one corner of the board, and tacked it against the south side of the Cabin, where I made reproductions of the cocoons. The nail had been left, and now it suggested the same place. A light stroke on the head of the nail, covered with cloth to prevent jarring, fastened the board on a log. Never in all my life did I hurry as on that day, and I called my entire family into service. The Deacon stood at one elbow, Molly-Cotton at the other, and the gardener in the rear. There was not a second to be lost, and no time for an unnecessary movement; for in the heat and bright sunshine those moths would emerge and develop with amazing rapidity.

Molly-Cotton held an umbrella over them to prevent this as much as possible; the Deacon handed plate holders, and Brenner ran errands. Working as fast as I could make my fingers fly in setting up the camera, and getting a focus, the second moth's head was out, its front feet struggling to pull up the body, and its antennæ beginning to lift, when I was ready for the first snap at half-past eleven.

By the time I inserted the slide, turned the plate holder and removed another slide, the first moth to appear had climbed up the board a few steps, and the second was halfway out. Its antennæ were nearly horizontal now, and from its position I decided that the wings as they lay in the pupa case were folded neither to the back nor to the front, but pressed against the body in a lengthwise crumpled mass, the heavy front rib, or costa, on top.

Again I changed plates with all speed. By the time I was ready for the third snap the male had reached the top of the board, its wings opened for the first time, and began a queer trembling motion. The second one had emerged and was running into the first, so I held my finger in the line of its advance, and when it climbed on I lowered it to the edge of the board beside the cocoons. It immediately clung to the wood. The big pursy abdomen and smaller antennæ, that now turned forward in position, proved this a female. The exposure was made not ten seconds after she cleared the case, and with her back to the lens, so the position and condition of the wings and antennæ on emergence can be seen clearly.

Quickly as possible I changed the plates again; the time that elapsed could not have been over half a minute. The male was trying to creep up the wall, and the increase in the length and expansion of the female's wings could be seen. The colours on both were exquisite, but they grew a trifle less brilliant as the moths became dry.

Again I turned to the business of plate changing. The heat was intense, and perspiration was streaming from my face. I called to Molly-Cotton to shield the moths while I made the change. "Drat the moths!" cried the Deacon. "Shade your mother!" Being an obedient girl, she shifted the umbrella, and by the time I was ready for business, the male was on the logs and travelling up the side of the Cabin. The female was climbing toward the logs also, so that a side view showed her wings already beginning to lift above her back.

I had only five snapshot plates in my holders, so I was compelled to stop. It was as well, for surely the record was complete, and I was almost prostrate with excitement and heat. Several days later I opened each of the cocoons and made interior studies. The one on the right was split down the left side and turned back to show the bed of spun silk of exquisite colour that covers the inner case. Some say this silk has no commercial value, as it is cut in lengths reaching from the top around the inner case and back to the top again; others think it can be used. The one on the left was opened down the front of the outer case, the silk parted and the heavy inner case cut from top to bottom to show the smooth interior wall, the thin pupa case burst by the exit of the moth, and the cast caterpillar skin crowded at the bottom.

The pair mated that same night, and the female began laying eggs by noon the following day. She dotted them in lines over the inside of her box, and on leaves placed in it, and at times piled them in a heap instead of placing them as do these moths in freedom. Having taken a picture of a full-grown caterpillar of this moth brought to me by Mr. Andrew Idlewine, I now had a complete Cecropia history; eggs, full-grown caterpillars, twin cocoons, and the story of the emergence of the moths that wintered in them. I do not suppose Mr. Hardison thought he was doing anything unusual when he brought me those cocoons, yet by bringing them, he made it possible for me to secure this series of twin Cecropia moths, male and female, a thing never before recorded by lepidopterist or photographer so far as I can learn.

The Cecropia is a moth whose acquaintance nature-loving city people can cultivate. In December of 1906, on a tree, maple I think, near No. 2230 North Delaware Street, Indianapolis, I found four cocoons of this moth, and on the next tree, save one, another. Then I began watching, and in the coming days I counted them by the hundred through the city. Several bushels of these cocoons could have been clipped in Indianapolis alone, and there is no reason why any other city that has maple, elm, catalpa, and other shade trees would not have as many; so that any one who would like can find them easily.

Cecropia cocoons bewilder a beginner by their difference in shape. You cannot determine the sex of the moth by the size of the cocoon. In the case of the twins, the cocoon of the female was the larger; but I have known male and female alike to emerge from large or small. You are fairly sure of selecting a pair if you depend upon weight. The females are heavier than the males, because they emerge with quantities of eggs ready to deposit as soon as they have mated. If any one wants to winter a pair of moths, they are reasonably sure of doing so by selecting the heaviest and lightest cocoons they can find.

In the selection of cocoons, hold them to the ear, and with a quick motion reverse them end for end. If there is a dull, solid thump, the moth is alive, and will emerge all right. If this thump is lacking, and there is a rattle like a small seed shaking in a dry pod, it means that the caterpillar has gone into the cocoon with one of the tiny parasites that infest these worms, clinging to it, and the pupa has been eaten by the parasite.

In fall and late summer are the best times to find cocoons, as birds tear open many of them in winter; and when weather-beaten they fade, and do not show the exquisite shadings of silk of those newly spun.

When fresh, the colours range from almost white through lightest tans and browns to a genuine red, and there is a silvery effect that is lovely on some of the large, baggy ones, hidden under bridges. Out of doors the moths emerge in middle May or June, but they are earlier in the heat of a house. They are the largest of any species, and exquisitely coloured, the shades being strongest on the upper side of the wings. They differ greatly in size, most males having an average wing sweep of five inches, and a female that emerged in my conservatory from a cocoon that I wintered with particular care had a spread of seven inches, the widest of which I have heard; six and three quarters is a large female. The moth, on appearing, seems all head and abdomen, the wings hanging limp and wet from the shoulders. It at once creeps around until a place where it can hang with the wings down is found, and soon there begins a sort of pumping motion of the body. I imagine this is to start circulation, to exercise parts, and force blood into the wings. They begin to expand, to dry, to take on colour with amazing rapidity, and as soon as they are full size and crisp, the moth commences raising and lowering them slowly, as in flight. If a male, he emerges near ten in the forenoon, and flies at dusk in search of a mate.

As the females are very heavy with eggs, they usually remain where they are. After mating they begin almost at once to deposit their eggs, and do not take flight until they have finished. The eggs are round, having a flat top that becomes slightly depressed as they dry. They are of pearl colour, with a touch of brown, changing to grayish as the tiny caterpillars develop. Their outline can be traced through the shell on which they make their first meal when they emerge. Female Cecropias average about three hundred and fifty eggs each, that they sometimes place singly, and again string in rows, or in captivity pile in heaps. In freedom they deposit the eggs mostly on leaves, sometimes the under, sometimes the upper, sides or dot them on bark, boards or walls. The percentage of loss of eggs and the young is large, for they are nowhere numerous enough to become a pest, as they certainly would if three hundred caterpillars survived to each female moth. The young feed on apple, willow, maple, box-elder, or wild cherry leaves, and grow through a series of feeding periods and moults, during which they rest for a few days, cast the skin and intestinal lining and then feed for another period.

After the females have finished depositing their eggs, they cling to branches, vines or walls a few days, fly aimlessly at night and then pass out without ever having taken food.

I have painted this moth from a newly emerged female, when all colouring was much stronger than after a few days of life. I have been careful to place the most minute line and trace the finest colour shading from lavender and rose madder at the apex of the wing, to terra cotta, black and white at the base. How perfectly the engravers can reproduce all these complicated markings remains to be seen.

Cecropia has several "Cousins," Promethea, Angulifera, Gloveri, and Cynthia, that vary slightly in marking and more in colour. All are smaller than Cecropia. The male of Promethea is the darkest moth of the Limberlost. The male of Angulifera is a brownish gray, the female reddish, with warm tan colours on her wing borders. She is very beautiful. The markings on the wings of both are not half-moon shaped, as Cecropia and Gloveri, but are oblong, and largest at the point next the apex of the wing.

Gloveri could not be told from Cecropia in half-tone reproduction by any save a scientist, so similar are the markings, but in colour they are vastly different, and more beautiful. The only living Gloveri I ever secured was almost done with life, and she was so badly battered I could not think of making a picture of her. The wings are a lovely red wine colour, with warm tan borders, and the crescents are white, with a line of tan and then of black. The abdomen is white striped with wine and black.

Cynthia has pale olive green shadings on both male and female. These are imported moths brought here about 1861 in the hope that they would prove valuable in silk culture. They occur mostly where the ailanthus grows.

My heart goes out to Cecropia because it is such a noble, birdlike, big fellow, and since it has decided to be rare with me no longer, all that is necessary is to pick it up, either in caterpillar, cocoon, or moth, at any season of the year, in almost any location. The Cecropia moth resembles the robin among birds; not alone because he is gray with red markings, but also he haunts the same localities. The robin is the bird of the eaves, the back door, the yard and orchard. Cecropia is the moth. My doorstep is not the only one they grace; my friends have found them in like places. Cecropia cocoons are attached to fences, chicken-coops, barns, houses, and all through the orchards of old country places, so that their emergence at bloom time adds to May and June one more beauty, and frequently I speak of them as the Robin Moth.

In connection with Cecropia there came to me the most delightful experience of my life. One perfect night during the middle of May, all the world white with tree bloom, touched to radiance with brilliant moonlight, intoxicating with countless blending perfumes, I placed a female Cecropia on the screen of my sleeping-room door and retired. The lot on which the Cabin stands is sloping, so that, although the front foundations are low, my door is at least five feet above the ground, and opens on a circular porch, from which steps lead down between two apple trees, at that time sheeted in bloom. Past midnight I was awakened by soft touches on the screen, faint pullings at the wire. I went to the door and found the porch, orchard, and night-sky alive with Cecropias holding high carnival. I had not supposed there were so many in all this world. From every direction they came floating like birds down the moonbeams. I carefully removed the female from the door to a window close beside, and stepped on the porch. No doubt I was permeated with the odour of the moth. As I advanced to the top step, that lay even with the middle branches of the apple trees, the exquisite big creatures came swarming around me. I could feel them on my hair, my shoulders, and see them settling on my gown and outstretched hands. Far as I could penetrate the night-sky more were coming. They settled on the bloom-laden branches, on the porch pillars, on me indiscriminately. I stepped inside the door with one on each hand and five clinging to my gown. This experience, I am sure, suggested Mrs. Comstock's moth hunting in the Limberlost. Then I went back to the veranda and revelled with the moths until dawn drove them to shelter. One magnificent specimen, birdlike above all the others, I followed across the orchard and yard to a grape arbour, where I picked him from the under side of a leaf after he had settled for the coming day. Repeatedly I counted close to a hundred, and then they would so confuse me by flight I could not be sure I was not numbering the same one twice. With eight males, some of them fine large moths, one superb, from which to choose, my female mated with an insistent, frowsy little scrub lacking two feet and having torn and ragged wings. I needed no surer proof that she had very dim vision.

"The Yellow Emperor"

SEVERAL YEARS AGO, Mr. A. Eisen, a German, of Coldwater, Michigan, who devotes his leisure to collecting moths, gave me as pinned specimens a pair of Eacles Imperialis, and their full life history. Any intimate friend of mine can testify that yellow is my favourite colour, with shades of lavender running into purple, second choice. When I found a yellow moth, liberally decorated with lavender, the combination was irresistible. Mr. Eisen said the mounted specimens were faded; but the living moths were beautiful beyond description. Naturally I coveted life.

I was very particular to secure the history of the caterpillars and their favourite foods. I learned from Mr. Eisen that they were all of the same shape and habit, but some of them might be green, with cream-coloured heads and feet, and black face lines, the body covered sparsely with long white hairs; or they might be brown, with markings of darker brown and black with white hairs; but they would be at least three inches long when full grown, and would have a queer habit of rearing and drawing leaves to their mouths when feeding. I was told I would find them in August, on leaves of spruce, pine, cherry, birch, alder, sycamore, elm, or maple; that they pupated in the ground; and the moths were common, especially around lights in city parks, and at street crossings.

Armed with this information, and spurred by my love of yellow, hours were spent when my cameras were focused on a bird nest, and I was waiting for my subjects to assume some desirable attitude, in searching for the moths in June, the caterpillars in August and early September, and when lifting wild roots for pupæ in the fall. Afield, when the light grew too dim for bird work, I hunted moths and secured them in larger numbers than I could use, and of many differing families, but never a yellow one.

Coming from a drive one rare June evening, I found Mr. William Pettis, a shooter of oil wells, whom I frequently met while at my work, sitting on the veranda in an animated business discussion with the Deacon.

"I brought you a pair of big moths that I found this morning on some bushes beside the road," said Mr. Pettis. "I went to give Mr. Porter a peep to see if he thought you'd want them, and they both got away. He was quicker than I, and caught the larger one, but mine sailed over the top of that tree." He indicated an elm not far away.

"Did you know them?" I asked the Deacon.

"No," he answered. "You have none of the kind. They are big as birds and a beautiful yellow."

"Yellow!" No doubt I was unduly emphatic. "Yellow! Didn't you know better than to open a box with moths in it outdoors at night?"

"It was my fault," interposed Mr. Pettis. "he told me not to open the box, but I had shown them a dozen times to-day and they never moved. I didn't think about night being their time to fly. I am very sorry."

So was I. Sorry enough to have cried, but I tried my best to conceal it. Anyway, it might be Io, and I had that. On going inside to examine the moth, I found a large female Eacles Imperialis, with not a scale of down misplaced. Even by gas light I could see that the yellow of the living moth was a warm canary colour, and the lavender of the mounted specimen closer heliotrope on the living, for there were pinkish tints that had faded from the pinned moth.

She was heavy with eggs, and made no attempt to fly, so I closed the box and left her until the lights were out, and then removed the lid. Every opening was tightly screened, and as she had mated, I did not think she would fly. I hoped in the freedom of the Cabin she would not break her wings, and ruin herself for a study.

There was much comfort in the thought that I could secure her likeness; her eggs would be fertile, and I could raise a brood the coming season, in which would be both male and female. When life was over I could add her to my specimen case, for these are of the moths that do not eat, and live only a few days after depositing their eggs. So I went out and explained to Mr. Pettis what efforts I had made to secure this yellow moth, comforted him for allowing the male to escape by telling him I could raise all I wanted from the eggs of the female, showed him my entire collection, and sent him from the Cabin such a friend to my work, that it was he who brought me an oil-coated lark a few days later. Throughout the summer in his drives across country he kept my work in mind, and frequently brought me another moth, a bird in distress from oil, or something I could use or save suffering. Now he is one of the men on whom I depend to watch for me, and bring anything there is even a hope I can use, or guide me to the haunts of birds he sees while about his business.

On rising early the next morning, I found my moth had deposited some eggs on the dining-room floor, before the conservatory doors, more on the heavy tapestry that covered them, and she was clinging to a velvet curtain at a library window, liberally dotting it with eggs, almost as yellow as her body. I turned a tumbler over those on the floor, pinned folds in the curtains, and as soon as the light was good, set up a camera and focused on a suitable location.

She climbed on my finger when it was held before her, and was carried, with no effort to fly, to the place I had selected, though Molly-Cotton walked close with a spread net, ready for the slightest impulse toward movement. But female moths seldom fly until they have finished egg depositing, and this one was transferred with no trouble to the spot on which I had focused. On the back wall of the Cabin, among some wild roses, she was placed on a log, and immediately raised her wings, and started for the shade of the vines. The picture made of her as she walked is beautiful. After I had secured several studies she was returned to the library curtain, where she resumed egg placing. These were not counted, but there were at least three hundred at a rough guess.

I had thought her lovely in gas light, but day brought forth marvels and wonders. When a child, I used to gather cowslips in a bed of lush swale, beside a little creek at the foot of a big hill on our farm. At the summit was an old orchard, and in a brush-heap a brown thrush nested. From a red winter pearmain the singer poured out his own heart in song, and then reproduced the love ecstasy of every other bird of the orchard. That moth's wings were so exactly the warm though delicate yellow of the flowers I loved, that as I looked at it I could feel my bare feet sinking in the damp ooze, smell the fragrance of the buttercups, and hear again the ripple of the water and the mating exultation of the brown thrush.

In the name—Eacles Imperialis—there is no meaning or appropriateness to "Eacles"; "Imperialis"—of course, translates imperial—which seems most fitting, for the moth is close the size of Cecropia, and of truly royal beauty. We called it the Yellow Emperor. Her Imperial Golden Majesty had a wing sweep of six and a quarter inches. From the shoulders spreading in an irregular patch over front and back wings, most on the front, were markings of heliotrope, quite dark in colour. Near the costa of the front wings were two almost circular dots of slightly paler heliotrope, the one nearest the edge about half the size of the other. On the back wings, halfway from each edge, and half an inch from the marking at the base, was one round spot of the same colour. Beginning at the apex of the front pair, and running to half an inch from the lower edge, was a band of escalloped heliotrope. On the back pair this band began half an inch from the edge and ran straight across, so that at the outer curve of the wing it was an inch higher. The front wing surface and the space above this marking on the back were liberally sprinkled with little oblong touches of heliotrope; but from the curved line to the bases of the back pair, the colouring was pure canary yellow.

The top of the head was covered with long, silken hairs of heliotrope, then a band of yellow; the upper abdomen was strongly shaded with heliotrope almost to the extreme tip. The lower sides of the wings were yellow at the base, the spots showing through, but not the bands, and only the faintest touches of the mottling. The thorax and abdomen were yellow, and the legs heliotrope. The antennæ were heliotrope, fine, threadlike, and closely pressed to the head. The eyes were smaller than those of Cecropia, and very close together.

Compared with Cecropia these moths were very easy to paint. Their markings were elaborate, but they could be followed accurately, and the ground work of colour was warm cowslip yellow. The only difficulty was to make the almost threadlike antennæ show, and to blend the faint touches of heliotrope on the upper wings with the yellow.

The eggs on the floor and curtains were guarded with care. They were dotted around promiscuously, and at first were clear and of amber colour, but as the little caterpillars grew in them, they showed a red line three fourths of the way around the rim, and became slightly depressed in the middle. The young emerged in thirteen days. They were nearly half an inch long, and were yellow with black lines. They began the task of eating until they reached the pupa state, by turning on their shells and devouring all of them to the glue by which they were fastened.

They were given their choice of oak, alder, sumac, elm, cherry, and hickory. The majority of them seemed to prefer the hickory. Part of them were kept in the house and fed on fresh leaves, and the remainder were placed on trees outdoors, and guarded from birds by a covering of scrim. They moulted on the fifth day for the first time, and changed to a brown colour. Every five or six days they repeated the process, growing larger and of stronger colour with each moult, and developing a covering of long white hairs. Part of these moulted four times, others five.

At past six weeks of age they were exactly as Mr. Eisen had described them to me. Those I kept in confinement pupated on a bed of baked gravel, in a tin bucket. It is imperative to bake any earth or sand used for them to kill pests invisible to the eye, that might bore into the pupa cases and destroy the moths.

I watched the transformation with intense interest. After the caterpillars had finished eating they travelled in search of a place to burrow for a day or two. Then they gave up, and lay quietly on the sand. The colour darkened hourly, the feet and claspers seemed to draw inside, and one morning on going to look there were some greenish brown pupæ. They shone as if freshly varnished, as indeed they were, for the substance provided to facilitate the emergence of the pupæ from the caterpillar skins dries in a coating, that helps to harden the cases and protect them. These pupæ had burst the skins at the thorax, and escaped by working the abdomen until they lay an inch or so from the skins.

What a "cast off garment" those skins were! Only the frailest outside covering, complete in all parts, and rapidly turning to a dirty brown. The pupæ were laid away in a large box having a glass lid. It was filled with baked sand, covered with sphagnum moss, slightly dampened occasionally, and placed where it was cool, but never at actual freezing point. The following spring after the delight of seeing them emerge, they were released, for I secured a male to complete my collection a few days later, and only grew the caterpillars to prove it possible.

There was a carnival in the village, and for three nights the streets were illuminated brightly from end to end, to the height of Ferris wheels and diving towers. The lights must have shone against the sky for miles around, for they drew from the Limberlost, from the Canoper, from Rainbow Bottom, and the Valley of the Wood Robin, their winged creatures of night.

I know Emperors appear in these places in my locality, for the caterpillars feed on leaves found there, and enter the ground to pupate; so of course the moth of June begins its life in the same location. Mr. Pettis found the mated pair he brought to me, on a bush at the edge of a swamp. They also emerge in cities under any tree on which their caterpillars feed. Once late in May, in the corner of a lichen-covered, old snake fence beside the Wabash on the Shimp farm, I made a series of studies of the home life of a pair of ground sparrows. They had chosen for a location a slight depression covered with a rank growth of meadow grass. Overhead wild plum and thorn in full bloom lay white-sheeted against the blue sky; red bud spread its purple haze, and at a curve, the breast of the river gleamed white as ever woman's; while underfoot the grass was obscured with masses of wild flowers.

An unusually fine cluster of white violets attracted me as I worked around the birds, so on packing at the close of the day I lifted the plant to carry home for my wild flower bed. Below a few inches of rotting leaves and black mould I found a lively pupa of the Yellow Emperor.

So these moths emerge and deposit their eggs in the swamps, forests, beside the river and wherever the trees on which they feed grow. When the serious business of life is over, attracted by strong lights, they go with other pleasure seeking company, and grace society by their royal presence.

I could have had half a dozen fine Imperialis moths during the three nights of the carnival, and fluttering above buildings many more could be seen that did not descend to our reach. Raymond had such a busy time capturing moths he missed most of the joys of the carnival, but I truly think he liked the chase better. One he brought me, a female, was so especially large that I took her to the Cabin to be measured, and found her to be six and three quarter inches, and of the lightest yellow of any specimen I have seen. Her wings were quite ragged. I imagined she had finished laying her eggs, and was nearing the end of life, hence she was not so brilliant as a newly emerged specimen. The moth proved this theory correct by soon going out naturally.

Choice could be made in all that plethora, and a male and female of most perfect colouring and markings were selected for my studies of a pair. One male was mounted and a very large female on account of her size. That completed my Imperialis records from eggs to caterpillars, pupæ and moths.

The necessity for a book on this subject, made simple to the understanding, and attractive to the eye of the masses, never was so deeply impressed upon me as in an experience with Imperialis. Molly-Cotton was attending a house-party, and her host had chartered a pavilion at a city park for a summer night dance. At the close of one of the numbers, over the heads of the laughing crowd, there swept toward the light a large yellow moth.

With one dexterous sweep the host caught it, and while the dancers crowded around him with exclamations of wonder and delight, he presented it to Molly-Cotton and asked, "Do you know what it is?"

She laughingly answered, "Yes. But you don't!"

"Guilty!" he responded. "Name it."

For one fleeting instant Molly-Cotton measured the company. There was no one present who was not the graduate of a commissioned high school. There were girls who were students at The Castle, Smith, Vassar, and Bryn Mawr. The host was a Cornell junior, and there were men from Harvard and Yale.

"It is an Eacles Imperialis Io Polyphemus Cecropia Regalis," she said. Then in breathless suspense she waited.

"Shades of Homer!" cried the host. "Where did you learn it?"

"They are flying all through the Cabin at home," she replied. "There was a tumbler turned over their eggs on the dining-room floor, and you dared not sit on the right side of the library window seat because of them when I left."

"What do you want with their eggs?" asked a girl.

"Want to hatch their caterpillars, and raise them until they transform into these moths," answered poor Molly-Cotton, who had been taught to fear so few living things that at the age of four she had carried a garter snake into the house for a playmate.

"Caterpillars!" The chorus arose to a shriek. "Don't they sting you? Don't they bite you?"

"No, they don't!" replied Molly-Cotton. "They don't bite anything except leaves; they are fine big fellows; their colouring is exquisite; and they evolve these beautiful moths. I invite all of you to visit us, and see for yourselves how intensely interesting they are."

There was a murmur of polite thanks from the girls, but one man measured Molly-Cotton from the top curl of her head to the tip of her slippers, and answered, "I accept the invitation. When may I come?" He came, and left as great a moth enthusiast as any of us. This incident will be recognized as furnishing the basis on which to build the ballroom scene in "A Girl of the Limberlost," in which Philip and Edith quarrel over the capture of a yellow Emperor.

But what of these students from the great representative colleges of the United States, to whom a jumbled string made from the names of half a dozen moths answered for one of the commonest of all?

"Hera of the Corn"

AT THE SAME TIME he gave me the Eacles Imperialis moths, Mr. Eisen presented me with a pair of Hyperchiria Io. They were nicely mounted on the black velvet lining of a large case in my room, but I did not care for them in the least. A picture I would use could not be made from dead, dried specimens, and history learned from books is not worth knowing, in comparison with going afield and threshing it out for yourself, in your own way. Because the Io was yellow, I wanted it—more than several specimens I had not found as yet, for yellow, be it on the face of a flower, on the breast of a bird, or in the gold of sunshine, always warms the depths of my heart.

One night in June, sitting with a party of friends in the library, a shadow seemed to sweep across a large window in front. I glanced up, and arose with a cry that must have made those present doubt my sanity. A perfect and beautiful Io was walking leisurely across the glass.

"A moth!" I cried. "I have none like it! Deacon, get the net!"

I caught a hat from the couch, and ran to the veranda. The Deacon followed with the net.

"I was afraid to wait," I explained. "Please bring a piece of pasteboard, the size of this brim."

I held the hat while the Deacon brought the board. Then with trembling care we slipped it under, and carefully carried the moth into the conservatory. First we turned on the light, and made sure that every ventilator was closed; then we released the Io for the night. In the morning we found a female clinging to a shelf, dotting it with little top-shaped eggs. I was delighted, for I thought this meant the complete history of a beautiful moth. So exquisite was the living, breathing creature, she put to shame the form and colouring of the mounted specimens. No wonder I had not cared for them!

Her fore-wings were a strong purplish brown in general effect, but on close examination one found the purplish tinge a commingling of every delicate tint of lavender and heliotrope imaginable. They were crossed by escalloped bands of grayish white, and flecked with touches of the same, seeming as if they had been placed with a brush. The back wings were a strong yellow. Each had, for its size, an immense black eye-spot, with a blue pupil covering three fourths of it, crossed by a perfect comma of white, the heads toward the front wings and the curves bending outward. Each eye-spot was in a yellow field, strongly circled with a sharp black line; then a quarter of an inch band of yellow; next a heliotrope circle of equal width; yellow again twice as wide; then a faint heliotrope line; and last a very narrow edging of white. Both wings joined the body under a covering of long, silky, purple-brown hairs.

She was very busy with egg depositing, and climbed to the twig held before her without offering to fly. The camera was carried to the open, set up and focused on a favourable spot, while Molly-Cotton walked beside me holding a net over the moth in case she took flight in outer air. The twig was placed where she would be in the deepest shade possible while I worked rapidly with the camera.

By this time experience had taught me that these creatures of moonlight and darkness dislike the open glare of day, and if placed in sunlight will take flight in search of shade more quickly than they will move if touched. So until my Io settled where I wanted her with the wings open, she was kept in the shadow. Only when I grasped the bulb and stood ready to snap, was the covering lifted, and for the smallest fraction of a second the full light fell on her; then darkness again.

In three days it began to be apparent there was something wrong with the eggs. In four it was evident, and by five I was not expecting the little caterpillars to emerge and they did not. The moth had not mated and the eggs were not fertile. Then I saw my mistake. Instead of shutting the female in the conservatory at night, I should have tied a soft cotton string firmly around her body, and fastened it to some of the vines on the veranda. Beyond all doubt, before morning, a male of her kind would have been attracted to her.

One learns almost as much by his mistakes as he profits by his successes in this world. Writing of this piece of stupidity, at a time in my work with moths when a little thought would have taught me better, reminds me of an experience I had with a caterpillar, the first one I ever carried home and tried to feed. I had an order to fill for some swamp pictures, and was working almost waist deep in a pool in the Limberlost, when on a wild grapevine swinging close to my face, I noticed a big caterpillar placidly eating his way around a grape leaf. The caterpillar was over four inches long, had no horn, and was of a clear red wine colour, that was beautiful in the sunlight. I never before had seen a moth caterpillar that was red and I decided it must be rare. As there was a wild grapevine growing over the east side of the Cabin, and another on the windmill, food of the right kind would be plentiful, so I instantly decided to take the caterpillar home. It was of the specimens that I consider have almost "thrust themselves upon me."

When the pictures were finished and my camera carried from the swamp, I returned with the clippers and cut off vine and caterpillar, to carry with me. On arrival I placed it in a large box with sand on the bottom, and every few hours took out the wilted leaves, put in fresh ones, and sprinkled them to insure crispness, and to give a touch of moisture to the atmosphere in the box, that would make it seem more like the swamp.

My specimen was readily identified as Philampelus Pandorus, of which I had no moth, so I took extra care of it in the hope of a new picture in the spring. It had a little flat head that could be drawn inside the body like a turtle, and on the sides were oblique touches of salmon. Something that appeared to be a place for a horn could be seen, and a yellow tubercle was surrounded by a black line. It ate for three days, and then began racing so frantically around the box, I thought confinement must be harmful, so I gave it the freedom of the Cabin, warning all my family to "look well to their footsteps." It stopped travelling after a day or two at a screen covering the music-room window, and there I found it one morning lying still, a shrivelled, shrunken thing, only half the former length, so it was carefully picked up, and thrown away!

Of course the caterpillar was in the process of changing into the pupa, and if I had known enough to lay it on the sand in my box, and wait a few days, without doubt a fine pupa would have emerged from that shrunken skin, from which, in the spring, I could have secured an exquisite moth, with shades of olive green, flushed with pink. The thought of it makes we want to hide my head. It was six years before I found a living moth, or saw another caterpillar of that species.

A few days later, while watching with a camera focused on the nest of a blackbird in Mrs. Corson's woods east of town, Raymond, who was assisting me, crept to my side and asked if it would do any harm for him to go specimen hunting. The long waits with set cameras were extremely tedious to the restless spirits of the boy, and the birds were quite tame, the light was under a cloud, and the woods were so deep that after he had gone a few rods he was from sight, and under cover; besides it was great hunting ground, so I gladly told him to go.

The place was almost "virgin," much of it impassable and fully half of it was under water that lay in deep, murky pools throughout summer. In the heat of late June everything was steaming; insect life of all kinds was swarming; not far away I could hear sounds of trouble between the crow and hawk tribes; and overhead a pair of black vultures, whose young lay in a big stump in the interior, were searching for signs of food. If ever there was a "likely" place for specimens it was here; Raymond was an expert at locating them, and fearless to foolhardiness. He had been gone only a short time when I heard a cry, and I knew it must mean something, in his opinion, of more importance than blackbirds.

I answered "Coming," and hastily winding the long hose, I started in the direction Raymond had taken, calling occasionally to make sure I was going the right way. When I found him, the boy was standing beside a stout weed, hat in hand, intently watching something. As I leaned forward I saw that it was a Hyperchiria Io that just had emerged from the cocoon, and as yet was resting with wings untried. It differed so widely from my moth of a few days before, I knew it must be a male.

This was only three fourths as large as mine, but infinitely surpassed it in beauty. Its front wings were orange-yellow, flushed with red-purple at the base, and had a small irregular brown spot near the costa. Contrary to all precedent, the under sides of these wings were the most beautiful, and bore the decorations, that in all previous experience with moths, had been on the upper surface, faintly showing on the under. For instance, this irregular brown marking on the upper side proved to be a good-sized black spot with a white dot in the middle on the under; and there was a curved line of red-purple from the apex of the wing sloping to the lower edge, nearly half an inch from the margin. The space from this line to the base of the wing was covered with red-purple down. The back wings were similar to the female's, only of stronger colour, and more distinct markings; the eye-spot and lining appeared as if they had been tinted with strong fresh paint, while the edges of the wings lying beside the abdomen had the long, silken hairs of a pure, beautiful red their entire length.

A few rods away men were plowing in the adjoining corn field, and I remembered that the caterpillar of this moth liked to feed on corn blades, and last summer undoubtedly lived in that very field. When I studied Io history in my moth books, I learned these caterpillars ate willow, wild cherry, hickory, plum, oak, sassafras, ash, and poplar. The caterpillar was green, more like the spiny butterfly caterpillars than any moth one I know. It had brown and white bands, brown patches, and was covered with tufts of stiff upstanding spines that pierced like sharp needles. This was not because the caterpillar tried to hurt you, but because the spines were on it, and so arranged that if pressed against, an acid secretion sprang from their base. This spread over the flesh the spines touched, stinging for an hour like smartweed, or nettles.

When I identified this caterpillar in my books, it came to me that I had known and experienced its touch. But it did not forcibly impress me until that instant that I knew it best of all, and that it was my childhood enemy of the corn. Its habit was to feed on the young blades, and cling to them with all its might. If I was playing Indian among the rows, or hunting an ear with especially long, fine "silk" for a make-believe doll, or helping the cook select ears of Jersey Sweet to boil for dinner, and accidentally brushed one of these caterpillars with cheek or hand, I felt its burning sting long afterward. So I disliked those caterpillars.

For I always had played among the corn. Untold miles I have ridden the plow horses across the spring fields, where mellow mould rolled black from the shining shares, and the perfumed air made me feel so near flying that all I seemed to need was a high start to be able to sail with the sentinel blackbird, that perched on the big oak, and with one sharp "T'check!" warned his feeding flock, surely and truly, whether a passing man carried a gun or a hoe. Then came the planting, when bare feet loved the cool earth, and trotted over other untold miles, while little fingers carefully counted out seven grains from the store carried in my apron skirt, as I chanted:

> "One for the blackbird, one for the crow,
> One for the cutworm and four to grow."

Then father covered them to the right depth, and stamped each hill with the flat of the hoe, while we talked of golden corn bread, and slices of mush, fried to a crisp brown that cook would make in the fall. We had to plant enough more to feed all the horses, cattle, pigs, turkeys, geese, and chickens, during the long winter, even if the sun grew uncomfortably warm, and the dinner bell was slow about ringing.

Then there were the Indian days in the field, when a fallen eagle feather stuck in a braid, and some pokeberry juice on the face, transformed me into the Indian Big Foot, and I fled down green aisles of the corn before the wrath of the mighty Adam Poe. At times Big Foot grew tired fleeing, and said so in remarkably distinct English, and then to keep the game going, my sister Ada, who played Adam Poe, had to turn and do the fleeing or be tomahawked with a stick.

When the milk was in the ears, they were delicious steamed over salted water, or better yet roasted before coals at the front of the cooking stove, and eaten with butter and salt,—if you have missed the flavour of it in that form, really you never have known corn!

Next came the cutting days. These were after all the caterpillars had climbed down, and travelled across the fence to spin their cocoons among the leaves of the woods; as if some instinct warned them that they would be plowed up too early to emerge, if they remained in the field. The boys bent four hills, lashed the tassels together for a foundation, and then with one sweep of their big knives, they cut a hill at a time, and stacked it in large shocks, that lined the field like rows of sentinels, guarding the gold of pumpkin and squash lying all around. While the shocks were drying, the squirrels, crows, and quail took possession, and fattened their sides against snow time.

Then the gathering days of October—they were the best days of all! Like a bloom-outlined vegetable bed, the goldenrod and ironwort, in gaudy border, filled the fence corners of the big fields. A misty haze hung in the air, because the Indians were burning the prairies to round up game for winter. The cawing of the crows, the chatter of blackbirds, and the piping bobwhites, sounded so close and so natural out there, while the crowing cocks of the barnyard seemed miles away and slightly unreal. Grown up and important, I sat on a board laid across the wagon bed, and guided the team of matched grays between the rows of shocks, and around the "pie-timber" as my brother Leander called the pumpkins, while father and the boys opened the shocks and husked the ears. How the squirrels scampered to the woods, and to the business of storing away the hickory nuts that we could hear rattling down every frosty morning! We hurried with the corn; because as soon as the last shock was in, we might take the horses, wagon, and our dinner, and go all day to the woods, where we gathered our winter store of nuts. Leander would take a gun along, and shoot one of those saucy squirrels for the little sick mother.

Last came the November night, when the cold had shut us in. Then selected ears that had been dried in the garret were brought down, white for "rivel" and to roll things in to fry and yellow for corn bread and mush. A tub full of each was shelled, and sacked to carry to the mill the following day. I sat on the floor while father and the boys worked, listening to their talk, as I built corncob castles so high they toppled from their many stories. Sometimes father made cornstock fiddles that would play a real tune. Oh! the pity of it that every little child cannot grow, live, learn and love among the corn. For the caterpillars never stopped the fun, even the years when they were most numerous.

The eggs laid by my female never hatched, so I do not know this caterpillar in its early stages from experience, but I had enough experience with it in my early stages, that I do not care if I never raise one. No doubt it attains maturity by the same series of moults as the others, and its life history is quite similar. The full-fed caterpillars spin among the leaves on the ground, and with their spines in mind, I would much prefer finding a cocoon, and producing a moth from that stage of its evolution.

The following season I had the good fortune to secure a male and female Io at the same time and by persistence induced them to pose for me on an apple branch. There was no trouble in securing the male as I desired him, with wings folded showing the spots, lining and flushing of colour, as described. But the female was a perverse little body and though I tried patiently and repeatedly she would not lower her wings full width. She climbed around with them three fourths spread, producing the most beautiful effect of life, but failing to display her striking markings. This is the one disadvantage in photographing moths from life. You secure lifelike effects but sometimes you are forced to sacrifice their wonderful decorations.

Leaving Home

"Shall We Save Natural Beauty?"

from *Let Us Highly Resolve*

Even while describing the natural world of the Wabash River, the Limberlost Swamp, and the farms around them, Gene Stratton Porter was noting the natural losses and the part that mankind played in these depletions. This plea was one of the moral essays written for her widespread audience, which she reached through various popular women's magazines. It joins an elegiac tone with the hortatory. Stratton Porter was ahead of her time in calling for a nationwide environmental movement.

WHEN I SHUT MY EYES and try to reconstruct the territory covered by the United States at the time of the arrival of the Pilgrim Fathers, it seems to me that in the whole world there was no equal amount of space having greater natural advantages in the matter of climate. We ranged from the snappy winters of Maine and Michigan to the temperate Central belt and on to almost tropical conditions in the South; both East and West coasts being affected by the adjacent sea, the Japanese currents having particular effect on the Pacific Coast. In contour, we had big mountains, medium mountains, and little mountains; plains, cañons, deserts, and rolling prairie country. We had great lakes, salt lakes, little lakes; big rivers, a network of streams, the whole country dotted with naturally flowing springs. The world has produced no bigger trees than the redwoods of California, and no better for commercial purposes than those in the hardwood belt extending across the country from Pennsylvania to Illinois and north to the boundary line. In the matter of unique formations, those things termed "wonders," the world has perhaps one waterfall to equal Niagara, none more delicately beautiful than the Bridal Veil and numbers of others. There are caves of entrancing beauty scattered here and there over the country, and most travellers are familiar with the petrified forests of Arizona. Then we have the boiling springs of several of the Northwest states, the Grand Cañon, the Yosemite Valley, and all of the other big, outstanding attractions; while scattered over all the country between these there are small lakes of indescribable beauty, little mountains watered by energetic streams, all sorts of unique and unexpected natural formations, and, over the whole, a wealth of plant and flower life not exceeded in beauty and rarity anywhere in the world. The same holds true of animal life, bird life, and the denizens of the water.

I have not been accustomed to considering myself among the oldest inhabitants; a fair degree of civilization had reached Indiana when I was born, yet, in my childhood, I was accustomed to Indians at the door, to wild turkeys, wildcats, and bear and deer in the woods not farther than Michigan from my home. We used to see wild pigeons come in such numbers that they broke down the branches of the beech, maple, and linden trees on which they perched at night. I was born at a period when, almost daily, huge wagons lumbered down our road, many of them drawn by oxen plodding a few miles each day on the way westward. The plains were covered with buffalo. We used the skins for sleigh robes, and they cost from ten to thirty dollars a piece, depending on the size and condition.

There was an abundance of game of every kind. The fish fairly crowded in the rivers, and one of the commonest sights of my childhood was the ascending smoke in all directions from the burning of uncounted log heaps. And oh! the pity of it! Those log heaps consisted of as fine trees as God ever made, felled where they stood and rolled together and burned *to get them out of the way!* Oak, hickory, beech, ash; elms that almost swept the sky; wild cherry, bird's-eye maple, black walnut—trees that to-day would be sawed into thin sheets and used for the veneering of less expensive wood; trees for which any lumberman would pay from six to twelve and fifteen hundred a trunk, felled and burned in order to clear the ground upon which they stood for the cultivation of corn and potatoes. The resources of the country were considered so vast that it never occurred to anyone to select the most valuable of these hard woods and store them for the use of future generations. Running across the ground surrounding Limberlost Cabin, there is a rail fence. Climbing it one day, I noticed the hardness and the beauty of the rails, and upon using a knife to scrape off the weatherbeaten surface, I discovered that the fence, for the length I examined it, was built of as fine black walnut as lumberman ever saw. At the prices of to-day, fences of black walnut, bird's eye maple, and cherry surrounding pioneer farms were worth millions of dollars. These valuable trees went into beams for the erection of outbuildings, houses and churches, much of the lumber being used indiscriminately, care being taken merely to select the woods known as "hard" for their endurance.

I have lived to see the enormous prices set upon furniture made from walnut, oak, cherry, and bird's-eye maple. While writing this article, I read of a black walnut tree just sold in Indiana from the stump of which alone four thousand dollars' worth of fine veneer was to be made, and if the trunk were solid and proved to be as finely marked as was hoped, it would swell the value to unbelievable figures for a tree. Who can estimate the appalling waste in the burning of those indiscriminate log heaps? I used to marvel at the gorgeous smoke ascending in wreaths and banners of lavender, pink, blue, red, gray from those green logs.

I have lived to see timber becoming so scarce that houses of stone, brick, and cement are resorted to through necessity rather than choice in many instances. I have lived to see the greater part of the springs dried up, the little streams drained from the face of the earth, and many of the rivers practically dry in the summer season, and the lake levels lowered, the fish, game, and fur-bearing animals practically exterminated. Since maturity I have seen but one wood duck—as exquisite a sight as ever rode the water. With one exception, the last wild pigeon I saw was confined in the zoological garden of Cincinnati, where it has since died and been mounted to preserve it for posterity. And when posterity looks upon this noble bird and reads its history, what will be said of us? About twelve years ago, in field work one day, one wild pigeon flew over where I was hidden in a fence corner with a set camera, and perched on a telephone wire above me. It was a male bird, gleaming in the light with metallic lustre, big and beautiful, its wings whistling in flight with the peculiar notes made by these birds. It seemed frightened and nervous. Its head erect, looking in all directions, it uttered a few call notes and then took a high and uninterrupted flight, so far as I could see, straight west. I never have seen another.

The deer and fur-bearing animals are practically gone from the country I knew, and the country farther west as well. Many of the Indians are nearly starving through scarcity of fish and game. The birds have been depleted in numbers until it is quite impossible to raise fruit of any kind without a continuous fight against slug and aphis, a war which birds in sufficient numbers would wage for us. With the cutting of timber has come a change in climate; weeks of drought in summer, destructive cyclonic windstorms, winters alternating from a condition so open as to freeze prematurely forced fruit and grain, and winters so stringently cold that the fruit trees are killed outright. The even temperature and the rains every three or four days which we knew in childhood are things of the past. Summer in these days means to scorch for weeks at a stretch with unalleviated heat; and in the same state in which I was born it has become necessary for the sons of the men who wasted the woods and the waters to put in overhead sprinkling systems in order to grow their garden vegetables, while windmills and irrigation are becoming common. In my childhood, my father planted grain with the same certainty of having a full crop that he had of having alternate day and night. To-day the farmer on my land has no more idea whether he will get a paying yield from the wheat, corn, and potatoes that he puts into the ground than he has as to whether the next cyclone will blow his house into the lake or pass a few yards on the other side of it. *We, as a nation, have already, in the most wanton and reckless waste the world has ever known, changed our climatic conditions and wasted a good part of our splendid heritage. The question now facing us is whether we shall do all that lies in our power to save comfortable living conditions for ourselves and the spots of natural beauty that remain for our children.*

If this is to be done, a nation-wide movement must be begun immediately. Our climate could be greatly bettered if every man owning land would do what he can to restore original conditions by fighting to save the water in his vicinity, and by planting all the trees for which he can possibly spare space. More water means more rain. A heavier growth of timber breaks up culminative winds and gives bird life, under rigorous protection, a chance to renew itself. Wherever there are plenty of birds, the inevitable spraying and fighting of insect pests is not necessary. In an individual way each man and woman should look this proposition squarely in the face. It seems incredible to me, when I remember the log heaps of my childhood, that to-day I am seeing builders use metal door and window casements and cement for the outside finish of houses.

It might be well even to consider the suggestion that there is a possible limit to the wealth of the interior of the earth. There may not be coal and iron, at the rate at which we are using it, to supply coming generations. Any thoughtful person realizes that there will not. Certainly to plant trees and to preserve trees, to preserve water, and to do all in our power to save every natural resource, both from the standpoint of utility and beauty, is a work that every man and woman should give immediate and earnest attention.

"Songs of the Fields"

from *Music of the Wild*

In *Music of the Wild* Stratton Porter closely describes the sights and the sounds of the Limberlost area, and in so doing also traces the human paths which have become a part of the landscape and which suggest the story of the agrarian society of her childhood. It is difficult to know whether the differences in the current names for the wildflowers Stratton Porter identifies are due to region or to time. The carrion vine or flower *Smilax herbacea* is a member of the lily family. *Dioscorea villosa* is called a "wild yam" and was cultivated by Native Americans for its medicinal properties, somewhat like those of modern steroids. What she calls "Wild Saffron" is now commonly called "Wild Senna"; it is a member of the pea family. Several of the hawthorns have red berries, including the small tree called the "Scarlet hawthorn." However, Stratton Porter may be describing the shrub "pasture hawthorn," the fruit of which is dry and mealy, albeit red.

Note: A "snake fence" is simply a split-rail fence that zigzags, as a snake moves, across the land. The angles give the fence its stability, and offer many nooks and crannies for the continued existence of "nuisance" plants which farmers would have tilled out of the pasture.

FROM THE FREQUENT OVERFLOWING of the river, that not only decays but washes away rails, one side of my oat field is profaned by a short stretch of wire fence. This is to be forgiven only because, as can be seen so clearly, it is necessary. Then, too, it is in such a damp, shaded place that no harm whatever results. The vines and bushes almost cover the wire, and queer long-legged water birds tilt and rock when they try to perch on it. Where it escapes the river the old rail fence still stands, and every year clothes it with richer beauty and brings it—alas! like all the remainder of the world—nearer the end.

I have cause for quarrel with scientists who named many of our flowers and vines. It seems at times as if they tried themselves, as witness: *monkey* flower, butterfly *weed*, jewel*weed*, *toad*-flax, and *carrion* vine. Of all the decorations that entwine these old fences none is more beautiful than the carrion vine. But what a name! Enough to prejudice any one. All because the ball of greenish-yellow bloom has a faint pungent odor that impressed Linnæus, or some other early writer, as slightly disagreeable. It can not be so very noxious, either, for the bees should know their business, and they gather its pollen eagerly. God put that pungent, almost sour odor in some flowers to cut the cloying sweetness of others, and make honey edible.

So this beautiful vine is disgraced, and there are so many more appropriate names it might have borne quite as well. It is difficult to understand why a slightly unusual odor of the flower should have been emphasized, while the exquisite cutting and texture of the leaves is overlooked. They are heart-shaped at the base, curving off to a long lance-point, of delicate texture, and of lovely shades of green that vary as the light falls on them. So why not name it "lance leaf" or "golden globe," either of which is quite as appropriate as carrion vine and not suggestive of anything objectionable.

Another common, but peculiar vine of my territory is wild yam, the dried seed pods of which form nature's best rattlebox. *Dioscorea villosa* is a great beauty. Its leaves are a perfect heart-shape as a heart is conventionalized, and so deeply veined that their golden-green surfaces catch the light in hills and hollows. Where the vine grows in bright sunlight along the road these leaves are so closely set they overlap like the scales on a fish. Its bloom is insignificant, the male flowers drooping clusters, the female spike-like heads. The seeds are small triangles, and a number of them are placed on a long stem. When these are dry and shaken by winter winds they make as good music as the hop tree.

Another old snake fence corner pet of mine, that flourishes in cultivation, and that is dignified and an artistic plant, is wild saffron. It bears transplanting well, and if its location and soil are at all congenial, in a few years it grows into a most attractive bush. It reaches from three to four feet in height, many shoots upspringing from the same root. The stems are round, smooth, and even, with a slight yellow tint to their green, that extends to the leaves also. These are set at different places, and point in all directions. They are very graceful, as each is made up of twenty small leaves set on a midrib. Approaching the top, the last nine or ten have a small spray of bloom branching from their bases.

These little bloom-sprays and the large crown of the plant are masses of small individual yellow flowers having five cuppy petals of unequal length, and anthers so dark-brown as to be mistaken for black at a casual glance. Both the leaves and the bloom-clusters help to give it a delicate, lacy appearance. I can not so describe the flowers as to paint an adequate idea of their richness. The separate sprays of the leaf bases appear lighter yellow than the massive head and show the individual flowers better. The crown is a conical mist of gold accented by touches of almost black. Saffron is a stately and distinguished plant of great beauty in the fence corners, where it has a struggle to preserve its individuality among the masses of growth around it. On a lawn its every feature of distinction would be enhanced.

One point that should be of especial interest to those who wish to try the cultivation of wild flowers and trees on their premises, is the range of color in the mid-summer and fall species. Many people relying on cultivated shrubs and flowers grow a mass of spring and early summer bloom, and have bare shrubs and leafless vines in fall and winter. The field flowers are a blaze of color all summer until frost, and there are several vines, bushes, and trees that are brilliant with seeds and berries throughout the winter.

Few words of our language are more suggestive of peace and comfort than "pasture." *Pastorem,* a green feeding-ground, according to the old Latins. And wherever there is a green feeding-ground you may be very sure you will find the shade of trees and bushes, and frequently there is running water. Wherever you locate these you hear a swelling bird and insect chorus. From the dawn of history men in travel and in burden-bearing have been very dependent on their beasts, and so have sought to make suitable provision for them. This setting off a space of growing food for stock is without date, and over and over the chroniclers of the Bible made use of the comparison of the care of men for their flocks with the care of God for men.

"The Lord is my Shepherd; I shall not want. He maketh me to lie down in green pastures; He leadeth me beside the still waters."

The bodily comfort we give to our beasts made the basis of a comparison with the spiritual comfort God gives us, in one of the most beautiful expressions ever portrayed in language, "He maketh me to lie down in green pastures." Before the eye rises the picture of a lush, green meadow sprinkled with daisies and dotted with buttercups; the lark overhead, and the full-fed cattle lying—pictures of contentment in the shade of the newly-leafing trees that ring with the songs of courting birds. The thought of a pasture is in some way connected with spring; perhaps because, as at no other time, the cattle cry for it, and beg piteously to be released to natural food. At that time the pastures are green; later they may not be. Then the cattle, dry-fed during the long winter, graze and graze until they become so fat the milk they give grows richer, and housewives make what they call "clover" butter.

When man treats the beasts that sustain and enrich him with the consideration he would like were he a beast, we have one of the very highest signs of the grace of God in the human heart. This study was made at almost four o'clock in the afternoon, when the cattle, after a day of grazing, were lying in fullfed content. It was so early in the season that hickory and late-leafing trees were bare, but already the stock sought for their resting-place the *shade* afforded by maple and elms.

There was no real necessity for shelter. The heat was not sufficient to worry them, but the inclination to lie in the shade was instinctive. Scattered around this pasture and in almost every fence corner there grows a tree for the express purpose of providing comfort for the stock and a choir-loft for field musicians. How the cattle appreciate this can be seen by their gathering to lie in the strip of light shade in the early spring! If they seek a sheltered spot when they really do not need it, what would become of them in the burning heat of July and August without it? How the birds love it they tell you in their notes of bubbling ecstasy.

Not far from this pasture are the grazing lands of some "progressive" farmers. These fields are enclosed in straight wire fences, guiltless of a leaf for shelter, so they offer migrant musicians no inducement to locate there. All the season tortured horses and cattle graze in early morning and evening, and at noontime stand in restless groups, striving to drive away the flies, and find shelter from each other's bodies; for neither cattle nor horses lie when they have finished grazing unless there is shade. To rest in the open would be to place themselves between two fires—the reflected heat from the earth and the direct heat from the sun.

"He maketh me to lie down in green pastures," I quoted, when passing such a field on a scorching August day.

"He sendeth His rain to the just as well as to the unjust," quoted my critic, in reply. "You know if I were He, I would not. I would send rain only to pastures with trees in them, and burn all the remainder."

So we agreed to keep watch as we drove across the country, making these illustrations, and see how much we could learn of the disposition of the farmers by the manner in which they provided for their stock and their birds. Soon it became apparent that the man who stripped a pasture of every tree treated his family with no greater consideration. There was scarcely a tree anywhere on his premises. In one place we counted four big stumps, all within a few rods of the house that the felled trees had shaded from noon until sunset. These trees had been cut within the past two years, and the house had stood for many. There was not a growth anywhere around it except a few scrub cedars, and not a bird note. It was bared to the burning heat.

What would it have meant to the women and children of that stopping-place, for there was no sign of home around it, to have had the tight paling-fence torn away from the few yards immediately surrounding the house; the shelter of those big trees, with an easy seat beneath them, and a hammock swinging between? I dreamed those trees were growing again and filled with bird notes, that fence down, a coat of fresh paint on the house, the implements standing in the barn lot sheltered, and one day's work spent in arranging the premises. Into the dream would come a vision of open doors and windows, the sound of the voices of contented women, the shouts of happy children, and the chirping of many birds.

Some farms belong to men my critic calls a "tight-wad." That is not a classic expression; but if you saw the lands from which every tree had been sold, the creeks and ponds dried and plowed over, the fields inclosed in stretches of burning wire fence to allow cultivation within a few inches of it, not a bird note sounding,—you would understand why the term is suitable as none other. Even if the Almighty did give the earth to the children of men, it scarcely seems fair to Him to efface every picture and hush all song. It is difficult to realize just what would happen were most men farming by this method. But we still have left some degree of comfort because there are so many of nature's gentle men: men who see the pictures, hear the songs, and wish to perpetuate them for their children.

I know a farm that has been for three generations in the same family, passing from father to son. The home—mark the word—is on a little hill in the middle of the land, obscured by surrounding trees from the road and its dust and travel. The quaint old house is a story and a half, and a porch extends the length of the front and both sides. That home even turns its back to the road. The front porch and door face the orchard in the center of the land, "where father always sat when he rested, so that he could hear the birds and bees sing," the son told me.

There are old beehives under the trees, and the grass is long and fine. One could look at that orchard in mid-winter and tell to a certainty just what music would swell there in June. The bluebird would claim the hollow apple tree, the catbird the plum thicket, the robin, jay, and dove the apple trees, and the ground sparrow the earth. The hens would mother broods there, the turkeys slip around warily, and the guineas clatter in the grass. Martins and swallows homing under the barn eaves would sail above the trees, and blackbirds from the creek would build on high branches. But no dream could encompass all the music that would swell there throughout the summer.

Any lover of sunshine, bird song, and orchard pictures almost could see the old man who finished his day's work and then rested himself with music, sitting beneath his trees, worshiping God in nature. I have known many men like him, and all of them had bodies as strong as their trees, music in their hearts if the birds failed to sing, and faces serene as summer skies.

The garden lies on one side of the dooryard, the barn lot on the other. The garden is a quaint commingling of use and beauty. There are raspberry, currant, and gooseberry bushes along the sides and across the foot, but on either hand at the front gate are flowers. Large clusters of white lilies grow by each post, and cinnamon pink, larkspur, ragged robin, and many sweet, old-fashioned blooms overflow the beds. Straight down the center is another big flower-bed, and at each side of it squares of radishes, onions, lettuce, salsify, spinach, strawberries,— everything edible, and all flower-bordered. In each corner is a peach tree, and there are others scattered here and there.

The dooryard is filled with pear, plum, apple, and some fine, big walnut trees. The barn is of logs; and at the door and all around the well and watering-trough are beds of crushed stone. Across the end of the house, facing the road, "father" built a schoolroom. It was fifteen feet wide and twenty long. There he taught the neighbors' children in winter and dried fruit in summer. Just back of the house a large meadow, tree-sprinkled, stretches down to the road, and in the corner next to the barn grow three willows so mighty that they called me to them,—and so I discovered a home, and "father" and "mother."

In a little dip in the meadow near the barn "father" planted those three willows thirty years ago. When they had grown to sufficient size to make enough shade, because the barn was low and hot, he built this big feed-trough under them, and then he carried corn and grain to it. The trough is six feet wide, eighteen long, and six inches deep. One of the trees is nine feet in circumference, one twelve, and one fourteen; and "all the birds of the heaven make their nests" in these boughs, while the trees sing unceasingly. The watering-trough, that father always kept filled, stands along the side of the yard fence next the barn. There must be forty acres of woods, from which trees have been taken only for fuel and to let in enough light to make the grass grow for pasture.

I never saw "father" and "mother." They were gone before the willows called me. Her son told me that "mother had big brown eyes and white hair, and her cheeks were always a little pink." Of course they were. Like the cinnamon pinks of her garden. So by the lilies and the ragged robins and her porch, facing *from* the dust and turmoil of travel, we know "mother." And by the schoolhouse he built with his hands, by the cultivation of beauty and music all around his home and entire farm, by the neatness of his barns and outbuildings, by the trees he spared and the trees he planted, we know "father." By these things we know where "father" is to-day. So when the last book is written and the last picture made, if I have done my work nearly so well as "father" did his, perhaps we will have a happy meeting.

I should love to tell him that his work lives as an example to his neighbors; how his willows have grown, and that they called me from afar, and I put them into a book for thousands to see, that they might learn of his great-hearted humanity. I shall want to tell him how many hours I have lain on the grass under the big pear tree at the corner of his house, of all the lunches I have eaten on the front porch looking into the orchard, of the cotton-tails that yet scampered there unafraid, and how one season a little red-eyed vireo built on a branch of the apple tree swaying across the end of the porch just above where "mother" always sat with her mending. Heaven is heaven because it will allow me to tell "father" and "mother" these things.

One of the beautiful trees this man spared for decorative purposes was the buckeye. I wonder if it was so named from the resemblance of the rich dark-brown nut to the eye of the deer. The trees grow more rapidly than some others, flourishing on upland, slightly sandy soil. The buds are large and open, to display vivid streaks of red and yellow in the spring. The colors are very rich. The flower is a long tassel, covered by tiny florets of greenish yellow. The leaves are oblong, deeply veined, and grow in clusters of four to the stem.

The fruit is a round nut, encased in a pulpy hull, dotted with warts of a bright tan-yellow in the fall. The nuts and hulls sometimes drop together, and sometimes the hull opens and the nut falls alone. The nuts are a rich dark-red mahogany, and in them lies the one objection to the tree. To some children they are poisonous, and also to grazing stock. Where these dangers can be avoided they are beautiful trees for ornamenting lawns.

Of all my country none is so truly mine as the old orchards. On almost every farm of the present day there is a deserted orchard. These trees are worthless commercially, but at times they bear fruit that can be used for cider at least; so their lives are spared. In some of these orchards the cabin of the father or grandfather who first wrestled with the forest yet stands. In many of them the home has fallen to decay or been torn down for firewood, but the apple trees remain even in plowed fields and amidst growing grain. These trees are monuments to a deeply-rooted objection to cutting a fruit tree, in spite of the fact that they produce small, sour, blighted, and wormy apples.

Almost without exception the old snake-fences surround them, weighted with loads of growing shrubs and vines, and on and under them home field mice, moles, rabbits, chipmunks, lizards, birds of low habit, night moths, and bugs and insects of innumerable species. The grass grows long, rank, and so silken fine it is delightful to lie and thread it through the fingers, and recite those exquisite lines of Walt Whitman's,—

> "I guess it must be the flag of my disposition,
> Out of hopeful green stuff woven."

Nearly all the old orchards are on the highest spot of a farm and near the center of the land. These pioneers had the English plan of an estate, with the residence in the middle, away from the annoyance of travel and the dust of the highway. But the inclination of their children seems to be to see how close to the road they can live. Indeed, many men owning several hundred acres of land covered with a half dozen valuable building sites, elevations that would insure a dry cellar, sanitary surroundings, all the breeze passing, and the seclusion that is due a family, build their homes solely with an eye to living on the road. If they are fond of surface water in their wells, which breeds typhoid fever, dust, heat, and constant trespass of travelers, no one can interfere, and the result is splendid for the birds and for me.

The farther away from the old orchard the new home is builded the surer am I of finding among the trees shy doves from river thickets, brown thrashers, warblers, and bright-eyed vireos, in addition to the catbirds, bluebirds, kingbirds, robins, and screech owls that habitually home there. Also the long grass invites the larks and ground sparrows to join the chorus. And what a song it is! The rough bark of old apple trees is a table spread for larvæ seekers, and the masses of bloom a far call to insect hunters, so that from earliest spring these beautiful old orchards are the veritable choir-loft of the Lord, and from them arises one constant volume of joyful praise and thanksgiving. Even in the night the orioles nestle contentedly on their perches, and you can hear them talk about the goodness of God in their sleep.

Fifteen feet high in the branches of one of these old apple trees a robin built her nest before leafage in the wet, cold April of 1907. There were two eggs when one morning found the cradle filled with snow, and I thought she would desert it, but later she returned. Surely brooding bird never had a more uncomfortable time. The tree had borne apples the previous year, and of course she thought it alive and expected protection from the leaves. It was quite dead, and never a sign of bloom or leaf appeared.

The weather changed abruptly each day. With no shelter whatever she sat through freezing night, snowy days, sleet, rain, and flashes of hot sunshine. When she had four babies almost ready to leave the nest, a terrific cold rain began on Saturday morning. By afternoon it poured, and she pointed her bill skyward and gasped for breath. I fully expected that she would desert the nest and seek shelter before morning, but she remained, although drenched and half dead. That rain continued all of Sunday, pouring at times, until Monday morning. Although I watched by the hour, not once from the time it began until rifts of sunlight showed Monday morning did I see her leave her nest or feed the young, or her mate bring her a morsel of food. For an hour at a stretch, several times a day, I thought she would drown. My ladder had been erected for some time before her location, and by noon Monday I resumed a series of pictures of her nesting history. There were several dozen of them, representing every phase of her home life, the one I use here being especially individual.

Both birds attended the young alternately, with the difference that when the father fed them he removed a fæces and flew away. When the mother arrived she performed the same operation, and then, setting her breast feathers on end, slowly moved over the young, who thrust their heads against her breast, and she brooded them until the male returned. I loved to see the young move toward her and watch the sudden swell of the feathers to admit them. Several times I was tempted to record it, but thought the act was too fast for my lens. However, as I had almost everything else, I decided to try, and that morning as I detected the impulse to lift the feathers with the snuggling of the young, I snapped. The bird that disdained shelter and kept his head out when the mother moved over the nest, left it before the day was done.

Robins are true orchard birds, wonderfully friendly, and great worm consumers; in fact such fabulous numbers are fed to young robins that many times over one is repaid for the few apples and cherries they pick later. They are invaluable aids in agriculture, and every robin nest a farmer finds in his dooryard or orchard is worth five dollars to him above all the birds possibly can destroy, and the music they make, especially the song they sing in the rain, should be above price. Robins are the alarm clocks of the fields, for almost without exception they wake the morning and all birds with their glad cry, "Cheer up!"

These old orchards home many big night moths, one that reminds me of the robin. The caterpillar feeds on apple leaves, and its cocoons frequently are spun on old trees either on a water sprout at the base or high among the branches. The predominant color of this moth is the steel-gray of the robin, shading darker and lighter, and it has prominent markings, half-moon shaped, on its wings, almost the color of the robin's breast. It is more gaudy than the bird, however, for it also has lines of white, faint lines of black, wider ones of tan, and dark-blue circles. It is the commonest of all large moths, and is around almost every country home at night, and frequents cities as well; but because it is a creature of darkness, many people live a lifetime where it is oftenest found and never make its acquaintance.

Of all the birds that frequent orchards near homes, and those rarer ones that settle in my deserted orchards, the kingbird is most appropriately named; for he is king, and his mate is queen, and the apple tree they select is a palace, and the nest is their throne-room. So ably do they defend it that never in all my life have I seen a pair conquered or their nest despoiled. The king is not such a large bird—smaller than a robin, of robin-gray, with a white throat and black tail having a white tip; but he is stoutly built, plump, and pugilistic, and of truly remarkable agility on wing. He has a smoky, black, rounding crest, and wings of the same color. Kingbirds give their young the worms that feed on grass blades, small flies, and moths that flutter close to the ground. They perform a variety of acrobatics on wing in search of food, poising over orchard and meadow hunting prey, and darting after it in headlong flight, with indescribable turnings and twistings of tireless wings.

This habit of food-catching in air prepares them for the battles they wage on wing, for so agile are they, so hardy, and of such unfaltering courage, that they attack anything threatening their nests. I have seen them chase crows, dusky falcons, and in one case a large hawk, in pell-mell flight across the sky, and their deft twistings enabled them to escape unharmed, while they darted savagely at heads and eyes and put their enemies completely to rout. With any bird close their own size—a mewling catbird or a jay wanting a newly-hatched nestling for dessert—they make quick disposal.

There is very little art in their nests, but their eggs are beautifully decorated. The young are colored similar to their elders, the families large and so cunning as to be irresistible. No bird is more useful in an orchard, unless, indeed, it be a cuckoo, which is of great value because it eats caterpillars. In protecting an orchard from jays, hawks, and crows, such a pair of fighters saves you dozens of more gentle timid birds that carry worms and bugs by the million from fruit trees. In consideration of this you should acknowledge their royalty and offer them every encouragement to reign over your premises.

As we regard harmony, the kingbird is the least musical resident of the orchard. Tilting on a lookout from the top of the tree in which his nest is placed, he uses what to me sounds like, "Ka-tic, a-tic, a-tic," for a tribal call and means of communication between pairs. His sustained song, if song it may be called, appeals to me as "Ka-tic, a-tic, querr, kerrr, kerrr!" but it is not composed of either mellow or musical tones, and is at all times inflected as if it were a continued call of defiance; so that the good folk who attribute to him a "sweet musical song, softly warbled," are the veriest romancers.

The picture here given shows a nest nearly fifteen feet high in one of these old orchards, around which I worked until the story of what I did with these birds would sound like romance of another variety, did I not have a picture just as good as this to prove every statement I make. Not a leaf of the location was touched, but as it was a second nesting for the season, and in July, the heat was so intense that despite the shade of her chosen location the mother bird often lolled on the nest, as in this picture. The wonderful thing about it is that after a few days I placed the camera on the top of a ladder opposite the nest and near enough to secure reproduction of this size. The old birds were so convinced of my good intentions that I obtained dozens of poses as good as this, and even better, of each of them. I took their young from the nest and photographed them every day for the last four days before they left home, replaced them, and they remained even a day and a half after I had finished.

It is a truth that I can prove amply by reliable people who watched the performance from afar, that both old birds sat in the top of their tree and never took flight or made a sound while the young were away from the nest, and at once went on feeding them when they were replaced. Of course, I handled those young from the time they were little pin-feathered things, and they had no fear of me. If they had cried, I fancy the old ones would have been alarmed. But that birds of their universally admitted pugnacious character would permit me to handle their young, and even remove them from the nest for a half hour at a time, proves they know enough to distinguish friends from foes. It shows that even the wildest creatures can be tamed to your will by persistent kindness and unlimited patience in approaching them.

These birds are never more beautiful and interesting than when on wing, food-hunting. The waving grass of the orchard is one ground for them; the shrubs covering the fence, another. Other writers have expatiated at length on the wild rose, alder, and goldenrod that grow along these old fences; I wish to call attention to the bloom of the scarlet haw. The kingbirds taught me to notice it. I followed them to learn what insect they hunted there. I found several differing flies and gnats, and sometimes a bee was snapped up.

The scarlet haw does not bloom in crowded clusters, as does its cousin, the red haw. I have found eight blooms to a cluster, again four or five, and ten times as often six, thus establishing an average and preserving detail. Each blossom has five exquisitely cut and cupped petals, dainty stamens and pistil, and long enough stem to display the full beauty of the flower without pushing it into the others. Neither are these clusters crowded on the bush so closely as to lose their individuality, and they bloom so late that while the leaves are yet tender and of paler green than later in the season, many of them are full size and dark enough in color to form a background that emphasizes the daintiness and purity of the blooms and makes them the beauties of the entire haw family. The fruit is scarlet in color and not good to eat. The flowers will set the joy-song singing in any appreciative heart, and their perfume calls up a choir of half-intoxicated, nectar-loving insects.

I have seen night hawks soaring late in the evening above old orchards, and heard whip-poor-wills cry there, but I think they only settled in flight for a time, as they might in any secluded growth of trees. The night bird that really homes, breeds, and lives there summer and winter is the screech owl. It would be the funniest thing in ornithology to see a plucked screech owl or parrot. Small owls are such comical creatures in their feathers, such caricatures of their great horned relatives of the forest!

Most familiar in the orchards are the little brown screechers, and slightly larger ones of a cool gray, tan, brown, and black coloring. I am very fond of them because I know so well how happy they are, how unusually secure in the hollow apple tree, and how successful their hunting. I believe they have *less* cause than many other birds to be unhappy over anything, and so, of course, their songs are of love and contentment.

The owl has been shuddered at for a sufficient length of time. Now for a change I wish to suggest that the people who write further history of him put themselves *in the bird's place and describe his song as it is sung, and not as it appeals to the interpreter's fancy.* I love to hear a screech owl screech. It means that he is having a hilarious time. His heart is bubbling over with the joy of cool, dim night life in the orchard, or throbbing with the exultation of the mating fever. He is a friendly, social bird. Every winter he comes around the cabin hunting food, and he will answer my repetition of his calls until I become uncomfortable and close the window. Every time he lifts his voice he is either locating his mate, happy enough to talk about it or pleading for a wife and home. He is the most contented bird of the orchard and almost without exception its only night singer.

A hollow apple tree is his favorite home, and from four to six the number of his children. I doubt if the anatomy of any bird contains a member more wonderful than the eye of an owl. The organ of vision is fixed in a socket so that the bird turns its head instead of its eyes, and they are surrounded by a reflector of fine, closely set feathers, while the composition of the ball is so intricate as to merit a volume by itself. The owl can enlarge the retina, in order to see more clearly as he enters darker places. The Almighty did few things more wonderful than to evolve the eye of an owl.

I love all the music of nature, but none is dearer to the secret places of my heart than the Song of the Road. The highways are wonderful. They appear to flow between the fields, climbing hills without effort, sliding into valleys, and stretching across plains farther than the eye or lens can follow. All of my roads have three well-defined wheel tracks. There are two strongly marked that every vehicle makes, and another only slightly outlined, made by those passing on the way. Tiny flowers of yellow sorrel, rank fennel, grass, dandelion, smartweed, and catnip grow to the fence corners, and these are filled with tall meadow rue, milkweed, poke berry, goldenrod, asters, thistle, saffron, teazel, and sumac sprouts. There are wild roses, alders, maple, oak, and elm shrubs, and the straggling old snake-fences are bound together and upheld by bittersweet, wild grape, honeysuckle, and moonseed.

I love the morning road, when the air is yet tinged with the dampness and mystery of night, when the foliage is sharply outlined against the reddening sky, and every bird sings his chant as if he just had mastered it for a sublime offertory to a sun that never arose before. Hope is so high in the morning. You are going to succeed where you failed yesterday. You are going to advance so far beyond anything already achieved. God is good to give to men a world full of beauty and ringing with music, and scarcely realizing it you resolve to be good as well. So you add your voice, and travel the long road in the morning with a light heart.

But after all the evening road is better, for it leads back to home and friends, and it is quite true that there is "no place like home." In the red glory of the setting sun there is the promise of light for another day; the peaceful fields appear satisfied with their growth; the birds sing vespers with a depth of harmony altogether devotional; the hermit thrush and the wood robin make your heart ache with the holy purity of their notes. And if the high hopes of the morning did not all come true, the peace of evening brings the consoling thought that perhaps you have grown enough during the day to accomplish them on the morrow; or perhaps it is best after all that success did not come. Intangible, but springing from everywhere, creeps the dark and the time of mystery; the screech owl and the whip-poor-will raise their quavering night songs, and without urging your horse lifts his tired head and breaks into a swifter trot, for night is coming, and he too is on the home road.

Many volumes could be filled with the history of old snake-fences, their inhabitants, and environment. Some of our rarest birds home in the shrub-filled corners or swing from branches above, and flowers of unusual beauty are found growing in them and all along the wayside. If you do not believe the birds are social and love the company of human beings, compare the number of oriole nests you can find in deep forest or open wood with those in fields, orchards, and along roads. In my country I always learn after the leaves fall that orioles in greater number than anywhere else to be found have swung over the road above my head in their pendant bags of hair and lint throughout the summer.

Of all the myriad flowers that distil sweets and call many insects to join in the song of the road none are more beautiful than blazing star. The stems, if not bent by pushing against something unyielding, grow straight toward heaven to a height of from two to three feet where the soil is dry, and by swampy and damper roads attain to four, and during the season of 1907 even five. The leaves are slender and sparsely set, alternating, and the blooms are exquisite. It is difficult to name their shade, because it fluctuates with the amount of moisture, exposure to sun, and the length of time the flower has been open, but it runs from pale violet to deep magenta-purple. The bloom, sometimes an inch across, is a head of fine petals, and reminds one of a painter's brush, filled with exquisite color. Each little flower is folded separately, and at maturity opens, one at a time, around the outer rim until the whole is a mass of shaggy, delicately colored petals. The seed slightly resembles larch fruit or Norwegian pine cones, on account of being similar in shape and covered with scales, but these are purplish-red.

One of these plants bears stamens, and another pistils, so that they are unable to reproduce themselves; and were it not for the work of the bees and butterflies in cross-fertilizing, they would become extinct. They have enough stamens and pollen to give a golden glow to the base of the petals, and are of sufficient perfume to attract bees and butterflies. Archippus, Cœnia, and Troilus do the work necessary in carrying pollen back and forth between plants.

The most exquisite roadside bird of which I ever have succeeded in making a series of studies is the goldfinch, commonly known in the country as the "wild canary," the "lettuce" and "seed bird." These are almost our latest migrants, wait until July to build, and bring off but one brood in a season. The nest is a dainty affair of intricate construction, and takes longer to complete than that of any other bird I know. I have seen a pair of orioles build their nest in three days; but the goldfinches work for a week, and sometimes longer. They use quantities of plant fiber stripped from last year's dead, dry weeds, and line copiously with thistle and milkweed down. Why such deliberate and dainty architecture is not conducive to neater home-life is difficult to say; for these exquisite little birds are the filthiest housekeepers I know intimately.

Nearly all songsters—almost every bird, in fact—with its bill removes from the young the excrement, carrying and dropping it far from the nest. The goldfinches have cradles filled to overflowing, five and six young to the brood, and the elders pay no attention to this feature of parenthood, so that in a short time their nests are as white outside with a rain of droppings as they are inside with milkweed down.

The females are olive-green and yellow birds, and the males are similar in winter. In summer they don a nuptial dress, that with the pure, bubbling melody of their song must make them irresistible. They wear a black cap and sleeves, have a tail touched with black and white, and a pure lemon-yellow waistcoat. They frequent gardens, deserted orchards, and roadsides. Their song is of such bubbling spontaneity that they can not remain on a perch to sing it, but go darting in waves of flight over fields and across the road before you, sowing notes broadcast as the wind scatters the seed they love. They have a tribal call that can be imitated so they answer it readily. The male cries. "Pt'seet!" and the female answers, "Pt'see!" The continuous song that they sow on the air with an abandon approaching the bubbling notes of the bobolink, and really having more pure glee in it, to my ears syllabicates, "Put seed in it! Put seed in it!"

Possibly I thought of this because they are always putting seed into themselves. Mustard, thistle, lettuce, oyster plant, millet, and every garden vegetable and wild weed that produces a seed, in time will bear a goldfinch singing as it sways and feasts.

One of the commonest plants of the wayside, dignified and attractive in bloom, and wholly artistic in seedtime, is the milkweed. This plant is inseparably connected in my mind with the goldfinch, that depends upon it for most of its nesting material, and with the monarch butterfly, the caterpillar of which feeds upon the leaves. Any plant that blankets a goldfinch family and nourishes a butterfly is an aristocrat of the first order. In touch of it grows our best-loved climber.

Because of its elegant leaves, its stout, twining stem, and brilliant and long clinging berries, the bittersweet is the very finest vine of the roadside. In winter it outshines all others, because the hulls of the yellow clusters open in four divisions and expose a bright-red berry divided sometimes into three, and again four parts, each containing a small oblong seed. The elegant vines cover fences, trees, climb poles, and spread over bushes all along the road. The berries retain their brilliant color during winter, so that on gray days they lighten the gloom, and on white ones they contrast with a brilliancy that is equaled only by the scarlet heads of the mountain ash.

Such pictures and music are the natural accompaniment of the old snake-fences. Whenever I come into country abounding in them my heart always begins softly to sing, "Praise the Lord!" For where these old fences are replaced by wire the farmers always make a clean sweep to the roadside, and not the ghost of a picture or the echo of a song is left to me. There are times when my disappointment is so great it is difficult to avoid a feeling of childish resentment. Sometimes I stop my horse and attempt to preach timber conservation and the laws of attraction as applied to moisture; but what has a passing woman to tell a lord of creation busily improving his field? He is providing a few more feet of space for corn and potatoes and enlarging his egotism over greater personal possessions. I notice that in making a field most men exhibit a sense of creation. It is where their work is made manifest. Yes, even to a greater degree than they realize, for sometimes when they arrogantly dismiss me and my theories I smile as a summer storm sweeps unbroken over their field to emphasize my assertions.

Then men must seek shelter and stand helpless while a stout hickory they thought could weather such conditions alone is wrung to ribbons. The great oak left because of its value is stripped of its heart, their stock falls dead, their barns and homes ascend in smoke or their crops are beaten down with the storm or carried away with the wind, and their buildings demolished. Blest and beneficent is most of the music of nature. But when there is a storm, and the earth trembles, the heavens appear to open before our eyes; when the wind-harps shriek, and the big bass-drum rolls its thunder,—all other notes are hushed and forgotten. When nature presses the bass pedal and plays fortissimo we acknowledge the grandeur and irresistible power of the storm. And we see its beauty also. No other picture equals the splendor of mountains of black massing clouds, the white flare of electricity, the falling sheets of glistening water. Most of us enjoy a storm with palpitant exultation, although it is one musical performance that seldom gets an encore. But there are times when it teaches man that if he had left a few acres of forest in the middle of his land, and a border of trees around the edge deep enough for a wind-break, he would have saved his summer's labor, his home, and provided music and shade for the highway.

The roads run systematically across the face of earth, singing the song of travel and commerce. Then there is a far sweeter song, sung by little streams of water, wandering as they will, in beneficent course, quenching the thirst of the earth, enhancing its beauty, and lulling us with their melody. Any one of these little streams is typical of all, but each nature-lover has his own particular brook that to him is most beautiful.

"I come from haunts of coot and hern,"

sang Tennyson of his. My Limberlost comes from the same haunts, and nothing can convince me that any running water on the face of earth is more interesting or more beautiful. I have read of the streams that flow over India's golden sands, down Italy's mountains, through England's meadows; but none of them can sing sweeter songs or have more interest to the inch than the Limberlost.

It is born in the heart of swampy wood and thicket, flows over a bed of muck or gravel, the banks are grass and flower-lined, its waters cooled and shaded by sycamore, maple, and willow. June drapes it in misty white, and November spreads a blanket of scarlet and gold. In the water fish, turtle, crab, muskrat, and water puppy disport themselves. Along the shores the sandpiper, plover, coot, bittern, heron, and crane take their pleasure and seek their food. Above it the hawk and vulture wheel, soar, and sail in high heaven, and the kingfisher dashes in merry rattling flight between the trees, his reflection trailing after him across sunlit pools. The quail leads her chickens from the thicket to drink, and the wild ducks converse among the rushes. In it the coon carefully washes the unwary frog caught among the reeds, and the muskrat furrows deeper ripples than the stones.

The lambs play on the pebbly banks and drink eagerly, the cattle roll grateful eyes as they quench their thirst and stand belly-deep for hours lazily switching their tails to drive away flies. Little children come shouting to wade in the cool waters, and larger ones solemnly sit on the banks with apple-sucker rods, wrapping twine lines and bent pin hooks, supporting their families by their industry, if the gravity of their faces be to-ken of the importance of their work. Sweethearts linger beside the stream and surprise themselves with a new wonder they just have discovered—their secret; but the Limberlost knows, and promises never to tell.

Perhaps that is what it chuckles about while slipping around stones, over fallen trees, and whispering across beds of black ooze. The Limberlost is a wonderful musician, singing the song of running water throughout its course. Singing that low, somber, sweet little song that you must get very close earth to hear, because the creek has such mighty responsibility it hesitates to sing loudly lest it appear to boast. All these creatures to feed and water; all these trees and plants to nourish! The creek is so happy that it can do all this, and if it runs swiftly other woods, thickets, fields, and meadows can be watered. Then the river must be reached as soon as possible, for there are factory wheels to be turned, boats to be carried, and the creek has heard that some day it is to be a part of the great ocean. When the Limberlost thinks of that its song grows a little more exultant and proud, bends are swept with swifter measure, louder notes are sung, and every bird, bee, insect, man, and child along the banks joins in the accompaniment. All the trees rustle and whisper, shaking their branches to shower it with a baptism of gold in pollen time. The rushes and blue flags murmur together, and the creek and every sound belonging to it all combine in the song of the Limberlost.

Sometimes it slips into the thicket, as on the Bone farm; for it is impartial, and perhaps feels more at home there than in the meadows, surely more than in cultivated fields, where the banks often are stripped bare, the waters grow feverish and fetid, its song is hushed, and its spirit broken. But in the thicket the birds gather very low above the surface, the branches dip into the friendly floods, and it nourishes such an abundance of rank growth as men scarcely can penetrate. Then the Limberlost and the thicket hold a long conversation, to tell each other how very content and happy they are. The bed of the Limberlost in the thicket is ooze and muck, so the water falls silent while slipping over the velvet softness, with only a whisper to the birds and trees; not so loud as the song of the flags, rushes, and water hyacinths that grow on the banks. The many trees and masses of shrubs lower their tones to answer the creek, and he who would know their secret must find for himself a place on the bank and be very quiet, for in the thicket the stream will sing only the softest lullaby, just the merest whisper song.

The big turtles in the water are quiet folk. So are the sinuous black snakes sunning on the bushes, and the muskrats homing along the banks. As if loth to break the dark, damp stillness with louder notes, the doves coo softly; for they, too, have a secret, the greatest of any bird in all the world. No wonder they keep together and live so lovingly, and coo and coo softly; those wild, tender, and—above all other—loving birds. One would think they would warble from the treetops and soar with the eagle, had not long years taught that modesty and tenderness are their most prominent characteristics.

For this is their secret. They are the chosen bird of Omnipotence. It was a dove that carried the news of release to the prisoners in the ark, and it was in the form of a dove that the Spirit of God is said to have materialized and hovered over the head of Jesus when He was baptized in the Jordan. What other bird bears honors high as these? Yet doves home in the thicket, on a few rough twigs they place their pearly, opalescent eggs, and in trembling anxiety brood and raise a pair of young that go modestly and lovingly through life, exactly the same as their parents. Nowhere else in all nature does the softly-uttered coo of a dove so harmonize with the environment as over a stream in a thicket; and no accompaniment to the murmuring voice of the Limberlost is quite so melodious as the love-song of this bird.

The thicket seems a natural home for almost every feathered creature. This because there are trees, bushes, and shrubs, with their berries, nuts, and fruits; vines and weeds bearing seed; every variety of insect and worm, and water with its supply of food, thus providing things to eat in a small space for almost every species. In spring and summer the birds have full sway; but in the fall, after the first black frost, come rugged country boys and girls and village children in search of fruit and nuts.

To some there is nothing so delicious as the black haw—white until almost ripe, then a day of mottled estate, and then such a luscious, shining black berry it has no equal; and if the birds get any they must be ahead of the boys and girls. The opossums must be before the boys at the persimmon tree, for few are left when they finish. The robins love wild grapes, and cedar birds the poke berries, and squirrels, hazelnuts.

Hazel bushes are beautiful. The leaf is something like the elm in shape, though the hazel is of finer cutting. They are nearly the same size, deeply grooved on top, and heavily veined underneath. The nuts grow from two to six in a cluster and are sheltered in a leafy, pulpy green cover with fringed edges, most artistic and, I should think, of great benefit to the decorator searching for an unhackneyed subject. There are many places where they could be used with fine effect in leather work, especially as the ripe nut is a good leather color. But the boy who reaches the hazel bushes before the squirrels gets up very early in the morning, and then only too often to find that the worms have been ahead of him; for when green the shells of hazelnut and chestnut are so very soft that beetles bore into them and deposit eggs that hatch, and the worm develops inside the shell, that hardens later. This explains why so often you crack a perfectly sound nut and find a wormy kernel.

When the Limberlost leaves the thicket and comes into the open again it does not spread, as it did on the bed of ooze; for in the firm clay soil of fields and meadows only a narrow channel is cut, and so with forces renewed by concentration it comes slipping across Bone's woods pasture. Through his fields, always tree-shaded, it flows, and then crosses farms whose owners I am glad I do not know; for here my creek is robbed of shelter, and left to spread ineffectually, and to evaporate in fetid, unwholesome pools. The trees are cut, and grazing stock by wading everywhere trample down the banks and fill the channel with soil; thus wantonly wasting water that in a few more years these land-owners will be digging ditches to reclaim. With broken heart it is dissipated by the sun, and a dry sob of agony is the only note raised as it painfully oozes across this land and beneath the road bridge.

Here the creek reaches deep-shaded channel once more, and bursts into song crossing Armantrout's pasture; for it is partly shaded, though many large trees on the banks are being felled. A happy song is sung on the Rayn farm, where it is sheltered by trees and a big hill. In full force it crosses the road again, slides below the railroad bridge, rounds the hill, chanting a requiem to the little city of the dead on its banks, flows through the upper corner of the old Limberlost swamp, hurries across the road once more, and so comes singing into Schaffer's meadow.

The low, open meadow covered closely with cropped velvet grass, "green pastures," where full-fed cattle lie in deep shade. Nowhere in its course to the river does the Limberlost "preen" and sing exultingly as when crossing this meadow. All the water babies travel with it, the kingfisher and the plover follow; the children play along the banks, and if it has any intuition at all, surely the creek can see gratitude in the eyes of the inhabitants of the meadow as they thrust their muzzles in the depths or stand cooling under trees. If the Limberlost loves admiration, here it receives a full share. The banks are covered with enough trees and bushes to make almost continuous shade for the waters, and a thing of beauty it goes laughing on the way to the Wabash. In fact it is so close the river here that big fish come adventuring and to spawn, and their splash is part of the music that the family living on the banks hears daily. Mr. Schaffer says that he can stand on his back porch, bait a fish, turn, and drop it into the frying-pan. This really could be done, but much as I have trespassed there I never have seen the fish on their way anywhere except to the river.

Aside from the song of the creek and the birds that follow, there comes an occasional wild duck, sometimes a loon lost in migration or slightly wounded by a hunter, and every spring and fall migrating wild geese pay a visit and add strange voices to the running chorus. Through Grove's meadow, adjoining, the creek is wilder and wider, and then gathering force in a last rush, with a glad song it goes hurrying to mingle with the Wabash.

The river, when swollen with the flood of spring rains, sings a sweeping, irresistible measure that carries one's thoughts by force; but this is its most monotonous production. There is little variation, and the birds are the strongest accompanists. Later, when it falls into the regular channel, it sings its characteristic song and appears so much happier and more content. I believe the river loves and does not willingly leave its bed. When a strong, muddy current it sweeps the surface from valuable fields, drowns stock and washes away fences; it works as if forced, and I like to think the task is disagreeable. At times it seems to moan and sob, while sucking around big tree trunks and washing across meadows and fields.

When it comes home again and runs in the proper channel it shouts and sings with glee the true song of the river. You can hear the water triumph as it swirls around great maple and sycamore roots, chuckle as it buffets against rocks, gurgle across shoals, and trill where it ripples over a pebbly floor. The muskrat weaves currents against its flow, the carp wallow in mucky pools, and the black bass leap in air as if too full of life to remain in their element.

The river is a house, the bed its floor, the surface its roof, and all the water-folk its residents. What a wonderful thing it would be if the water were transparent, that we might see the turtles, eels, and catfish busy with the affairs of life; bass, pickerel, and suckers maintaining the laws of supremacy, and water puppies at play! When the purple tints on its banks fade, tree-bloom baptizes it with golden pollen, and a week later showers it with snowy petals of wild plum, thorn, crab, and haw. All summer the trees drop a loosened leaf here and there, with Good Samaritan results; for these make lifeboats on which luckless wasps, bees, and worms fallen from blooming trees ride to safety and dry their drenched coats and weighted wings. Trees are the great life-saving service of the river, especially in the fall, when the water is covered with crisp, dead leaves. Many of them are needed, for the cool nights chill the insects so that they fall easily, the winds blow with unusual violence, and there are three times as many victims drowning as in summer.

Throughout the season many blooms decorate the river bank, but two stand pre-eminent: the redbud borne on a small tree, the mallow on a shrub. The tree flower is remarkable because it is almost the first color shown, and it breaks all over the branches like a severe attack of measles, when not the hint of a leaf is in sight. These come later in beautiful heart-shaped design, and the flowers are replaced by long, wine-red seed pods. The tiny blooms are shaped like the separate flowers of a locust spray, and of a shade our mothers spoke of as red analine. The blunt point of the bloom once was called a "pink tinted tear" by a poet, and this color flushes stronger until it becomes a deep magenta at the base, while the cup that holds it is reddish-brown.

This shade must be the rarest in all God's workshop, because He uses it so very sparingly. It is found on flower faces and in nature less often than any other. How He prizes it is proven by its appearance among the very first, at a time when we are eager for the color and perfume of spring. Our grandmothers taught us to love it on the petunia faces bordering olden flower beds. I delighted in it early on the Easter eggs my mother colored for me. It is one of the most ancient and popular of manufactured colors, chosen for reproduction, without a doubt, because nature is so miserly in its use; for only in hints and suggestions does it fleck the face of creation. First we see it on the redbud beside the river. Then as the poke berry matures it stripes the thrifty stem with gorgeous color to attract the bibulous cedar bird. In mid-summer you find hints of it on wayside blazing star, and in the fall New York asters and ironwort suggest it in their bloom.

But its time of greatest glory is in the first appearance, when anything else that may be in flower is white or faint pink and lavender, and only serves as a background for its tones of positive color. This hint of nature should be remembered well by lovers of the redbud. It is extremely choice about its setting. It refuses to tolerate color other than green, white, or modifications of its own shades. The trees are numerous along the Wabash and in the woods, so that—blooming before leafage and almost first, and seeming to commingle with the mist and haze of early spring—they touch the horizon with a faint purple that melts into the blue of the sky and the lazy white clouds.

Then comes the time to worship the river. Not even when decorated in the gold of tree bloom is it so exquisitely lovely, so delicate to look upon. Few leaves are unfolded, and those a faint greenish-yellow; the magenta masses on the banks, the water singing loudest at high tide, the purple mists in the air, and fleecy clouds over all. Returning birds are warbling in a craze of joy at home-coming, and we look and listen with eyes and ears hungering for just this after the long days of winter.

To the accompaniment of water voices are added songs of birds on the banks, bushes, and trees, and the animals that live beside it. The sun bird—the oriole—with breast and heart of gold, flashes above it; the cardinal, with shrill whistle, nests beside it; the catbird and jay, the robin, thrush, dove, and chat, all home along its banks, and in them nests the typical bird of the river, the kingfisher.

> "No wonder he laughs so loud,
> No wonder he looks so proud,
> There are great kings would give their royalty,
> To have one day of his felicity."

Thus sang Maurice Thompson, the sweetest musician the Wabash ever knew. Six feet the birds tunnel into a pebbly, firm embankment; on the ground deposit at least six oblong, white eggs, and the mother walls them in with regurgitated fish bones heaped around her as she broods. One family to a season is the rule, and the young remain long in the nest before they become self-supporting and add their voices to the chorus of the river.

The kingfisher is one of the birds of most ancient history, and very interesting. A large volume could be filled with tradition and story concerning it. This proves that people of all time have found it worthy of consideration. Its song is not musical according to our standards, but it is the gayest, most care-free, rollicking bird of the river, and one whose presence is almost universally respected. In all my work afield I never have found a kingfisher wantonly shot, or heard of such a thing. There seems to be an understanding that they are not suitable for food, and do not interfere with other birds; so they are unmolested. They fly in dashes and perch at short intervals, making it a task for any one so disposed to harm them. The only depredation I have known them to suffer is from snakes entering their nests.

The animals that join their grunting, sniffling, and snarling with the voices of the river are the opossum, ground hog, muskrat, coon, and fox. I do not mean that all of these are river animals, but that their species home close the water, go there to quench their thirst, prey upon its denizens, and mingle their voices with its song.

Of all vegetation along the river, mallows are the typical flowers, the blooms we see most often, and love best. The masses of spring color that line the river as a rule belong quite as much to the fields, fences, and thickets as to the water. They are generally everywhere that a shrub remains. The mallow is a true water flower, and grows in greater beauty and blooms in a profusion unknown to its swampy relatives. The plants flourish so close to the water that half the roots are washed in the river.

The succulent stems are pithy and of a golden-green color. The leaves are olive-green above and whitish underneath, slightly resembling maple foliage, but they are more artistically cut.

The buds are incased in a big, loose, heavily veined covering that opens to permit their exit, and this cover is set in a fringed cup, adding an artistic touch. The rosy, delicate, pink bloom emerges in a crumpled, folded state, and slowly opens and stretches to a smooth trumpet-shaped flower, as the wings of a moth expand and grow even; and it appears in late July and August, when it has a solid green background to emphasize its beauty and scarcely a rival to attract attention from it. There are five petals of the bloom, maroon at the base, abruptly shading to delicate pink at the edges, and strongly veined with maroon color on the outside. The flowers measure from four to six inches across and closely resemble pink hollyhocks. At the base the stamens and pistils combine in a tube that spreads in a pollen-covered tip and attracts bees and all sweet-lovers to the plant. When the petals fall, the case that opened for their exit closes again, and the seeds ripen inside. From pods that I gathered beside the river I have two mallow plants growing at my well curb. They were kept during winter and planted in early spring. Mallows bear cultivation easily in sufficiently damp places, but they can not have too much water.

The river with its accompanying voices forms a characteristic part of the Song of the Fields; a pure, liquid note tinged with serene and tranquil melody sung from a perfect setting, and perhaps draws a larger audience than any other music of the open. Because the fields are the scene of man's greatest activity, the voice of toiling humanity is their dominant note.

The roar of great cities, the screaming of lake, river, and railroad traffic, and the busy hum of workers in the fields combine in the song of life. But bare and unadorned existence is an ugly, sordid thing, so some men have kept all the beauty they could. That part of the original gift of the Lord to the children of men that they themselves have preserved furnishes every picture it rests our weary eyes to see and every note our tired ears care most to hear—the divine and unceasing Song of the Fields.

On the Banks of the Wabash in Winter

"When the Geese Fly North"
"The Bride of Red Wing Lake"
"The Lost White Wild Strawberries"

from *Tales You Won't Believe*

Like the first piece in this collection, these last three tales are from the period when Gene Stratton Porter lived in "Wildflower Woods," the home she built north of Geneva, Indiana. Her first home is now the Limberlost State Historic Site. A small portion of the vast area of swamp which Stratton Porter explored and wrote about from 1895 to 1913 is being restored as wetland. Wildflower Woods is now the Indiana State Historic Site Limberlost North. This more rustic location features guided walks through the woods and grounds Gene Stratton Porter cultivated. Both sites are open from early spring through late fall.

The rural life and natural wonders which Gene Stratton Porter celebrated are not as easily preserved as are her houses. Even in these tales, written during the 1920s while she lived in California, there are elegiac notes as she looks back at her past and at a culture made forever different by World War I.

"When the Geese Fly North"

WHEN THE SOUND of hammers had ceased and the workmen had removed the last load of débris from the vicinity of Limberlost Cabin, it became my delightful task to induce the birds and every other living creature of the woods and water of northern Indiana to come to my small one hundred and twenty acre preserve and make themselves at home. I could guarantee that they would not be bothered by guns, by dogs and cats, or by thoughtless tourists. I could not guarantee that they would not prey upon each other, that they would not live out their lives in accordance with the ancient instincts of the wild.

I clothed myself in a dull olive khaki, and with every equipment for field work made as inconspicuous as possible, I went about the business of making friends with my wild neighbours.

I had an unique location. Quite forty acres of the one hundred and twenty I had purchased were covered with a splendid growth of original timber. I had broad, open fields, deep ravines, and over a mile of swampy, winding lake shore from which in many places the land rose abruptly, almost the entire length of the shore being thickly covered with trees and bushes bearing fruit, nuts, and berries. Predominant among these were every variety of oak tree known to that region, huge giants of the forest, many of them ranging from twenty to fifty feet to the first branches, straight trunks, tall and proud, every autumn full-fruited, so that literally bushels and bushels of acorns fell from their cups and rolled down the steep embankments into the shallow shore water.

The lake upon which I located in northern Indiana is owned and controlled by the State. There is a practice every fall of lowering the water to a degree that will protect the docks and boathouses which, at the settled end of the lake, stand before every one of the cottages which house a summer population frequently exceeding five thousand.

While the lake was covered with ice and the shore line with snow, every day I saw big gray squirrels and the smaller red ones, and 'coons on gray days, going down to the shore to burrow under the snow and feed on acorns, the hulls of which were thoroughly water soaked, the meat, however, seeming not be the least affected.

Across the front of the second story of the Cabin that I built for my convenience while engaged in field work ran a big sleeping porch. The hillside upon which the Cabin stood sloped rather abruptly to the lake. The front foundations were four or five feet in height and this threw the sleeping porch among the branches of the great trees closely surrounding the Cabin. From this point of vantage I had almost the same opportunity for watching and studying the lives of the wild as if I really had been in the trees themselves. I had made a practice even while the building was under construction of keeping out quantities of food for the squirrels and birds, and on the east side of the Cabin I had built an open porch with a cement floor and broad window seats upon which I constantly kept food for the wild, as well as suet baskets on the logs of the building and the trunks of the near-by trees. All over the location I had many vantage points for watching and studying the birds, the sleeping porch being one of the best.

Equally as fine was a cedar boat in which, in unobtrusive clothing, I could follow the lake shore, quietly nosing like a drifting log into marshy nesting grounds and swampy bayous. Lying in this boat at night, facing the sky, it was a most interesting thing to watch the spring and fall migrations. From an unbelievably early period in the spring until the last goldfinch of June, at almost any hour through the night I could hear the little feathered hosts going over. Sometimes it was bluebirds that were talking to each other as they crossed my lake. Sometimes it was swifts or martins. Sometimes it was big flocks of warblers, sometimes vireos, orioles, or robins.

From the first year of my residence on the lake there were always waterfowl going north and coming south. Usually these were in scattered flocks. Once I counted seventeen wild geese in one flock that had alighted on the water not far from my boathouse. Always there were a few flocks of grebe and galinules, all of which usually remained, as well as a plentiful sprinkling of killdeer, plover, shitepoke, bittern, and heron. Sometimes we had gulls on the lake for a pause in migration, but none ever remained. During the past three years there has been one pair of coots that has nested and remained throughout the season. I once saw Father Coot proudly leading down the lake past the Cabin nine young ones, while Mother Coot brought up the rear.

I learned from all these birds in their trips back and forth that they had no fixed time for migration, and it often seemed as if even their instincts were misleading. The records of the vicinity frequently show heavy bird disasters occurring over Lake Michigan, which was near my location. Large flocks of birds gathered for migration and attempted to cross the lake in heavy winds, or when the first snows and the icy breath of winter were in the fall air, with the result that for days the bodies of small birds would be washed ashore and piled in heaps on the sand.

These fatalities seemed to occur mostly in fall migration, but there were times when the birds caused themselves much suffering and loss of life by attempting a northern migration too early. Birds tender from their winter in the South, in Central America, and some that travel even so far as Patagonia, came to us in late February and early March. At that time the ground would not be sufficiently thawed to furnish worms for the meat eaters, the seed stalks were blown bare of food supplies by heavy winter winds, and skifts of snow sometimes covered the earth to the depth of several inches for days at a time, so that the birds were almost starved. I very frequently had bluebirds, lark, quail, and robins come up to the out-buildings and the Cabin in search of food.

In the latter part of February, 1915, about two o'clock in the morning, I was awakened by the voice of wild geese. My first impression was one of intense surprise that the geese should be going over so early in the season. The lake was still covered with ice. A few days of sunshine had melted the snow on the slanting banks facing the east on the Cabin shore line.

My next impression was one of wonder as to where the birds could be. The sound of their voices was not coming down from the sky as was usual with geese in migration, but it seemed to rise to my windows from below. I threw back the covers, and standing on the waist box in front of a window beside the fireplace in my indoor sleeping room, I looked down on the lake shore. At first I could see nothing, but I could hear the voices of what seemed to me to be a whole world full of wild geese. Thinking to better the view, I slipped into the adjoining room where there was no porch outside the windows and from that point I saw one big, gray wild gander with a black ring circling his neck come around the corner of the boathouse and head down my lake shore. He was alternately gabbling and gobbling acorns. To right and to left he snatched them, keeping straight down the shore line, and behind him, in steady formation, clearly defined by the ice of the lake shore, there came through the moonlight, marching in orderly procession varying from three to five abreast, geese and yet more geese, all of them busy picking up acorns and talking continuously.

As the procession of geese rounded the corner of the boathouse their voices came up clearly, but back of that there rolled an indistinguishable chatter that seemed to reach over unbelievable space. I was seized with a feeling, perhaps a throw-back to primitive days—after all, they were wild geese, fat and juicy and on their northern migration—a sort of obsession that it was a pity that all of them should go north. Someone should wake up and secure for us at least a pair of those big, gray geese where there seemed to be geese by the hundreds.

I turned and cried to Mr. Porter: "Oh, Dad! Wake up! Come here and see what is happening!"

In a sleepy voice he retorted: "Well, what *is* happening?"

"Don't you hear?" I cried. "There is a whole world of wild geese down on the shore line passing the Cabin!"

After an instant he said: "Yes, I hear them. There must be a big flock of them, but I am chilling with a cold, and I wouldn't get out of bed for all the geese in the universe."

I realized that goose hunting on a raw February night might not be the best medicine for a cold, so I replaced the sash and slipped back to my own room. I drew the blankets from my bed, and turning on the light, took the time from my dressing table clock. It was fifteen minutes after two. Then I put out the light, wrapped myself in the blankets, and stood where I could watch the passing flock.

In a steady stream the geese came on. Sometimes one would venture out of line and come a short distance up the embankment in search of an acorn. Sometimes one would try to work a bite from under the ice coating of the lake, but as a rule the great body of the flock kept in orderly procession, and it kept moving, in a hurried trot following around the shore line. On down past the big wild flower beds of close an acre each which in spring were masses of red and blue and yellow and pink bloom, they went, out of sight into the deepest depths of the cove on the Sower land adjoining mine, and then out again into the moonlight where it beat full and fair on the eastern side of Pleasant Point below us, and so marched around the Point.

When the last goose had passed my window it was slightly past fifteen minutes after three o'clock. I was so cold that I could scarcely creep back to bed and gather the covers around me. I had watched from the time the gander in the lead rounded the boathouse until, with a shrill honking, he had taken wing somewhere in the region of Sponhauer Island below Pleasant Point. I could hear the muffled beating of wings and the answering screams of ganders down the line when the migratory flight was resumed, but in so far as I could judge, each member of the enormous flock followed the shore line and went on feeding to that point at which the leading gander took wing. I could see them when they rounded Pleasant Point, and I could see the bow they formed as they lifted and arched up against the sky following the lead of the gander across the lake and due north.

After breakfast in the morning I put on my boots and heavy field clothes, and, taking a stout walking stick, I went down to the shore line. I followed it south and east to the deep bay on my side of the clubhouse at the head of the lake, around coves and curves, all the way back through the woods until I reached the point at which the flock had taken wing. I was simply dumbfounded. I went back to the library and before I began work I tried to tell my secretary and Mr. Porter how many geese there had been in that flock. They laughed at me.

About ten o'clock there arrived, unexpectedly, at the Cabin the entomologist of the State of Indiana, Mr. Frank N. Wallace. Mr. Wallace had been a friend of mine for a number of years. He had been employed by me to remove the dead wood and to fill the cavities in the trees surrounding the Cabin before and during its erection. For a number of years he had been assisting me in collecting the trees, the shrubs and vines, and the flowers native to northern Indiana from the swamps and the woods, and helping me to find a homing place for them in the wild flower sanctuary I was working to establish. He was thoroughly familiar with my methods of keeping my records and with the work that I was doing. His standing in my home came very close to being that of a beloved brother. He was not only my business associate, he was my friend, and he had cemented his friendship by marrying a young woman who for seven years had been a highly prized secretary of mine. I had expected that of all the world this lean, grave Scotch friend of mine would weigh my words and accept my findings.

He evidently did that very thing, but my word that day weighed so heavily that his credulity was taxed to the uttermost. He looked at me speculatively, as if he were searching for signs of fever, and when I saw the doubt in his eyes and the uncertainty on his countenance, I said to him: "At least my word is not altogether lacking in confirmation. I can give you the time at which the gander in the lead rounded the corner of the boathouse. I can give you the time at which the last of the flock went out of sight toward the north. It was slightly over one hour. During all that time, from three to five abreast, a steady procession of feeding geese went hurrying around our shore line."

And then I added: "This morning I put on my boots and took my walking stick and followed them from where the first of the flock alighted to where they arose. If you want to get an idea better than my word can give you as to how many hundred geese followed this lake shore last night, make the same trip yourself. Their tracks are not obliterated and their droppings dot the lake shore like a fall of hail."

I waved my friend toward the door and with incredulity on his face he went. An hour later I met him on his return. There was no incredulity on his face now. Rather it was bathed in a sort of awed wonder. He said to me softly: "My God! I had not supposed there were that many wild geese in the whole world!"

"The Bride of Red Wing Lake"

HAVING SPENT MY CHILDHOOD in the country and being by six years the youngest of the family, I learned at an early age to amuse myself with the outdoors rather than in play with other children. So, from the earliest moment that I was allowed to wander at will, I made friends with the birds, with the flowers, with the trees, with anything and everything with which I came in contact. Perhaps my very dearest playmates of all were three streams of running water that crossed our land. One of them, in the northern section of the land, was broad for a brook even in those days; shallow; and it had mucky banks where grew all kinds of sedges and swamp grasses, cat-tails and bul-rushes, and great beds of blue flag. Willow trees grew on its banks in one shaggy patriarch of which a scarlet tanager nested almost every year, and the male bird, a thing of blood-red and coal-black colour, sang from the top branches and performed his share of tanager family life in near prox-imity to the flag bed which in bloom time was a sheet of blue that at-tracted both the wild and the domestic bees and the sweet-loving humming birds and the butterflies. In this same tree an oriole always swung its pendent purse of lint, plant fibre, and string from the door-yard. A thrilling riot of colour ensued when a bird of blood red and an-other of sun yellow began the activities of feeding two nests filled with clamouring young above a bed of blue wild iris beside a brook that threw rainbow shadows and had many secrets to whisper and sing and chuckle over. On all the land which Father owned there was not a spot more ex-quisite than the small promontory on which grew the tanager and oriole willow, not even in deep wood where the other small brook that ran from west to east passed the red flame of *Monarda didyma* and white violets climbed down the bank until they could see themselves in the water.

That brook was narrow, contrary in its flowing; when it came into the open it was too lovely for words. It, too, had borders of fancy grasses with big, rough heads like burrs and sprays of clotted gold-brown lace and the stately cat-tails and slender, graceful bulrushes. A favourite spot on its banks was under a wild cherry tree and the ground all around was full of wild leeks and ramps, and sometimes when the cattle came down to drink, they browsed on these and spoiled the flavour of the milk and butter. This brook had a pebbly bed which could be waded with safety almost all the way. Every bird common to the ornithology of the Central States came to it for a drink or to nest in the shrubs and trees along its banks, or paused for a choir loft in the big forest trees homing on the steep bank above it. There were wonderful little fish that played in its wa-ters, tiny minnows with white tummies and silver sides and gray backs and darker fins, and the loveliest little things not more than an inch and a half or two inches in length, white underneath, silvery on the back with blood-red dots down the sides and tiny dark freckles on their faces. There was great excitement in the family when one of the boys found a six-inch catfish with its yellow under parts and its dark, velvety back, its peculiar mouth formation and its big head. He ran all the way from the brook to the house with it in his hat and nobody scolded him a particle because no one ever had seen such a fish before. We called it the "black velvet fish" and we kept it in a big glass jar filled with rain water and fed it angle worms and bread crusts.

Flowing from the north to the south was the biggest brook of all. The other two were its tributaries. This stream was in a hurry to reach the Wabash River. It ran a straighter course, cut a deeper bank, because it carried a heavier volume of water and there were places in it where I was cautioned to be careful because they were so deep that I might go in over my head and drown. This brook, as it entered our land, was flanked by a high hill where big stone faces cropped out, decorated with queer lichens of gay colours and dainty little ferns and mosses grew between them, and queer water grasses at the base. I almost always went to this spot to start playing in that stream. It was large enough that any water-loving wild bird came to it. The killdeer loved it. They ran along its banks with their quavering, grieving soft cries. If one had trusted what they said and translated their tones into a human way of thinking, one would have believed that these birds were not having a very good time. But after watching them carefully for several years, I found out that Mr. and Mrs. Killdeer were particularly congenial and happy about their home life and that they took the best possible care of their four youngsters. Their queer nests in the cornfield were so carelessly constructed that they were scarcely nests at all. The hen birds brooded on four big, darkly speckled eggs, so sharply pointed that Father explained to me that Mother Killdeer was too lazy to build a for-sure nest; so she shaped her eggs with points so that they would whirl as if on a pivot instead of rolling away if anything disturbed them.

It was while playing beside these brooks, spending days in watching the growing things and the living things that homed in the waters or came to them for refreshment, that I learned in the beginning to love to be alone, to love to be out of doors, to love to tuck down unobserved in a secluded spot and watch how the ground puppies played at the water's edge, how the muskrats managed their home life, how the 'coons came from their hollow trees in the deep woods, slipping along in the early evening, to catch frogs. And I learned, too, how neat 'coons were by watching them go out on a stone or a log and repeatedly scour and rinse the slime from the luckless frogs they caught for their food. I learned to know the water birds particularly well and all the small fish, and I developed a love for the music of running water, for the living things habituated to it, that has never left me.

I had heard of lakes; I knew what they were; but the first real lake that I ever saw with my very own eyes was that one lying in northern Indiana called Sylvan Lake at the northern end of which lay the little railroad station called Rome City—exactly why, it would take a philosopher to tell, since it had nothing in the world to do with Rome and it was so tiny that it scarcely deserved the name of "village" when I first became acquainted with it. This was a peculiar lake, spreading into broad sheets of water in places and then narrowing to high banked channels; widening into marshy places having all sorts of water growth; lying shallow over mucky beds where yellow water lilies bloomed, and growing deeper where the white ones lifted to the sky faces of beauty unsurpassed by any flowers that ever grew anywhere. There were many places where large patches of forest growth, big hardwood trees belonging to that belt which runs across New York state, southern Michigan, and northern Ohio and Indiana, reached the perfection of as lovely trees as the world has to offer in oaks, elms, maples, beeches, lindens, every tree habitual to that location and some which were rare. This stretch of magnificent forest had, for good measure, two or three unusual oaks and Kentucky coffee trees, frequent specimens of burl maple and walnut and wild cherry, and among the bushes customarily found with such forests there was the music of the castanets of the hop tree and the cymbals of the wafer ash. There was the lace of chionanthus, the bloody berries of the northern holly; there was in profusion the pale velvet of the wild rose and the snow of the massed heads of alder with dogwood in the early spring, and before that, the purplish tints of the Judas tree. Vines ran everywhere, among them Dutchman's pipe and bittersweet and ground nut with its brown and lavender velvet clusters of bloom, and *Discorea villosa* with its exquisite leaves, and moonseed with its purple and blue fruit and leaves more beautiful than English ivy.

The lake made its way southward for leisurely miles, and to these woods that surrounded it were added every vine and shrub and the very rarest of the wild flowers that botanists knew. On the shores of this lake I have found Hooker's orchid, rattlesnake plantain, and twenty-three other orchids ranging from pink snake's mouth to "three birds." The gold lady slipper was at home on many a stretch running to the water. Sometimes they were so luxuriant they grew a pair of these exquisite flowers proudly upheld side by side. From the south end, which was the highest, the water flowed north set in a current by many springs around the shore line and by the outlet of the Little Elkhart, and naturally all this wild life with the white and gold lilies and the blue flags of the shore line for added attractions, lured every bird and butterfly and dragon fly native to that part of the country.

The first time I ever visited that lake had not an hour that does not stand out distinct in my memory. I had dreamed of a place like that. My brooks in childhood had taught me what might be expected when truly deep wood and large bodies of water met in loving conjunction. The first time I ever visited this lake I was left in a peculiar degree to my own devices. I had come as the guest of the sweetheart of one of my elder sisters. It was a habit of theirs to rent a boat, row it to some particularly attractive place on the bank, and amuse themselves with conversation, reading, and discussing their own interests. In the meantime, I might take the boat and exercise my muscle on experiments in rowing, and upon investigating the shore line. Nothing in all this world could have suited me better. There was a Chautauqua assembly convening on a big island in the lake where the best talent of the country was engaged in delivering lectures, giving concerts and plays. There was a huge pipe organ and particularly fine music, but so long as I could get the oars of a boat in my fingers and the freedom of the lake and the banks at my command, neither the music nor the best that Henry Ward Beecher and De Witt Talmadge and Sam Jones had to offer made any difference to me. At night I dutifully listened to the music and thought over the lectures, but during the daytime I worked on perfecting myself in rowing and exploring the lake shore.

My first day out in a boat happened to be with a middle-aged man who was the brother of my landlady. Just why he took a youngster in short skirts and first year high school attainments in the way of education into his charge and spent a day teaching her to master every trick possible to a boat, is beyond my conception. His sister told me that he was an expert oarsman, that he had been familiar with the water all his life, that he would take good care of me and would be pleased to teach me to row. So with all the confidence in the world I went with him, and my confidence was in no way misplaced. The day we spent together on Sylvan Lake was wonderful. The weather was perfect. God never made a lake more beautiful. Spring and summer were just merging. The birds were still singing with courting enthusiasm and it was my first day in a boat on water. I was permitted to sit in the oarsman's seat and take those oars in my strong young hands and make that boat walk the water backward or forward or turn at my bidding. I very speedily learned how to manipulate it and I took the utmost pride in being an apt scholar, in watching so carefully that I never had to be told but once. I tried to consider every movement, to make it a graceful and an efficient movement, and I had the physical strength to do anything I chose with a boat; so I rowed for uncounted miles around the lake shore, pausing for my raptures over lilied pools. We loitered through the shadows of great trees and floated with the current down deep channels where we went a reasonable rate with no exertion whatever. By and by noon came, and then we did an exceedingly reprehensible thing. We realized that we were many, many miles from home and we were annoyingly hungry. While we were figuring on whether there would be any chance of finding something to eat at one of the farms that ran down to the water's edge, we came around a cove and above us we heard resounding voices. We discovered that a Sunday School picnic was in progress in a beautiful beech wood which ran down to a cove bordered with bushes and cat-tails.

As we softly edged our way under the shadow of the bushes and over the lily pads, we caught sight of a number of clothes baskets—big, deep, broad, oblong baskets such as I was accustomed to seeing used in the country where families numbered from a dozen up—and I knew what those baskets contained, and so did my escort. I looked at him and he looked at me, and kneeling forward, he crept down the centre of the boat and motioned me to change places with him. Then he took the oars and with extreme expertness he nosed the prow of the boat up to within a few feet of those baskets, and I softly stepped from the boat, and under the cover of the sheltering branches, made a raid on them. When I came back I had fried chicken for two and hard-boiled eggs and cookies and bread and butter and a pie and every blessed thing that ever went into clothes baskets groaning with food in the days when all the world was fertile and everybody had so much food that they fattened the pigs on the excess from the table and gave bountifully to every passerby on the road. Just as I arose with my plunder and started for the boat, some sharp-eyed individual espied me and set up a yell. It was a frantic dash that I made and a mighty leap that I took to my end of the boat. The impact of my weight shot it far into the water and I dropped on the seat while a skillful oarsman put distance between us and that bank at a rate that was amazing. Then we rowed back around the lake shore until we thought we were secure and acknowledged ourselves to be the blackest of sinners. We had stolen. We had taken things that did not belong to us. But we were really hungry; it was a holiday; it was June; while there were baskets and baskets of food, and our contrition was not of the brand that could even be designated "skin deep." So we finished a wonderful day and when it was over I was pronounced sufficiently skillful to take a boat and row it safely anywhere I chose. My mind was so filled with blue skies across which swallows and water birds were skimming, with great forests and bloomful bushes and vines, with water flowers new and strange to me, with exultation over my new prowess in being able to make a boat walk the water at my will, that when I went to bed I could not go to sleep. I had only to close my eyes in order to see, as clearly as I had seen at any time during the day, the slant of the sunshine on the water, to hear the voices of laughing, happy people, the roll of the great pipe organ on the island, and the bird songs, to recall the quackings of the ducks in the sedgy places, and the chattering of coot and grebe, while my ears were fairly glutted with the notes of the red wings. All day long I had heard them and seen their blood and orange wings for the first time. They never had deigned to stop, when coming up from southern migration, at any of my small brooks. They always had come farther north to the still waters and the open spaces of the lakes.

This was my first introduction to this lake which many years afterward I named to suit myself, in honour of these birds, Red Wing. In the years that ensued, winter became a time of effort during which, by some hook or crook, I must amass enough money to pay my fare and supply me with food for another period at Sylvan Lake. And so the years crept on, one after the other, and each year, in some way, I managed, sometimes for a whole glorious month, to make a field trip to the lake. In their passing the years had brought to me a home of my own and a youngster I was doing my best to rear in the way I thought she should go. But I had not reached the place, and I never shall reach it, where I will give up devoting some part of each day to the stiffest effort I can make at personal improvement. I had been taught from childhood to count that day lost on which I had not learned something that I did not know before, on which I could not paint a little better picture than I had painted the previous day, upon which I could not execute a piece of music with a slight degree more facility in some particular than I had done on the yesterday.

Again it was early June. With my family I was staying at Triplett's Hotel on Sylvan Lake. I had reached the place where self-expression had become a material thing and I had accumulated from my work sufficient funds to make me financially independent. I was looking for a location upon which to build a workshop in the most available territory I could find for my natural history productions, and in all my search in northern Ohio, southern Michigan, northern Illinois and Indiana I had been able to find no one spot that so suited me for my individual purposes as Sylvan Lake. The thought I had in mind at the time was to buy a cottage far toward the head of the lake surrounded by over an acre of ground, heavily wooded, and there, among its birds and lily pools and its stretches of fern and robin's plantain and blue-eyed grass, I would carry on my work from early spring until late fall drove me back to the Cabin I had built on the Limberlost.

It was while I was wavering over this purchase and trying to make up my mind as to whether it was exactly the thing I required for my work that an experience came to me which stands out in sheer beauty past almost any other in a lifetime that, by the grace of God, has given to me opportunity to know much of exquisite beauty. I had been studying the violin and I had brought with me to the lake a beautiful instrument especially made for me by an old master musician in one of the big musical instrument factories of Cincinnati. I did not want to bother any one at the hotel with my own particular brand of violin music, so every morning I slipped from bed before my family was awake and taking my instrument, I crept softly from the hotel, went to the boathouse, and taking my boat, rowed to some of the coves at the end of the lake and there, with the prow backed into the embankment sufficiently to hold steady, I would do my practicing for the edification of the muskrats and the groundhogs of the bank, for the birds that were flying through the trees and nesting around the water, and grinning early farmer boys.

This particular morning in June I had slipped out earlier than usual. I had taken a new route. When I left the channel running from Triplett's Hotel into the broader waters toward the southern end of the lake, instead of turning to the right, as had been my usual practice, I turned to the left and rowed past the shore line of the place I coveted where the blue-eyed grass winked among the roots of the big oaks; and rounding a small promontory, I pulled back into a large bay on the banks of which there now stand a number of cottages. At that time there was no building anywhere near except the stone house on the large island which is the summer residence of the Episcopal bishop of the diocese of northern Indiana. The residence was not yet opened. There was not much sign of life on the surrounding farms, the homes of which lay far away bordering the roads. I had a big bay, teeming with sheer beauty, all to myself. There were the usual hardwood trees climbing the embankments around the water. There was the usual line of shrub and bush border, and beyond were cattails and sedges, and spreading over the surface, the flat circular lily pads, while in the prime of their beauty the gold lilies, the white lilies, and the blue of water hyacinths and of iris outlined the shore, and here and there white arrowheads lifted their graceful, lacy sprays of bloom, back of them the fine lace of cardinal flower, the gold cornucopias of touch-me-not, and among the bank bushes, wild rose satin and alder lace.

Softly I pushed my boat among the lily pads until the prow of it was firmly anchored in the bank. Then I sat there, listening and absorbing. I have told you that it was June. I have told you that it was a world practically unspoiled by man in that region. I have no words in which to tell you what I got from that location or from that morning. I could fill half-a-dozen books with the natural history that was a legitimate perquisite of that one bay, just as Thoreau said that he could live and write for one long lifetime concerning the wonders of Walden Pond. I am very familiar with Walden Pond as Thoreau saw it and it had not the beginning of the riches that lay in that lilied bay, with its hardwood forest and its bush, vine, and sedge decoration, in the heart of northern Indiana.

I had been watching a bittern standing like a soldier at attention and waiting for a luckless frog or water puppy to come sufficiently close to his beak for a spear-like thrust, when suddenly out of the clear sky there came winging from some of the trees of the shore line, straight down to the water within a few rods of my boat lying like a log (I must have so blended that I was not discernible from the bushes and the growth around me) the most wonderful wild bird that I ever have seen in freedom in all my life. Instantly I knew, from talk that I had heard since childhood, that it was going to be my rare and unique privilege to see in a haunt native to it what very probably was the last remaining specimen of that bird, which on account of its unparalleled beauty Linnæus called "the bride." And I knew, too, that with the species the "bride" was really the groom. The bride herself was not one half so gaudy and at that minute was probably in some hollow tree bordering the lake shore brooding on a nestful of eggs, and the groom, who had stolen the bridal robes, and taken the name, had come down to the water to disport himself for my edification.

Repeatedly my father had told me of this bird and from my earliest remembrance he had bewailed the fact that because of its exquisite beauty and the delicacy of its flesh it was supposed to be practically extinct. He had not hoped, the last time he talked with me concerning it, that I ever would be able to see more than a mounted museum specimen, and here I sat in the gray and gold of a June dawn when the world was waking to life all around me, while there landed, splash! on the water in front of me, so close that not a feather marking was obscured, a male wood duck. And the male wood duck is a bird so variously and so gorgeously marked that no other bird in the ornithology of the whole world can surpass it in intricacy of pattern and design, in multiplicity of colour and in grace. I had not rather have seen for myself Mearn's quail with its totem-pole face, or the scissor-tailed swallow of the West.

My bird struck the water daintily, making a landing by a slowing-down wing movement and extended toes. He sailed down and alighted on the water as he might have alighted on the earth, while as his feet went under and his breast struck, he folded his wings with a flirt and sailed before me like a boat. The first thing he did was to throw up his head with a queer clucking call as if he were crying back to his mate: "I am here all safe. Don't worry about me." Then the head shot forward and the beak plunged under the water and in one movement he encompassed the acts of washing his face and taking a drink, because he threw up his head and put his bill in the position of a drinking bird, and instantly afterward shook it to throw the water from his face. He breasted me straightly and the beak that he had thrust into the water had a hooked tip that came very close to being black. On each side of the base there was a triangle that was red as blood and from that a wide, irregular marking of pale yellow ran down the sides to the tip. I saw the bill as it lifted from the water with all of the colours exaggerated by freshness. In the deepening gold of the morning, as the first sun rays struck down on him across the shrubbery, the top of his head was exquisite to behold. There were greens that seemed to keep their integrity, yet they were of several different shades, and between them was a bronze maroon mingled with a bronze green, an iridescent sort of combination that I have never seen equalled. Springing from the red at the base of the beak were white lines running about the eye on each side and stretching to the end of a long crest that hung in fringes far down the back of the head. A line of white started at the back angle of the eye and the crest was also decorated with a white line meeting the other at the tip. The eyes were big and liquid with wide circles of blood red around the iris. The cheeks and the side of the head were a gleaming dark bronze, while I have never seen any snow whiter than the white of the throat. This white rounded the cheek, curved up to the eye in a narrow tip, dropped again in a circle which rounded the side of the head and met on each side in a point at the crest. The white patch extended down the throat and stopped short with an even circling line, while the breast abruptly changed to the loveliest shade of maroon imaginable, much lighter than that on the head, yet it had the same bronzy tint. This broad band covered the back of the neck below the shoulders where it was darker. The lightest, most exquisite shading came immediately over the crop and here he was flecked with triangular markings so tiny that they were almost invisible. They were white at the top; widening and falling farther apart and growing larger as they met the under parts—an exquisite little marking laid on as if pencilled with the most exacting art. At the wing butts was a narrow band of white facing the maroon, then one twice its width of jetty black, and next were delicate pale yellow feathers, fine traceries of black and broad bands of black and white. His back was green overlaid with maroon and hints of yellow with a wide white band crossed the tail base, the tail itself being very long for a duck, green above, the deepest shade of the lovely maroon at the sides.

After I had breathlessly watched him a few seconds, I picked up a music score lying in the bottom of the boat and from my case slipped a pencil and on the score I jotted down the colours, going over them repeatedly to make sure that I was right.

The bride paid not the slightest attention to me. Not for a minute did he differentiate me from any other object of the shore line. In the careless abandon of utter freedom, he was disporting himself according to his habit. He stood on the water, stretched his body to full height, and flapped his wings, looking like a mass of rainbows and jet and ruby and diamonds and emeralds and soap bubbles all rolled into a jumble. Several times he disappeared and came up swallowing some weed or worm that he had found on the lake bed and after every such performance he leaned forward, swishing his face back and forth through the water to make it perfectly clean, shaking his head from which the drops of water rolled as if it were greased, as indeed it was, and time and again taking the plunge of bath between the courses of his breakfast. Around him spread the big circling emeralds of the lily pads. White as the white of his throat were the white lilies, and gold as the gold of his beak and his back were the yellow, and bloody as the blood of his beak was the cardinal flower on the shore line.

With the exception of securing the pencil and the music score, I made not the slightest movement. Time did not enter into consideration. I have no idea how long he remained breakfasting and bathing. As I sat watching him I kept thinking back to a time when my father told me of having found a nest on the shore of a lake in the side of a large tree from which a branch had been wrenched by storm. He had made his way up to it and found that it contained eleven eggs nested in down that must have been pulled by force from the breast of the mother bird. He saw her, but she was not so brilliant nor so beautiful by far as the male. He had not seen the male on the water but he did see him walk the length of a large limb, seemingly as expert as any bird. I had inquired at that time if he had webbed feet, and Father said he had not been close enough to determine. I was watching breathlessly to find out for myself, but I could not tell. I thought so from the way he sustained himself when he stood on the water to stretch to full height and exercise his wings, while I remembered that the illustration of several of my books on birds seemed to indicate that the feet were webbed, and I recalled reading not long before about how a man in the East claimed that he had located a nest. He had watched for days to see how the young negotiated the twenty feet of height between the nest and the water. He said that when the day came, the mother bird carried the young down, one at a time, in her beak and deposited them on the water. This immediately had called forth criticism. In the next issue of the magazine in which the statement appeared it was claimed that the young rode down to the water on the back of the mother, while another man who testified to having been an eye witness, pronounced both former historians inaccurate. What he had seen was that the mother uttered a sharp cry and made an abrupt dive at the nest, and that with one accord, all of the young had rushed from the hole and tumbled, some to earth, some to the water below the nest; that all of them landed on their feet, those on earth at once running to the water, and immediately all of them surrounded the mother and swam away. From a lifetime of close observation of bird life this is what I think would and did happen.

With anxious eyes I searched the lake shore. I decided that I would make it my business to examine every tree for a mile in either direction anywhere near the water in the hope that I, too, might see the nest of the most beautiful bird the water had left of which to boast.

After I had completed my colour analysis and worked it down to the finest degree possible to me, I still sat watching the bird, sometimes for a fleeting minute, studying the shore line, until as suddenly as he came, he uttered his call again, spiralled up in the sky and sailed over Round Island away to the south as if he had no intention of stopping until he reached Panama. Then I picked up the oars and softly worked my boat through the lily pads and down the lake. I knew whom I meant to ask to come with me the following morning to watch for the bird and to help me hunt his nest. I could scarcely wait to get home to tell my family what a wonderful thing had happened, yet they were so accustomed to my coming home with a tale of the most exquisite sight I ever had seen that they were not nearly so enthusiastic as I had hoped they would be. It did not seem to make any particular difference to them that a bird which I never had hoped to see alive and in freedom had materialized and given an intimate performance of his morning rites for my sole benefit.

The next morning I was on hand with the party I had selected to accompany me. An hour and a half by the clock we sat motionless in the boat and waited, but no bird came. The next morning, when the invitation was again extended, it was flatly declined; so I went alone, and alone I witnessed a repetition of the performance; and while I was intent in going over my colour diagnosis, in soaking into my soul every shade and tinge and iridescent evanescence of beauty that flashed over the oiled, wet feathers of the jewelled bird, almost from across my shoulders, nearly in line with my head, there came a sharp crack of a gun and the bride whirled over on the water, struggled an instant, and floated out still.

Then there was a rush of oars; the boat I had not seen sped across the water in a scurry to secure the prize before it should sink. I was left sitting in my boat speechless with indignation while the tears of rage and of pity and of excitement were streaming down my cheeks. Just two perfectly decent men who lacked education! When my boat came on the scene bearing a woman having a face that I know was white and stained and troubled, and I tried to tell them what beauty like that should mean to the world, they were filled with contrition. They were so sorry; they had been floating as they fished, they merely saw the flash of colour, knew it was a duck and fired on the instant. The fact that June was the time for nesting; that they had broken the laws of man when they killed the mate of a brooding bird; that they had broken the laws of God when they took the life of intense interest and exquisite beauty; that they had broken the laws of decency when they disappointed me and spoiled my plans (because I very well knew that when her mate did not respond to her cry the female would leave her nest and seek her kind elsewhere)— none of these things had occurred to them.

So the laws of man were broken, and the laws of God and the laws of decency, and the laws of the wild, and there was real suffering for the brooding bird and for me, and a real loss to humanity; and it all harked back to the fact that two men had not been properly trained in their childhood. They had not been taught to respect the rights of the wild or of other people. They had not been taught that beauty is not so common in this world that it may be sacrificed wantonly. They had not been taught to be kind or to be considerate, and both of them were ashamed and red-faced and apologetic. I fear I was not so courteous as I should have been when they expressed their sorrow and one of them said to me: "We did not know that there was such a lovely thing among the ducks of the country. We did not know that they were in this locality at all. If it will do you any good, we will faithfully promise never to shoot another one so long as we live."

That was where I perhaps lacked courtesy, for I could not help saying to him: "No. I am quite sure you never will, because in all the field work I have ever done in the woods and around the water, this is the only wood duck that I have ever seen, and I am perfectly confident that none of us will ever see another."

And so far as I am concerned, I never have, neither have I ever been able to learn of any one else who has.

"The Lost White Wild Strawberries"

T HE LAST WORKMEN left Wildflower Woods in February. From then until spring there was leisure to plan the laying out and planting of the grounds. This was a business which did not give me much concern. There was only one thing to do and that was to let Nature take her course. There was no place in which to put the red bed except to make it parallel with the west line of the property, beginning at the garage, running down the hill to the blackest piece of swamp the lake shore possessed, including about an acre. Nature had already planted more reds in that locality than anywhere else around the shore line, and this was the hint to me that if I wanted to grow a red bed successfully, I must plant red flowers where the signs were propitious for red. The bloody berries of the wild bittersweet draped the shore line from tangles of vines; here and there, a few yards farther in, grew the red wood lilies; columbine, almost blood-red, was waving on a slope halfway up the hill; Jack-in-the-Pulpit was holding aloft bloody fruit at a slightly higher elevation; next the lace and fruit of ginseng; and on top of the hill in front of the garage there was wonderful soil, the accumulated riches of ages, waiting for anything the locality afforded.

For several years I had been locating and marking wild specimens in northern Indiana. I knew where to find bittersweet to load the western fence. I knew where elders, with berries of red velvet, flourished. I knew where wild tiger lilies bordered swamp after swamp and euonymus ran riot. I knew where burning bush, mountain ash, and red and scarlet haws were to be had. I knew where to find *Monarda didyma*, cardinal flower, and fox fire. I had already tucked in the man-like divided roots of the ginseng. There was not a flower or a fruit or a berry of bloody red in this hunting ground of mine that I had been working over since I was a school girl in short skirts, that I had not located and ready to hand.

I had a corps of five field men, fairly well trained from the previous season, one of whom, a year or two later, became the entomologist of the State of Indiana, a friend of mine of Scotch extraction, Mr. Frank N. Wallace. Equipped with a good car and all necessary field paraphernalia, we bloodied that hill in one season. I discovered that around the mountain ash and the northern holly at the top of the upward slope from the lake, in front of the far side of the garage, between the clumps of cardinal flower and fox fire, there was quite a bit of space left bare. So one day we made a trip to West Lake and from the corner of a field I remembered we brought in a modest little offering of five hundred wild strawberries. *Fragaria Greyana* were the kind we set, with their coarsely serrated leaves and hairy stems. For years I had known of this big red bed of delicious wild strawberries, the fruit large, blood-red, the seeds deeply embedded in pits; not such fine ones anywhere else in all my hunting grounds. For years I had shared them with the birds and squirrels and perhaps country children. We scattered red strawberries all the way from the dry land fern bed down the hill between the other plants to the borders of the ginseng bed with its flaming red berries. We set them from the feet of the red trumpet creepers and honeysuckle that we ran up the trees to close proximity with the Indian turnips and the spikenard's brilliant clusters of berries. Frank said it was an even toss as to whether we should put them in the red bed or in the white, since the flowers were white. I decided on the red because the spot where I wanted to put them was true wild-strawberry territory, and I thought there would be quite a bit of enjoyment in eating the berries under burning bush and holly to the accompaniment of cardinal flower and fox fire.

When we had finished with the red bed, we advanced on the white, which we placed adjoining as the soil was best suited for lilies of the valley, arrowhead lilies, white adder tongue and trillium, and the white violets; because it was full of dogwood and white asters and every wild thing that grows in the woods of northern Indiana. Following such lines of reasoning, we advanced around the lake shore, allotting an acre to each of the big beds of pink and blue and mauve until we reached the Cabin and circled it with a sheet of yellow even larger. We worked so hard that season that by the following spring, when bloom time came, every bed was fairly well outlined in its own colour to begin with.

The fame of my wild-flower garden had begun to spread over the state, and not only that, but the whole United States, and it reached to the ends of the earth as well. There were blessed people who wanted to help. The first was a doctor in Colorado who sent me a bundle of pasque flowers. He sent them with a guilty conscience, because in his haste to get them to me, he had torn up his wife's kitchen apron in order that the roots might be wrapped in something that would hold moisture. Then a schoolgirl in Maine sent a bunch of partridge berries for Thanksgiving decorations. She had snipped the little sprays two or three inches in length. Remembering the art of my mother in growing wild things, I tried to do what I thought she would have done. After the partridge berries had decorated my Thanksgiving table, I pinched the berries from the top, made a fresh cut of the diagonal stems, and stuck them in trays containing a mixture of woods' earth and sand, mostly sand, moistened it, and let my cuttings have sunshine through a glass. By spring I had enough rooted partridge berry to cover a large space under one of the oaks of the red bed.

For years Frank Wallace shipped to me uncounted baskets filled with very carefully named and numbered specimens—rare violets, wild larkspur, shooting star, commelina, dozens of the beauties of Brown County that did not occur so far north as Wildflower Woods.

A schoolboy in western New York sent me a packet of seed and a cigar box filled with roots of *Monarda didyma* which helped to bloody up the red bed considerably, and at the present time it has spread until it covers nearly a quarter of an acre.

A girl in Georgia sent me jasmine. A man from California sent me several large packets of Payne's wild-flower seed with which I covered one entire hill with almost every wild bloom that was annual in that state, and some of these clarkia, metzelia lindleyi, and the California poppies stood the winter. Two of them are still flourishing, but the mentzelia could not endure the bitter winter of 1914.

There were half-a-dozen packets of roots from a flower lover near Medicine Hat, including a spool box containing one tiny evergreen tree which is growing beautifully to-day. There were wild red iris from Russia and an exquisitely dainty and beautiful blue iris from France; hardy ivy from an old abbey in England, and exquisitely beautiful white asters from a woman in Norway—asters having smooth stems covered with the overlaying frost that botanists call "bloom" on the reddish stems. The slender leaves were perfectly smooth, the colour of young oats, and daintily covered with the "bloom" also. The flowers were lacy white with gold centres.

Away from South Africa came golden wattle and many packets of seed. And there were packages of seed from a school teacher in New Zealand, and others from India and from the Bermudas; and so it went on for very nearly the circle of the globe. One man, a minister in a Pennsylvania church, offered to make a queer bargain with me. If I would furnish him botanical Biblical material for a lecture, he would collect roots for me of wild flowers that I lacked. I did my level best on his lecture and he added to my collection the painted trillium, a yellow wood lily, three orchids, azaleas and rhododendrons, but in the growing of the two latter I failed because the soil of my woods was not right. Minnesota contributed more pasque flowers and northern Michigan sent trailing arbutus and wintergreen, but perhaps the greatest thrill of the entire collection came when I received a packet containing half-a-dozen wild strawberries, guaranteed to bear white wild strawberries, from the home grounds of General Lew Wallace.

When those half-dozen white strawberry plants were put into my hands, I felt that keen joy which any collector feels over a new specimen. To say that I was delighted is putting the matter mildly. I was absolutely thrilled. These plants had a history. General Wallace, who was a great flower lover, had found them growing wild in the woods near his beautiful home in Crawfordsville. I had visited this home; I knew the proportions of the great beeches which grew for the General in the most elaborate manner, truly lordly beeches with wide-spreading arms of gray moleskin, great velvet trunks and branches almost sweeping the ground. On these trees the General had lavished in tree surgery what was considered by most of us a fortune in those days, and through the grasses beneath them there grew a world of violets, mostly blue, but there were a few of the white and the yellow. The General's home was a big, spacious place with an air of leisure and quiet and contentment and the love of growing things in evidence, things that grew as if they loved the man who lived there and would show their appreciation of the time and money he lavished upon them by wide gestures of luxuriance.

I never have been able to account for exactly how the General found these wildings. In the East, Britton and Brown report them as having been brought in from Europe, but I have a strong suspicion that in the Middle West and North they are natives. I cannot prove this, but I believe it. They must be extremely rare because in all the years during which I have spent much time on my knees in the woods of Ohio, Illinois, Indiana, and Michigan, I never have found wild white strawberries for myself, nor have I met any one else who did with the exception of these discovered by General Wallace.

I walked the space allotted for white from the lake shore to the garage, back and forth, searching for soil that came the nearest to matching that around the roots that had been sent me. I used particular care as to the degree of light and shade and then I got upon my knees and carefully, with my own fingers, I tucked in the roots of the white strawberries from the wild flower collection of a great general, to whose brain could be attributed a book that I considered one of the greatest historical romances in all the world, a book that few people mentioned, so busy was every one with the salvos of applause that greeted "Ben Hur" in his spectacular passage from the galleys to the arena and the presence of kings, a book that is one of the sheerest, cleanest pieces of writing, with a fine degree of literary flavour, with a subject so entrancing that, to my way of thinking, "Ben Hur" could not compare with it—"The Fair God," a book that I had read and re-read until I could quote pages of it in all its colour and splendour and romance. I fairly worshipped the genius of the man who wrote that book and I thought of all these things and a great many others, not forgetting "The Prince of India." I was proud and I was pleased to the depths of my soul that some of these plants from the grounds of General Wallace should come to me.

When the holes had been properly dug and fertilized and a bit of water added, and the roots had been tucked in and covered according to their running habit, and everything was finished, came the minute when Frank Wallace caught me at a lifetime habit of mine. He was standing where he saw my face as I knelt up after planting the white strawberries that this very talented and very great warrior had sent me, and he said to me softly: "Mrs. Porter, while you are planting these rare wild things you pray, don't you?"

And I said: "Yes, Frank. I do everything in my power for them, and then I ask God to please do what lies in His power to give them life and beauty so that the youngsters who come after me may learn to appreciate these lowly, delicate little growing things, may learn to be reverent and tender and loving with them, so that they may get the fine flavour of the very best things that life has to give."

So I prayed my prayer to the God of Growing Things over the white strawberries, and for four or five years I had the feeling that my prayer was answered. They not only grew, but they grew abundantly. They ran and they spread from the roots, and they seeded down, and by and by my six plants had multiplied to dozens and at bloom time they whitened a wide space and at berry time they remained equally white. The berries were large and they were delicious and they were like pearls in colour. Of all the thousands of visitors that came to the Cabin and walked down past the bed, not one had ever seen a white wild strawberry, so they were one of the wonders and the marvels of the grounds. Happy was the person who came in fruit time and had the treat of the ovoid-conic berries of pearly white, with the seeds lying so even on the surface that they could be easily brushed off. There was not one of those visitors who did not know the history of the warlike deeds and the literary fame of the great man who had found and given thousands the chance to see and to taste white wild strawberries.

Then came the bitter cold winter of 1914, that first year of the war when it seemed as if the wrath of the Ice King expended itself on all the world, northern Indiana having, to my way of thinking, the monkey's share. That winter the snows drifted almost as high as the fences and lay there for weeks; that winter the ground froze so deep that we could not bury our dead for weeks at a time. We all remember that dreadful winter when our hearts were filled with fear and anxiety for those who must remain, as well as for those who must go. And when spring came and the rain fell and the sun shone warm again, I found that great havoc had been wrought in the woods. Many an orchid had lost its life in the bitter weather; many a fern had been frozen past endurance; many a wilding that I had thought securely acclimated and habituated to its place did not put in its appearance. Not a trace of trailing arbutus remained, and among others, the white wild strawberry bed was wiped out as completely as if it never had been. There was not one plant left.

The General had made his crossing and he was learning what Heaven has in store for men who fight a good fight and who use their brains for the benefit of others, and I was wondering if I might appeal to his son for even one plant in case the originals, which lay considerably farther south than my grounds, had not been so severely punished by the cruel weather, because in all the time since I had first heard of the white wilding, I had looked for them everywhere in my hunting grounds and not even the ghost of a white one had I ever found, and in all my questionings among the farmers and the country folk whose swamps and woods I invaded, none had ever heard of a wild white strawberry.

That spring I found that one of my big beeches across the driveway and several yards from the white strawberry bed was dead. I was not much surprised. Mr. Wallace and I had taken a long chance on tree surgery with this specimen. It was a huge beech, fairly a shell, the branches dead for forty or fifty feet. It was almost a foolhardy chance that we took in trying to save it. But it graced an isolated spot, it was a lordly tree, its crown was beautifully shaped, its trunk was mast-straight and velvet-fine. We were on the spot in an effort to save every one of these giants of the forest that possibly could be saved. If General Wallace watched me from beyond, I wanted him to see that my beeches were having the same chance that he had given his. We took an expensive risk on this one because it ate cement by the barrel and when we got it filled, we realized that we would probably have our pains and our expense for nothing because the heat of summer suns shining upon it would so heat the cement that the bark would become sap bound, and if that did occur, the cold of the first severe winter would be disastrous. Between heat and cold, the thing happened.

Then came the problem of how to get that great, wood-encased cement monument down and out of the wild garden. It was a problem that required some time and considerable expense in the solving, but at last the tree was felled, the wood removed from it, the big cement trunk rolled back in the swamp and buried from sight. We discovered when we removed the trunk that even the larger roots were hollow and many squirrels had been homing among them. They had burrowed under the cement from root to root and made their winter quarters. With the beech removed, we filled the hole, raked it over, and considered that expensive job ancient history.

Now we reach the unbelievable part of this story, the thing that seems incredible, and yet things are so very simple when Nature is left to her own devices. The following year, coming through the woods and taking a short cut past the location of the beech, I was dumbfounded one day in early June to discover a big circular bed of wild white strawberries spreading over every inch of ground that the beech tree had occupied. There could be no mistake about them. There was a shiny gloss on the white strawberry leaf, its green not so deep as the red, the veinings were more deeply grooved, the edges cut in deeper serrations, the leaf slightly different in shape, there was a pure whiteness, a waxy texture in the bloom and it lifted higher than the leaves. There lay a nice big circular bed of white wild strawberries in the neighbourhood of ten feet in diameter, plants of a thrift and vigour the tiny bed I had set had never attained. There they were and the question was how did they get there? There was only one answer that could be made in all the world to that question and the answer was that the squirrels had been feeding on the white strawberries and that they had sowed the seed all through and over the location and when the tree was removed and the earth was raked smooth, and when the snows blanketed it and the sun shone and the rains fell, all these little seeds in their fertilized coats germinated and sprang up and gave back to me my lost and dearly loved wild white strawberry bed. Nature returned to me my lost gift from the wildings of the great general.

Gene Stratton Porter Chronology

1863   August 17. Geneva Stratton is born in Wabash County, Indiana, the youngest of twelve children born to Mary and Mark Stratton.

1874   The Stratton family moves into town of Wabash, where Geneva attends school.

1881   Geneva spends her first summer at Sylvan Lake.

1884   Geneva Stratton meets Charles Dorwin Porter, age 34, at a chautauqua on Sylvan Lake, Indiana.

1886   In April, "Gene"—as she is now called by Charles—marries Charles Porter.

1887   In August, Jeannette Porter is born.

1894   Gene and Charles visit Chicago Exposition, where Gene gets the inspiration for "Limberlost Cabin," which they have built, and occupy beginning in 1895.

1900   The first of her articles appear in *Recreation* and *Outing* magazines.

1901   Publication of "Laddie," a short story about her childhood, in *Metropolitan* magazine.

1903   *The Song of the Cardinal* published.

1904   Approached by Edward Bok of *Ladies Home Journal* to do a series on birds. These articles become *What I Have Done With Birds.*

1909   Jeannette marries G. Blaine Monroe.
A Girl of the Limberlost published.

1912   The clearing of Limberlost Swamp prompts Gene to buy a cottage on Sylvan Lake.

1914   Move to "Wildflower Woods," the home which Gene has had built on Sylvan Lake.

1916   Publication of *Morning Face*—a children's book dedicated to Jeannette's daughter Gene—unusual at time for its humor and the suggested activities for parents and children, designed to encourage appreciation of the natural world.

1917   Motion picture (which Stratton Porter felt unsatisfactory) made from novel *Freckles*. Jeannette and her two daughters undergoing difficult divorce.

1918   Visit to a sanitorium in upstate New York. The author claimed this visit was for a physical examination, which she felt she needed at her age. Biographers have discussed her possible emotional exhaustion.

1920   Move to Los Angeles, California. Jeannette, finally divorced, takes children to live with Gene.

1921   Incorporation of Gene Stratton Porter Productions. This movie company eventually produced versions of her novels *Michael O'Halloran, A Girl of the Limberlost, Laddie,* and *Keeper of the Bees.*

1923   Jeannette marries James Leo Meehan.

1924   *Keeper of the Bees* (published posthumously) written at the Stratton Porter home on Catalina Island, California.

1924   December 6. Gene Stratton Porter fatally injured in an automobile accident in Los Angeles, California. She is buried at Hollywood Memorial Park.

1926   Death of Charles Dorwin Porter.

1929   August 20. Auction of Bel-Air home of Gene Stratton Porter. Publication of Jeannette Porter Meehan's novel *Freckles Comes Home.*

1946   "Wildflower Woods" (Limberlost Cabin North) on Sylvan Lake becomes Indiana State Memorial. Now designated a historic site, Limberlost North encompasses twenty of the original 150 acres, and includes the gardens, arbor, orchard, and scenic paths.

1945   Limberlost Conservation Association, Inc., gives home in Geneva to state of Indiana for Gene Stratton Porter Memorial.

1977   November 7. Death of Jeannette Porter Meehan in Los Angeles.

Select Bibliography

An attempt has been made to list all of Gene Stratton Porter's novels, non-fiction books, poems, and short stories, as well as the articles which are part of her oeuvre as a nature writer, including her notes on photographing nature. The editorial pieces which appeared in *McCall's* and were collected in the volume *Let Us Highly Resolve* are not listed separately, with one exception (*) included for its pertinence to the study at hand. The nature essays collected in *Tales You Won't Believe* are listed separately. The separate chapters of serialized novels are not listed. Only a partial selection of the editions are listed for the frequently reprinted novels *Freckles* and *A Girl of the Limberlost*. Materials listed as Critical Studies were selected for their relevance to the study of Gene Stratton Porter's nature writing.

Novels

The Song of the Cardinal. Indianapolis: Bobbs-Merrill Co., 1903.

Freckles. New York: Doubleday, Page & Co., 1904; Bloomington: Indiana University Press, 1986; New York: Dell Publishing Co., 1988, afterword by Jean Craighead George.

At the Foot of the Rainbow. New York: The Outing Publishing Co., 1907.

A Girl of the Limberlost. New York: Doubleday, Page & Co., 1909; Dell Publishing Co., 1986, afterword by Patricia Reilly Giff; Signet Books, 1988, afterword by Joan Aiken.

After the Flood. Indiana Society of Chicago, *The Hoosier Set*, vol 8. Indianapolis: Bobbs-Merrill, 1911. Privately reprinted, Muncie, Indiana: Rollin King, 1975.

The Harvester: Garden City, New York: Doubleday, Page & Co., 1911.

Laddie: A True Blue Story. Garden City, New York: Doubleday, Page & Co., 1913.

Michael O'Halloran. Garden City, New York: Doubleday, Page & Co., 1915.

Morning Face. Garden City, New York: Doubleday, Page & Co., 1916.

A Daughter of the Land. Garden City, New York: Doubleday, Page & Co., 1918.

Her Father's Daughter. Garden City, New York: Doubleday, Page & Co., 1921.

The White Flag. Garden City, New York: Doubleday, Page & Co., 1923. Serialized in *Good Housekeeping,* April through November 1923.

The Keeper of the Bees. Garden City, New York: Doubleday, Page & Co., 1925. Serialized in *McCall's,* February through September 1925.

The Magic Garden. Garden City, New York: Doubleday, Page & Co., 1927. Serialized in *McCall's,* October 1926 through March 1927.

Poetry

"A Limberlost Invitation." In *An Invitation to You and Your Folks from Jim and Some More of the Home Folks.* Indianapolis: Bobbs-Merrill, 1916, for the Indiana Historical Commission.

"Peter's Flowers." *Red Cross Magazine,* April 1919, 2–4.

"Symbols." *Good Housekeeping* 72:12 (January 1921).

"Blue-Eyed Mary." *Good Housekeeping* 72:52 (May 1921).

The Fire Bird. Garden City, New York: Doubleday, Page & Co., 1922.

Jesus of the Emerald. Garden City, New York: Doubleday, Page & Co., 1923.

"Euphorbia." *Good Housekeeping* 76:10–13 (January 1923); 76:24–27 (February 1923); and 76:42–45 (March 1923).

"Field O' My Dreams." *Outdoor America* 3(5):26–27 (December 1924).

"Whitmore's Bull." *McCall's* 53(9): 8–9 ff. (June 1926).

Non-Fiction

What I Have Done With Birds. Indianapolis: Bobbs-Merrill, 1907. Serialized in *Ladies' Home Journal,* April through August 1906.

Birds of the Bible. Cincinnati: Jennings and Graham, and New York: Eaton & Mains, 1909; Cutchogue, New York: Buccaneer Books, 1986.

Music of the Wild. Cincinnati: Jennings and Graham, and New York: Eaton & Mains, 1910.

Moths of the Limberlost. Garden City, New York: Doubleday, Page & Co., 1912, reprinted 1914, 1916, 1921, 1926. Reprint (without photographic illustrations) Greenport, New York: Harmony Raine & Co., 1980; Cutchogue, New York: Buccaneer Books, 1986.

Friends in Feathers. (Revised and enlarged edition of *What I Have Done with Birds*) Garden City, New York: Doubleday, Page & Co., 1917; Nelson Doubleday, 1922.

Homing With the Birds. Garden City, New York: Doubleday, Page & Co., 1919, 1920; Cutchogue, New York: Buccaneer Books, 1986.

Tales You Won't Believe. Garden City, New York: Doubleday, Page & Co., 1925. Serialized in *Good Housekeeping,* January 1924 through February 1925.

Let Us Highly Resolve. Garden City, New York: Doubleday, Page & Co., 1927. Essays previously published in *McCall's* as "Gene Stratton Porter's Page" January 1922 through December 1927.

Articles and Short Stories

"A New Experience in Millinery." *Recreation* 12 (2): 115 (February 1900).

"Camera Notes." (Bylined column) *Recreation* 12(2): 159–60 (February 1900); 12(4): 323–28 (April 1900); 13(1): 77–82 (July 1900);

14(1): 77–79 (January 1901); 14(2): 159–61 (February 1901); 14(3): 244 (March 1901); 14(5): 405–7 (May 1901).

"Why the Biggest One Got Away." *Recreation*, April 1900, 265–68.

"In the Camps of Croesus." *Recreation*, July 1900, pp. 21–22.

"From the Viewpoint of a Field Worker." In *The American Annual of Photography and Photographic Times Almanac for 1902*, edited by Walter E. Woodbury, 214–26. New York: Scoville Manufacturing Co., 1901.

"Bird Architecture." *Outing* 38:437–42 (July 1901).

"Bird Architecture." *Outing* 38: unnumbered (September 1901).

"Laddie, the Princess, and the Pie." *Metropolitan Magazine* 14:416–21 (September 1901). [See Note]

"Photographing the Belted Kingfisher." *Outing* 39:198–202 (November 1901).

"How Laddie and the Princess Spelled Down at the Christmas Bee." *Metropolitan Magazine* 14:739–53 (December 1901).

"A Study of the Black Vulture." *Outing* 39:279–83 (December 1901).

"Under My Vine and Fig Tree." In *The American Annual of Photography and Photographic Times-Bulletin Almanac for 1903*, edited by W. I. Lincoln Adams, 24–34. New York: Scoville Manufacturing Co., 1902.

"The Birds' Kindergarten." *Outing* 40:70–74 (April 1902).

"When Luck is Golden." *Metropolitan Magazine* 15:440–45 (April 1902).

"Sight and Scent in Animals and Birds." *Outing* 40:295–98 (June 1902).

"The Real Babes in the Woods." *Metropolitan Magazine* 16:201–13 (August 1902).

"The Music of the Marsh." *Outing* 40:658–65 (September 1902).

"Bob's Feathered Interloper." *Metropolitan Magazine* 17:192–203 (November 1903).

"The Camera in Ornithology." In *The American Annual of Photography and Photographic Times-Bulletin Almanac for 1904*, edited by

W. I. Lincoln Adams, 51–68. New York: Scoville Manufacturing Co., 1903.

"Freckles' Chickens." *Ladies Home Journal* 21:9–10 (November 1904).

"The Call of the Wayside." In *The American Annual of Photography and Photographic Times-Bulletin Almanac for 1906,* edited by W. I. Lincoln Adams, 186–92. New York: Scoville Manufacturing Co., 1905.

"The Making of a Great Ranch." *Country Life in America* 11:298–302 (January 1907).

"Character Sketches of Twelve Birds." In *Biennial Report of the Commissioner of Fisheries & Game for Indiana.* Indianapolis, 1908.

"Why I Wrote *A Girl of the Limberlost.*" *World's Work* 19:12545–47 (February 1910).

"Hidden Treasures: Moths of the Limberlost." *Country Life in America* 22:29–36 (June 1912).

"The Gift of the Birds." *The Youth's Companion* 88:47–48 (March 19, 1914); and 88:159–60 (March 6, 1914).

"Hundred, Not Six." *New York Times Magazine* 4:14–15 (September 5, 1915).

"My Work and My Critics." *Bookman* [London], 49:147–55 (February 1916).

"My Life and My Books." *The Ladies' Home Journal* 23 (September 1916).

Untitled selection for April 30th in *The Hoosier Year.* Indianapolis: Max R. Hyman [1916].

"Why I Always Wear My Rose-Colored Glasses." *American Magazine* 88:36–37ff. (August 1919).

"My Ideal Home, Part 4." *Country Life of America* 40:40 (October 1921).

"My Great Day." *Izaak Walton League Monthly* 1(2) (October 1922).

"All Together, Heave!" *Izaak Walton League Monthly* 1(4): cover (December 1922).

"Tales You Won't Believe: A Miracle and a Marvel." *Good Housekeeping* 78:16–17 ff. (January 1924).

"Tales You Won't Believe: When the Geese Flew North." *Good Housekeeping* 78:18–19 ff. (February 1924).

"Tales You Won't Believe: The Bird that Needs a Champion." *Good Housekeeping* 78:44–45 ff. (March 1924).

"Tales You Won't Believe: Singers of Immortality." *Good Housekeeping* 78: 22–23 ff. (April 1924).

"Tales You Won't Believe: The Gold-Medal Flower." *Good Housekeeping* 78:30–31 ff. (May 1924).

"The Dog That Will Never Be Kicked Again." *Literary Digest,* May 24, 1924, 59–63.

"Tales You Won't Believe: The Miracle Moth." *Good Housekeeping* 78:34–35 (June 1924).

"Tales You Won't Believe: The Bride of Red Wing Lake." *Good Housekeeping* 79:34–35 ff. (July 1924).

"Tales You Won't Believe: The Last Passenger Pigeon." *Good Housekeeping* 79:54–55 ff. (August 1924).

"Tales You Won't Believe: The Lost White Wild Strawberries." *Good Housekeeping* 79:52–53 ff. (September 1924).

"Tales You Won't Believe: The Search for 'Three Birds.'" *Good Housekeeping* 79:37 ff. (October 1924).

"Tales You Won't Believe: The Phlegmatic Bluebird." *Good Housekeeping* 79:51–52 ff. (November 1924).

"Tales You Won't Believe: The Fire Bird." *Good Housekeeping* 79:26–27 ff. (December 1924).

"Tales You Won't Believe: The Bird of Invention." *Good Housekeeping* 80:32 ff. (January 1925).

"Tales You Won't Believe: Grass." *Good Housekeeping* 80:17 ff. (February 1925).

"What My Father Meant to Me." *American Magazine* 99 (February 1925).

"The Healing Influence of Gardens."* *McCall's,* December 1927, 120.

Biographical and Bibliographic Studies

"An American Bird Woman." *Chambers Journal* 46:636 ff. (October 1, 1914).

Banta, Richard E., ed. *The Hoosier Caravan: A Treasury of Indiana Life and Lore.* Bloomington: Indiana University Press, 1951, 478.

Clothier, Anastasia. *Limberlost Cabin and Wildflower Woods.* Pamphlet, n.p., 1936.

King, Rollin Patterson. *Gene Stratton-Porter: A Lovely Light.* Chicago: Adams Press, 1979.

Long, Judith Reick. *Gene Stratton-Porter: Novelist and Naturalist.* Indianapolis: Indiana Historical Society, 1990.

———. "Gene Stratton-Porter: The Hum of Life." *Traces of Indiana* 2(3) (Summer 1990): 40–47.

MacLean, David G. *Gene Stratton-Porter: A Bibliography and Collector's Guide.* Decater, Indiana: Americana Books, 1976.

Meehan, Jeannette Porter. "My Mother." *McCall's* 52 (January 1925).

———. *The Lady of the Limberlost: The Life and Letters of Gene Stratton-Porter.* Garden City, New York: Doubleday, Doran & Co., 1928.

"Mrs. Porter and Nature." *Bookman* 35 (August 1912): 587–89

Richards, Bertrand F. *Gene Stratton-Porter.* Boston: Twayne Publishers, 1981.

S. F. E. *Gene Stratton-Porter: A Little Story of the Life and Work and Ideals of the Bird Woman.* Garden City, New York: Doubleday, Page & Co. [1915]. [Attributed to both Eugene Francis Saxton and Samuel F. Ewart.] Reissue, with slight emendations by H. E. Maule. Garden City: The Country Life Press, 1919. Appended to 1925 edition of *The Keeper of the Bees.*

Critical Studies

Bakerman, Jane S. "Gene Stratton-Porter: What Price the Limberlost?" *Old Northwest* 3, no. 2 (1977): 173–84.

———. "Gene Stratton-Porter Reconsidered." *Kate Chopin Newsletter* II, no. 3, Winter 1976–77, 3–4.

Brooks, Paul. "Birds and Women." *Audubon* 82 (September 1980): 88–97.

Cooper, Frederic Taber. "The Popularity of Gene Stratton-Porter." *The Bookman,* August 1915, 671.

Dahlke-Scott, Deborah, and Michael Prewitt. "A Writer's Crusade to Portray the Spirit of the Limberlost." *Smithsonian* 7 (April 1976): 64–69. Reprinted in *Backpacker* 4 (August 16, 1976): 28 ff. as "Elder of the Tribe: Gene Stratton-Porter."

Finney, Jan Dearmin, ed. *Gene Stratton-Porter, the Natural Wonder: Surviving Photographs of the Great Limberlost Swamp by Gene Stratton-Porter.* Indianapolis: Museum Shop, Indiana State Museum [c.1983].

Hill, Herbert R. "Limberlost Author: Gene Stratton-Porter." *Outdoor Indiana* 33 (April 1968): 26–27ff.

Hoekstra, Ellen. "The Pedestal Myth Reinforced: Women's Magazine Fiction, 1900–1920." In *New Dimensions in Popular Culture,* ed. Russel B. Nye. Bowling Green, Ohio: Bowling Green University Press, 1972.

Ifkovic, Edward. "The Garden of the Lord: Gene Stratton-Porter and the Death of Evil in Eden." *Journal of Popular Culture* 8, no. 4 (1975): 757–66.

"In Memoriam Gene Stratton-Porter." *McCall's,* February 1925, 27.

Lillard, Richard G. "The Nature Book in Action." *English Journal* 62, no. 4 (1975): 537–85.

Mann, Ruth J. "Botanical remedies from Gene Stratton Porter's *The Harvester.*" *Journal of the History of Medicine,* October 1975, 367–84.

Mighetto, Lisa. "Science, Sentiment, and Anxiety: American Nature

Writing at the Turn of the Century." *Pacific Historical Review,* 54(1): 33–50.

Obuchowski, Mary DeJong. "Gene Stratton-Porter: Women's Advocate." In *Midamerica: The Yearbook of the Society for the Study of Midwestern Literature,* 1990.

Overton, Grant M. "Naturalist vs. Novelist: Gene Stratton-Porter." In *American Nights Entertainment,* New York: D. Appleton & Co., 1923.

Phelps, William Lyon. "The Why of the Best Seller." *The Bookman,* December 1921, 298–302.

Phillips, Anne Kathryn. "Domestic Transcendentalism in the Novels of Louisa May Alcott, Gene Stratton-Porter and Jean Webster." Ph.D. diss., University of Connecticut, 1993.

Presley, Kathryn Thompson. "Neglected Popular Fiction of the Gilded Age: A Quest for Certainty." Ph.D. diss., Texas A & M University, 1991.

Schmitt, Peter J. *Back to Nature: The Arcadian Myth in Urban America.* New York: Oxford University Press, 1962.

―――. "Wilderness Novels in the Progressive Era." *Journal of Popular Culture* 3, no. 1 (1969): 72–79.

Schumaker, Arthur W. *A History of Indiana Literature: With Emphasis on the Authors of Imaginative Works Who Commenced Writing Prior to World War II.* Indianapolis: Indiana Historical Bureau, 1962.

Wallace, Frank N. "Gene Stratton-Porter and Her Studies of Native Plants." (1925) Typescript in Indiana State Library.

―――. "Afield with Gene Stratton-Porter." *McCall's,* June 1926, 10ff.

Note: During her lifetime, and until quite recently, the earliest acknowledged fictional works of Gene Stratton Porter were stories of her family's life in rural northeastern Indiana, published in *Metropolitan Magazine* in 1901 and 1902. In 1984, Judith Reick Long, a Stratton Porter biographer, published an article arguing for the attribution to Stratton Porter of the short story "A Strike at Shanes." This story, published in 1893 by the American Humane Education Society, is a tale about a group of farm animals who strike against a cruel farmer. There is no record of Stratton Porter acknowledging this piece, although she makes veiled references to early works which she discarded or "lost."